# ARE WE LIVING IN THE END TIMES?

## Tyndale House books by
## Tim LaHaye and Jerry B. Jenkins

**The Left Behind series**
*Left Behind®*
*Tribulation Force*
*Nicolae*
*Soul Harvest*
*Apollyon*
*Assassins*
*The Indwelling*
*The Mark*
Book 9—available fall 2001

**Left Behind®:** *The Kids*
*#1: The Vanishings*
*#2: Second Chance*
*#3: Through the Flames*
*#4: Facing the Future*
*#5: Nicolae High*
*#6: The Underground*
*#7: Busted!*
*#8: Death Strike*
*#9: The Search*
*#10: On the Run*
*#11: Into the Storm*
*#12: Earthquake!*

**Tyndale House books by Tim LaHaye**
*Are We Living in the End Times?*
*How to Be Happy Though Married*
*Spirit-Controlled Temperament*
*Transformed Temperaments*
*Why You Act the Way You Do*

**Tyndale House books by Jerry B. Jenkins**
*And Then Came You*
*As You Leave Home*
*Still the One*

# Are We Living in the
# END TIMES?

## TIM LAHAYE
## JERRY B. JENKINS

Tyndale House Publishers, Inc.
WHEATON, ILLINOIS

Visit Tyndale's exciting Web site at www.tyndale.com

Discover the latest about the Left Behind series at www.leftbehind.com

Copyright © 1999 by Tim LaHaye and Jerry B. Jenkins. All rights reserved.

Designed by Melinda Schumacher

Permission is granted to Bible teachers and pastors to reproduce the charts in this book for use as a teaching aid only, not for resale. In addition, beautiful transparencies for use with an overhead projector are available from Visualize-It Productions, 4263 Alta Mira Dr., La Mesa, CA 91941.

Charts adapted from *Rapture Under Attack,* © 1992, 1998 by Tim LaHaye. Used by permission of Multnomah Publishers, Inc.

Published in association with the literary agency of Alive Communications, Inc., 7680 Goddard Street, Suite 200, Colorado Springs, CO 80920.

Unless otherwise indicated, all Scripture quotations are taken from the New King James Version. Copyright © 1979, 1980, 1982 by Thomas Nelson, Inc. Used by permission. All rights reserved.

Scripture quotations marked KJV are taken from the *Holy Bible,* King James Version.

Scripture quotations marked NIV are taken from the *Holy Bible,* New International Version®. NIV®. Copyright © 1973, 1978, 1984 by International Bible Society. Used by permission of Zondervan Publishing House. All rights reserved.

*Left Behind* is a registered trademark of Tyndale House Publishers, Inc.

**Library of Congress Cataloging-in-Publication Data**

LaHaye, Tim F.
  Are we living in the end times / Tim LaHaye and Jerry B. Jenkins.
    p.  cm.
  Includes bibliographical references.
  ISBN 0-8423-0098-8 (hc)
  ISBN 0-8423-3644-3 (sc)
  1. Rapture (Christian eschatology)  2. Tribulation (Christian eschatology)  I. Jenkins, Jerry B.  II. Title.
BT887.L28  1999                                    99-41424
236′.9—dc21

Printed in the United States of America

08  07  06  05  04  03  02  01  00
9   8   7   6   5   4   3   2

*To the millions of readers of the Left Behind series,
with the prayer that this book will help them gain a clearer
understanding of end-time Bible prophecy*

# CONTENTS

# INTRODUCTION

## *How Close Are We?*

THESE are easily the most exciting days to be alive, not just because of breathtaking advances in technology and science, but because we twenty-first-century Christians have more reason than any generation before us to believe that Christ will return to take us to His Father's house.

We are not the first generation to think like this, of course, for history reveals that many interpreted the events of their day as fulfillments of end-time prophecies. In some cases their date setting and speculation turned off more people than it inspired, but at least they were studying the Scriptures in an attempt to properly discern the times. Many of them sincerely longed for Christ to end the moral corruption and deterioration of their age by ushering in His kingdom of righteousness. All Christians consider such a possibility an infinite improvement on this war-weary and sin-cursed world.

We should not be surprised that those of past generations were confused about end-time events, for even Daniel, one of the greatest of the Hebrew prophets, was commanded to "shut up the words, and seal the book until the time of the end" (Daniel 12:4; the "time of the end" refers to the days just before the beginning of the Tribulation, up to and including the second coming of Christ).

One reason for their confusion is that the sealing of end-time events made it more difficult to understand the "signs of the times." The "unsealing" or ability to understand end-time prophecy, according to Daniel, would wait until "many shall run to and fro, and knowledge shall be increased" (Daniel 12:4, KJV). Hardly anyone doubts that ours is a day when people are "running to and fro" and knowledge has increased. Both secular knowledge and the knowledge of prophetic truth have increased tremendously in this century alone. We believe we are on the verge of obtaining even greater prophetic insights than at any other time in the last two millennia.

I (Tim) have been a student of prophecy for over fifty years and can tell you there has never been more interest, both secular and Christian, in knowing about the future than there is today. The amazing success of our Left Behind series—over ten million copies sold in the first four and a half years of publication alone—proves that. Our Web site (www.leftbehind.com) receives an average of more than eighty thousand hits a day. Thousands of readers have written to express their appreciation, ask a question, or tell of some spiritual dedication that the series inspired.

In fact, it is those letters (and especially the questions in the letters) that have prompted this book. We have two main objectives:

1. To provide a basic companion outline of the end-time events and scriptural verification of the personages fictionalized in the Left Behind series;
2. To show that we have more reason than any generation before us to believe Christ may return in our generation.

The recent proliferation of books, tapes, and videos on the fulfillment of end-time prophecy further spurred this book. Recently I received in the mail a new film and two new informational videos on signs of Christ's soon return. Truly there is an increase in knowledge on this subject—one of the many signs that we are rapidly approaching "the time of the end."

That others before us were wrong about the nearness of the Lord's return should not deter us from searching the Scriptures, now that some of the end-time prophecies are being unsealed. The ability to rightly evaluate the signs in our times is increasing almost daily, from Israel being reestablished as a nation, to the hatred of Israel by Russia and her Arab allies, to the emergence of China, and many other events—all part of the end-time prophetic tapestry.

The technological capabilities of this generation permit us to see the fulfillment of events that were impossible just one generation ago. Christ could come today, and no prophecy of the end times necessary for His coming would go unfulfilled.

Of course we cannot *guarantee* that Christ will come in our generation. In His mercy He may tarry one more day, which in His economy is a thousand years (2 Peter 3:8). But we insist that we have more reason than any generation before us to believe He will come in our generation. And we think that by the time you finish this book, you will agree.

# PART ONE

## *Context*

# ONE

## *Prophecy 101*

GOD must have wanted His followers to learn Bible prophecy, because He dedicated almost 30 percent of His Scripture to it. Not only does prophecy teach us about future events, it also assures us that God keeps His word and His promises.

For example, the Old Testament features more than one hundred prophecies regarding the coming of the Messiah to the earth. Through these prophecies we know that Jesus was truly the Messiah, for He fulfilled every one of them. That is also how believers can be so confident that He will return physically to this earth to set up His kingdom, because He promised He would—five times more frequently than He promised to come the first time! Since His first coming is a fact of history, we can be at least five times as certain that He will come the second time.

## PROPHECY FOR NEW CONVERTS

Another reason we know that God wants Christians to study and understand prophecy is that one of the earliest New Testament books is 1 Thessalonians, a letter filled with teaching about end-time events. Every chapter contains a reference to the second coming of Jesus Christ. The apostle Paul, the man God used to set the pattern for local churches throughout the world, taught the details of Bible prophecy to that new Thessalonian church during its first three weeks of existence. (We know this because he was driven out of town before his fourth Sabbath.) Yet even a casual reading of the book shows that he spoke freely about the Second Coming, the Rapture, the Antichrist, the wrath to come, and other future events. Those are the very subjects we'll be considering in this book.

## PROPHECY IS NOT SO DIFFICULT

During the past three decades there has been a dearth of prophecy teaching in both our seminaries and our churches. Many seminary professors educated in secular graduate schools were often humiliated by their humanist professors for believing "the fundamentalist approach" to Scripture. Taking the Bible literally was ridiculed, and these students were led to believe that prophecy was confusing and difficult to understand.

Consequently, when these men became seminary professors instructing the future ministers of the nation, they failed to teach the prophetic portions of the Scriptures, suggesting that prophecy is "too controversial." Since no one can teach what they do not know, thousands of our churches today never enjoy a prophetic message or sermon—not because the pastor doesn't believe in it, but because he doesn't know much about it.

One pastor, asked how he handled a controversial prophetic subject said, "I just don't deal with it."

*What?* He doesn't deal with almost 30 percent of the Bible? Often, laypeople who buy prophetic books or attend prophecy conferences or subscribe to prophetic magazines know more about the prophetic portions of the Scriptures than do their pastors.

The pastor of one of the most prestigious churches in America, a popular author, recently invited me to coauthor a new book on prophecy with him. He explained that his publisher had approached him with the idea, in light of the renewed interest in the subject due to the rapidly approaching new millennium. My friend added, "I have never made a study of prophecy and don't feel qualified to do so. I have read enough of your material to know we agree on the basics and think it would be good if we attempted the project together." I encouraged him to do a study of the subject and write the book himself, for prophecy is just not that difficult.

Anyone can understand the major events of Bible prophecy if they spend a little time comparing Scripture with Scripture and if they avoid the temptation to spiritualize anything that at first seems complex. A good rule of thumb when studying any Scripture is found in the golden rule of biblical interpretation:

> When the plain sense of Scripture makes common sense, seek no other sense, but take every word at its primary, literal meaning unless the facts of the immediate context clearly indicate otherwise.
> —Dr. David L. Cooper

If you follow this rule, it is relatively easy to understand Scripture; if you ignore it, you will always be in error. That is particularly true of the prophetic sections of Scripture. In recent years a number of teachers have concluded that prophecy should usually be interpreted symbolically. Consequently, a number of conflicting teachings have brought such confusion to the church that many have given up on the subject, even though to do so they abandon an important part of God's Word.

After I have spoken on the Second Coming at a church or prophecy conference, it is not uncommon for individuals to tell me that they have not heard a single message on the Second Coming in twenty-five years. One minister wrote to say he felt convicted for never having preached a sermon on the second coming of our Lord. He said, "I have now dedicated myself to God to study and preach more prophecy." If he does, his church will come to life, his attendance will pick up, and his church will be spiritually vitalized. There is no more challenging and motivating subject in the Bible than the study of prophecy.

## THE HISTORICAL EFFECTS OF PROPHECY

Properly taught, prophecy emphasizes the "imminent" return of Christ—that He could come at any moment. This has proven to be one of the most spiritually motivating forces in church history. For whether it is the church of the first three centuries or that of the last two centuries, prophecy has had three effects on the church:

1. It has challenged believers to holy living in an unholy age;
2. It has given Christians a greater challenge to evangelize; and

6

3. It has caused the church to be more missionary minded as the church has realized it must fulfill the great commission before Christ returns.

## THE FOUR PIVOTAL EVENTS OF HISTORY

Each of the most significant events in history has marked the end of an age. Three are past; one is yet to come. All were titanic conflicts between God and Satan for the devotion of mankind; all left a significant impact on the generations that followed. The first three are Creation, the Flood, and the first coming of Christ, including His death and resurrection for the sins of mankind. The fourth and final pivotal event is the second coming of Christ to this earth.

### Creation

According to the first chapter of Genesis (which means "beginnings"), the Creation highlights the origin of that very special creature, man, who is composed of not only a body and a mind but also an eternal soul. This crucial event is covered in the first three chapters of Genesis. The effects of the Fall—that is, the sin of Adam and Eve, who were created holy but used their free will to disobey God—plunged the world into sin and corruption, producing a pre-Flood population that became so wicked in only one thousand years that God destroyed them all, except for Noah and his family.

### The Flood

The worldwide Flood, described in detail in Genesis 6–8, shows how God repopulated the earth from only eight people. This monumental event is mentioned in the literature of various peoples of the ancient world, providing compelling evidence of its universality. If the scientific community recognized that fact, a spike would be driven into the heart of the theory of evolution, along with the theory of "theistic evolution" (God-guided evolution). But humanistic man would rather believe the unscientific theory of evolution than the truth of Scripture that God created man and will hold man accountable for the way he lives.

## The Cross

The third pivotal event of history was the crucifixion of Jesus Christ. The cross as a symbol includes His virgin birth in fulfillment of prophecy, His sinless life, His sacrificial death, and His resurrection. When He as God's only begotten Son gave Himself to die on that cross for "the sins of the whole world," He ended the age of law and introduced the age of grace. From that time on, individuals have been able to be eternally saved "through faith" by repenting of their sins and calling on Christ to save them. That is why it is called "the age of grace." That age will end with the next pivotal event. . . .

## The Second Coming

The second coming of Jesus Christ, and the many lesser events leading up to it and following it, is what prophecy is primarily about. It is doubtless the greatest story of the future to be found anywhere. No religion, no culture, and no literature offers such a sublime concept of future events that lead into an even better eternity. Once understood, these thrilling events prove so exciting and inspiring that many have turned from their sins to find Christ as their Lord and Savior—a good reason for all Christians to know about them, particularly as we see so many of these events fulfilled in our lifetime.

There are other important events in history, but none of greater significance than these four. They are highlighted on the following chart, which also locates these pivotal events on the time line of man's pilgrimage on earth, separating the ages past from the ages to come.

## The Four Pivotal Events of History

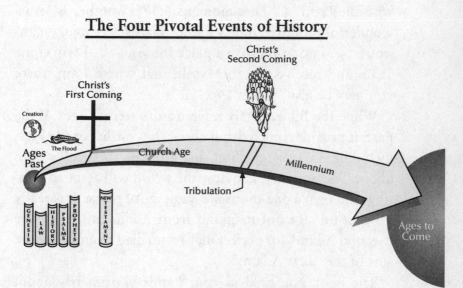

For some reason known only to God, the Bible says very little about the ages past or the ages to come. God seems most interested in man's understanding of his own past—so 50 percent of the Bible's sixty-six books cover human history. It contains a wealth of historical information that has been documented by archaeologists during the last two centuries. The sixty-six books of the Bible are mostly about man's existence in the period we call "time," from Adam and Eve through the coming kingdom age of Jesus Christ.

Twenty-five percent of the Bible contains instruction on how to live in the present and how to treat others.

And 28 percent is prophecy, some of which has already been fulfilled in Israel and the first coming of Christ. The Scriptures mention briefly our entrance into His heaven for eternity and also reveal some comforting words about our future. One example is: "And thus we shall always be with the Lord" (1 Thessalonians 4:17). Another is Jesus' wonderful promise "In My Father's house are many mansions. . . . I go to prepare a place for you. . . . I will come again and receive you to Myself; that where I am, there you may be also" (John 14:2-3).

While the Bible merely refers to the eternal ages of the past, it provides much detail about the conflict of the ages, including Satan's rebellion, his attempt to deceive man about God, eternity, and how the world will come to a fitting climax in a one-thousand-year age of peace. It is really a beautiful story of mankind from Adam to Christ, the "second Adam" (or perfect man) who died to atone for the sins of the "first Adam."

The book you hold in your hands is primarily about God's wonderful plan for man's future events in relation to this earth prior to that age of peace. Failure to understand God's plan, from the coming of the "first Adam" to the second coming of Christ to establish His kingdom, will keep you from answering the big philosophical questions of life: *Why am I here? Where am I going? How do I get there?* Only a study of prophecy adequately answers all of these questions.

The basic time line of human history just developed will be used throughout this book to introduce the many prophetic passages that fill in details of the future. It is most helpful to relate all prophetic teachings to this timeline.

## THIS PRESENT CHURCH AGE

Jesus not only promised His followers that He "will come again" and take them to His Father's house (John 14:1-3), He promised to "build [His] church, and the gates of Hades shall not prevail against it" (Matthew 16:18). He built that church through the ministry of the Holy Spirit working in His apostles and in those who became believers through them. For twenty centuries His church has been persecuted by religions, kings, and dictators, yet today it is stronger than ever. That in itself is a testimony to His promise, for although the church has been the most consistently hated group on earth, it is still growing and will continue to do so until He takes it out of this world. Church growth experts estimate the current number of Christians at over *one billion* and growing.

The church age, starting with the day of Pentecost in Acts 2 through the present day, corresponds to the age of grace on the chart on the following page. Jesus described it in Matthew 13, and the apostles, particularly Peter, John, and Paul, spent the rest of their lives building and instructing that church. Revelation 2 and 3 outline it, and the New Testament, particularly the epistles, describes how its activities should be conducted.

## ON THE USE OF CHARTS

An ancient Chinese proverb suggests that "a picture is worth a thousand words." If that is true, good charts are worth a thousand words about prophecy, for they pinpoint the timing of the events described and show prophetic events in relation to each other. For many years I have used charts in churches and prophecy conferences to make difficult concepts easy to understand. Charts are a basic ingredient of my six other books on prophecy. Throughout this book we will resort to using them for clarity.

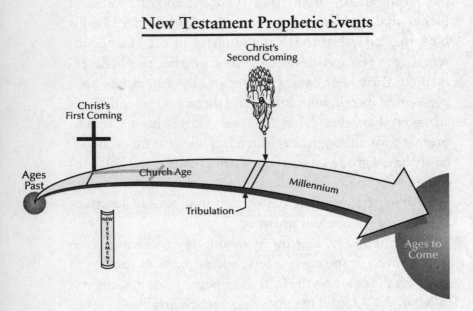

## New Testament Prophetic Events

As you look at the above chart of man's past and future sojourn on this earth, we hope you are struck with at least three significant facts.

## THE CROSS

The most famous symbol in human history marks the most significant event of all time. When Jesus Christ died on that cross for the "sins of the whole world," He reached back to Adam and Eve and forward to the last person who will be born during the Millennium—the thousand-year reign of Christ on new Earth—to atone for their sin. He redeemed all the acts of faith on the part of those before Him and offered to all after Him, by the simple act of faith, a means of escaping the consequences of Adam's fall into sin (and subsequently our own). This miracle of salvation was made possible because of who He was, the sinless Son of God. The Crucifixion was not merely a man dying for the sins of man, but "the only begotten Son of God" dying for the sins of mankind.

### All humankind has a choice to make

Every person in every generation has a choice: to obey God or to do his own thing. In Old Testament days obedient faith required men and women to sacrifice an innocent lamb in obedience to the instruction of God. Since the finished work of Christ on the cross, that act of faith is the bending of one's knees before the cross and calling on the name of the Lord. In this sense, each individual determines where he will spend eternity—with God or without Him. Those are the only two choices.

### You have a choice to make

Search your own heart to see if you have made such a decision. Have you personally called on the name of the Lord? If not, we urge you to pause from your reading and do so now. In case you would like some help in the wording of your prayer, we suggest the following:

> Dear Heavenly Father, I confess that I have sinned against heaven and in your sight and need forgiveness. Thank you for sending your Son Jesus to die

on the cross for my sins, according to the Scriptures, and I thank you for raising Him from the dead. Today I ask Him to come into my heart to cleanse me from my sin and become my Lord and Savior. I give myself to you. In Jesus' name I pray. Amen!

# TWO

## *What Are the Last Days?*

WHAT does the Bible mean by its many expressions for the last days? At first glance there are several terms that seem interchangeable, but in reality they may not always be so used. Confusion results if you do not examine the context carefully to verify that the term really means what you think it means.

Some terms for the "end times" include "the latter days," "the last times," "the latter years," or Daniel the prophet's favorite term, "the time of the end." Our Lord started His Olivet discourse (Matthew 24:1-8) by answering His disciples' question "What will be the sign of Your coming, and of the end of the age?" He often referred to that time as "the end," or "then shall the end come." Most people automatically think such terms are interchangeable because, generally speaking, they all have to do with the end of the Tribulation when Christ returns physically to the earth to set up his millennial kingdom (see chapters 14 and 15). We have found over fifty uses of such terms in Scripture and are confident there are probably many more.

## A COMMON ANALOGY

Prophecy scholar Thomas Ice, my colleague in the Pre-Trib Research Center, makes this interesting analogy:

> Sometimes Christians read in the Bible about the "last days," "end times," etc., and tend to think that all of these phrases all of the time refer to the same thing. This is not the case. Just as in our own lives, there are many endings. There is the end of the workday, the end of the day according to the clock, the end of the week, the end of the month, and the end of the year. Just because the word "end" is used does not mean that it always refers to the same time. The word "end" is restricted and precisely defined when it is modified by "day," "week," "year," etc. So it is in the Bible, that "end times" may refer to the end of the current church age or it may refer to other times.[1]

It is not difficult to locate the time meant by the biblical author for each of the above expressions, *if* the reader studies the context to make certain whom the prophet is addressing, the church or Israel. Most of the uses of these terms in the Old Testament and by our Lord have in focus the end of the Tribulation. (Most of these references merge the end of the Tribulation and the Glorious Appearing.) The uses of these terms in the epistles sometimes have in mind the end of the church age. This, of course, will occur simultaneously with the gathering of ourselves (the church) together with Christ in the Rapture (see chapter 9).

There are at least two exceptions to that general rule: Hebrews 1:1-2 and 1 John 2:18. In the Hebrews passage the Holy Spirit said, "God, who at various times and in different ways spoke in time past to the fathers by the prophets, has in *these last days* spoken to us by His Son, whom He has appointed heir of all things, through whom also He made the worlds" (emphasis added).

This evidently refers to the days in which they were living, for in their lifetime God had sent His Son to reveal His great love for mankind by dying for our sins. That act of divine mercy spelled the end of the Old Testament sacrificial system, which was being replaced by the new and better covenant made possible by the blood of God's Son.

In 1 John the apostle speaks of "the last hour." He is referring here to the new economy of God's grace, warning that even in this church age there would be "many antichrists . . . by which we know that it is the last hour." He was right: For two thousand years the church age has not been without false christs and antichrists sent by Satan to deceive the saints.

## THE PRIMARY USE OF END-TIME TERMS

In most cases the terms for the "last days" or "end times" refer to a period that may encompass no more than seven to ten or so years. We cannot pinpoint it more accurately because we are not certain how much time will elapse between the Rapture, which ends the church age, and the beginning of the Tribulation, begun by the signing of the covenant between the Antichrist and Israel (Daniel 9:27; see also chapter 13). Some prophecy scholars think it will be just a matter of days, but some estimates go as high as fifty years (though that opinion was written over seventy-five years ago. We are confident that if that writer were living today he would shorten his estimate to about one to three years, in view of the many new signs of the end that have come to light during our lifetime).

If we assume that the Antichrist's covenant with Israel follows the Rapture by a very short time, our estimate of three to ten years is reasonable. The following chart locates the time addressed and the relatively short period it covers.

## The Second Coming of Christ

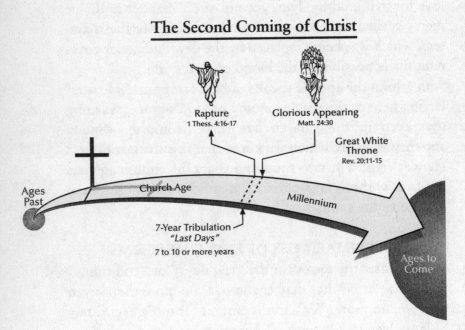

A similar expression ("afterward") from Joel 2:28-32 refers to that same period of time. It is included here because it is so significant, for it prophesies that during those "last days," just before and during Israel's seventieth week (the Tribulation), from the Rapture to the Glorious Appearing, the Holy Spirit will again be poured out on the earth like on the day of Pentecost, leading millions to the Savior. Like the other passages, one must examine the context to see what is meant. In this case we can expect the Holy Spirit to move on the hearts of people at the beginning of the Tribulation and culminate with the second coming of Christ. This outpouring will occur during the ministry of the 144,000 Jewish witnesses of Revelation 7 (see chapter 24) who see "a great multitude which no one could number" come to faith in Christ.

In short, the "last days," "end times," the "latter days," or even "afterward," usually refer to any point from just prior to the Rapture to the Glorious Appearing itself. While some references may refer to trends during the church age, most of them point to the seven to ten or more years, a period that pinpoints the end of "the times of the Gentiles" (see chapter 5) to the end of the "Great Tribulation" (see chapter 14). It is not difficult to discern what the writer of one of these many end-time references means if the reader pays close attention to the context.

"The last days," "the time of the end," and "the end of the age" are terms leading up to the seven-year tribulation when this age as we know it comes to the end. It is preceded by the Rapture and followed by the Glorious Appearing.

# THREE

## *Are These the Times of the Signs?*

EVER since Jesus Christ warned His followers that He would leave them to go to His Father's house in heaven and promised that He would "come again and receive [them] to [Himself]" (John 14:1-3), Christians have asked the $64,000 question: "When will you return, and what will be the sign of your coming?" The fact that Jesus did not rebuke the disciples for asking those two questions indicates that He approves of our watching for signs of His return. Daniel, the great Hebrew prophet, asked similar questions about end-time events in the twelfth chapter of his book.

A study of prophetic literature from the first century right up to our own day will show that Bible-believing Christians have always been interested in "when?" and the "signs." Admittedly, some commentators have come up with bizarre theories and conclusions that were proven wrong by the passage of time. Some have set ill-advised dates. In other cases, such as the Millerites in 1844, individuals have brought great embarrassment to the church. Most, however, have been humble teachers of the Word who watched for signlike events in their day in a vain hope that theirs would be the generation to see Christ return.

That hasn't been all bad. While some people became discouraged and quit studying prophecy because Christ had not yet returned in their lifetime, others were driven to restudy the Scriptures and became more conscious that Christ *could* return in their generation. This in turn made them more conscious of holy living in their unholy age, more evangelistic, and more missionary minded. Frankly, I think that is why God Himself, through His Son Jesus, His disciples, and others who were inspired to write the Scriptures, gave us 318 promises of Christ's return and made 28 percent of the Bible prophetic in nature. (For more information, see *The Beginning of the End* by Tim LaHaye, Tyndale House Publishers, Inc., 1972, 1991.)

History shows that whenever the church has lived as though her Lord could return at any moment, her members have tended to live for God and to energetically evangelize the lost. The golden days of the church and personal evangelism were days of teaching that Christ could soon appear. Such teaching usually involved a detailed examination of the "signs" of His return that believers thought were being fulfilled in their lifetime. The fires of revival that have come and gone throughout church history have often been associated with Second Coming teachings, including the "signs of the times."

## A WORD OF CAUTION ABOUT SIGNS
The Bible teaches us, "Let your moderation be known unto all men" (Philippians 4:5, KJV). A study of "signs" of

the end of the age or the return of Christ should always be undertaken with a degree of restraint. Date setters are to be ignored or, even better, rebuked as false teachers. It mystifies us that men would try to set dates for the return of Christ in view of the warning of our Lord Himself:

> "Of that day and hour no one knows, no, not even the angels of heaven, but My Father only." (Matthew 24:36)

> "It is not for you to know times or seasons which the Father has put in His own authority." (Acts 1:7)

Those two verses alone should warn us that anyone who suggests a date for the return of Christ is wrong. However, the Lord *did* say in the parable of the fig tree that we *can* know the general time of His coming. As Jesus said, "So you also, when you see all these things, know that it is near, at the doors" (Matthew 24:33).

One popular suggestion is that the coming of Christ, which will come suddenly when many are not ready for Him, will occur when those who know their Bible have good reason to believe He could come in their generation.

We really do have some powerful reasons for supposing that our generation has more reason than any before us to believe He could come in our lifetime! Still, although there are several signs of the end in existence today, we refuse to set limits on the season. But we will point out that some of these signs did not exist even a half generation ago.

At the outset, however, we wish to state categorically that we refuse to predict that Christ *will* come in our lifetime, for

He may delay His coming another fifty years or more. Still, we believe the evidence is to the contrary. We will quote secular scientists and others who see no possibility for the continued existence of this world. With the avalanche of problems that already exists, some significant voices have declared their doubts that our troubled planet has a future beyond the next twenty-five to fifty years.

We find it significant that today's Bible prophecy scholars have come to almost the same point in time as their counterparts in the secular world. Comparing the conclusions of these two disparate groups leads us to surmise that these "times of the signs" indicate rather startlingly that "the end of the age" is upon us; the time for Christ to return to set up His kingdom appears to be drawing near. The reason should be obvious: He is the only one who can unsnarl the mess man has made of this world.

## SOMETHING SIGNIFICANT IS ABOUT TO HAPPEN

For more than nineteen hundred years God has largely refrained from unmistakably intervening in the affairs of men as He did in the days of ancient Israel. There have been many miracles in that time, of course, but they have been confined mostly to believers, and even then He has not always intervened in a way that would cause skeptics to acknowledge His existence. During these years He has confined His expressions of His existence primarily to creation, the Scriptures, His Son's life and teachings, and the power of the Cross as it changes the lives of those who come to Him in faith.

While we hear a lot about the shortcomings of the church today, there are thousands in the body of Christ who are doing a good job of getting His message out to the peoples of the world. That is why there is such an incredible turning to God today in many parts of the world. The church is considered the "lampstand," or light of the world, in this age, and some in the church have done an extraordinary job of fulfilling their destiny.

That is about to change as we enter "the time of the end." As soon as the church is raptured (see chapter 9), God will again begin to visibly intervene in the affairs of mankind. Russia and her allies will go down to destroy the nation of Israel but will themselves be destroyed supernaturally by God (Ezekiel 38–39; see chapter 8). No one knows for sure whether that precedes or follows the Rapture; a case can be made either way. One thing is apparent: Russia's attack and the Rapture are the number one and two end-time events. They are followed by the rise of Antichrist (see chapter 21), the day of God's wrath (see chapters 12–14), the two witnesses (see chapter 23), the 144,000 Jewish evangelists (see chapter 24), and many other acts of divine intervention during the Tribulation. There will be so many signs that atheism will not be widespread during that period; amazingly, it will be supplanted by open and blatant rebellion against God.

The Tribulation will be followed by the majestic intervention of God in the glorious return of Christ to the earth (see chapter 15) to set up His thousand-year kingdom (see chapter 16), followed by heaven or eternity (see chapter 19).

The "time of the end" as Daniel called it, or "the last days" as the apostles referred to it, is that short period of seven to ten or more years of enormous change for this world as almighty God brings this age to an end by His supernatural intervention. God's people need to study the prophetic Scriptures so they can both be prepared themselves and help others prepare for His coming.

The good news is that this world will not end in chaos as the secularists predict. The Bible says Christ will come to solve the world's problems by introducing the greatest period in world history, the millennial kingdom of Jesus Christ. And while we are not certain it will occur in our lifetime, we have more reason to believe it might than any generation in the history of the church.

## MORE SIGNS OF CHRIST'S RETURN EXIST TODAY THAN AT ANY TIME IN HISTORY

Jesus rebuked the people of His day for failing to recognize the "signs of the times" that heralded His first coming (Matthew 16:3), calling them "a wicked and adulterous generation." They should have discerned the times, for centuries before, Daniel and other Hebrew prophets had predicted His coming. Simeon and Anna, mentioned in Luke 2, found in their studies of these prophecies sufficient cause to prompt them to go to the temple where they found the Christ child.

How much more reason do we have today to recognize the signs of His second coming! We are surrounded by so many obvious signs that one would have to be blind not to see them—yet some fail to recognize them even when they are called to their attention. So many signs exist today that you could write a book about them. In fact, I did, *The Beginning of the End,* first published in 1972 and then again in 1991. Many changes in the twenty-seven years since that book's first publication have only brought further confirmation that we are indeed living in "the times of the signs." Never in history have so many legitimate signs of Christ's return existed.

We say *legitimate* signs, for there is a difference between true signs of His coming based on Scripture and those that are inferred or imagined. In 1996 a popular TV preacher wrote a best-selling book, prompted by the cruel assassination of Israeli statesman Yitzhak Rabin. The book, based on some imagined significance of Rabin's signing the peace accord two years before, considered Rabin's untimely death to be a sign of the end. The truth is that the death of Rabin or any other world leader signifies only the anarchy predicted by the Bible for the end of the age. No significant Scripture links any specific leader to any peace treaty until the Antichrist is revealed and signs a seven-year peace accord with Israel (Daniel 9:27; see chapter 12). That *would* be a sign of the end—but not the assassination of Yeltsin, Arafat, Clinton, or any other current world leader, no matter how prominent.

## SIGNS ARE LIKE TIME CLOCKS

Over thirty years ago the cover of a national science journal featured a clock with hands set at five minutes to twelve, the editors' way of dramatizing that civilization was rapidly approaching the midnight hour of self-destruction. Subsequent issues of that journal have shown the minute hands of the clock inching ever closer to midnight. Some like-minded writers even popularized the phrase "the end of history." They meant the death of earth through pollution, overpopulation, nuclear annihilation, or some other catastrophe beyond the power of world leaders and governments to solve.

We would like to use that same graphic device to highlight the signs that have been proliferating ever since the first one burst on the world scene over eighty years ago. The hands of our clock will start at 11:00, to highlight how very close we could be to "the end of the age." Each time you see this symbol, look for information about another "sign" that shows the world is fast approaching the "end" when Christ shall come.

**Israel 1948**
Ezekiel 37

Two signs predicted by the Hebrew prophet Daniel for "the time of the end" should be obvious to all—the increase in travel and the increase in knowledge. Since 1914, when the average speed of cars and trucks was fifteen to twenty miles per hour, un-

**Increase in Travel
& Knowledge**
Daniel 12:4

til today, when rockets and satellites average twenty-four thousand miles per hour, man has had an explosion in knowledge. Why are these two signs mentioned together? Because they are interrelated. The speed of travel is dependent on the increase in knowledge. More than in any age before this one, men are "running to and fro on the earth"—just as the Bible predicted for "the time of the end."

# FOUR

## *The Sign of His Coming*

IT IS almost impossible to exaggerate the importance of our Lord's Olivet discourse found in Matthew 24–25 (with abbreviated versions in Mark 13 and Luke 21). We not only consider it to be the most important prophecy of future events, we believe it provides an outline of the future to which all other prophetic sections should be related. It is like a clothesline from which all other prophecy should be hung. An understanding of this passage is essential to a right understanding of the Bible's other prophetic passages.

### A UNIQUE HISTORICAL CONTEXT
While every part of the Olivet discourse provides a remarkable preview of the future, the first few verses of Jesus' sermon give us a unique historical context that enables us to sense when the great events it describes are about to unfold:

Then Jesus went out and departed from the temple, and His disciples came to Him to show Him the buildings of the temple. And Jesus said to them, "Do you not see all these things? Assuredly, I say to you, not one stone shall be left here upon another, that shall not be thrown down."

Now as He sat on the Mount of Olives, the disciples came to Him privately, saying, "Tell us, when will these things be? And what will be the sign of Your coming, and of the end of the age?" And Jesus answered and said to them: "Take heed that no one deceives you. For many will come in My name, saying, 'I am the Christ,' and will deceive many. And you will hear of wars and rumors of wars. See that you are not troubled; for all these things must come to pass, but the end is not yet.

"For nation will rise against nation, and kingdom against kingdom. And there will be famines, pestilences, and earthquakes in various places. All these are the beginning of sorrows." (Matthew 24:1-8)

## SHOULD WE TAKE IT LITERALLY?

Sometimes when individuals seek to understand prophetic texts, they are unsure whether they should read the biblical passages in a literal or in a more symbolic way. We can be grateful that our Lord's Olivet discourse began with a "test case" by which we can determine how we ought to read the rest of His sermon.

In the first two verses of Matthew 24 the disciples are seen proudly showing off the temple buildings to their Master. No doubt they expected Him to ooh and ahh along with them. But to say our Lord was unimpressed with what He saw is something of an understatement. "Do you not see all these things?" He asked His disciples, no doubt pointing to the gleaming structures around them. "Assuredly, I say to you, not one stone shall be left here upon another, that shall not be thrown down."

Note carefully this important test case. In these verses Jesus prophesied not only that the temple would be destroyed, but that its ruin would be so complete that not even one stone would be left standing upon another.

History records that our Lord's words were fulfilled *to the letter* in A.D. 70. In that year the Roman army under the command of Titus destroyed the city of Jerusalem. Fires raged through the city and in the temple area itself. After the flames burned themselves out, the soldiers saw that large amounts of gold had melted and flowed into the crevices of the blocks of the temple. In order to recover the precious metal, the Romans had to take the buildings apart, stone by stone. And so Jesus' prophecy was fulfilled literally; not one stone was left upon another.

Some of those stones were later used to erect the wall we see standing today near the edge of the temple mount. Every time you see pictures of the Wailing Wall in Jerusalem—a shrine that can be seen every day on the Internet (www.thewall.org)—you see the pinpoint accuracy of Jesus' prediction. And you get a big hint about how the rest of the Olivet discourse ought to be interpreted.

## WHAT SHALL BE THE SIGN?

We are indebted to the disciples for asking Jesus the crucial question "What will be the sign of Your coming, and of the end of the age?" In His answer our Lord unfolded several significant "signs" that will characterize life on earth just before His return. We believe some of these signs already have been fulfilled and that the time of the end could well be soon, even within our generation.

It is important to notice the first two warnings Jesus gave His disciples (and us) in Matthew 24:4-26:

1. "Take heed that no one deceives you. For many will come in My name, saying, 'I am the Christ,' and will deceive many."
2. "You will hear of wars and rumors of wars."

Let's consider both of these warnings, starting with the first one.

## 1. The "sign" of deception

The end times will be filled with deception—count on it. Jesus Christ predicted it. At least six times in His Olivet discourse our Lord warned His disciples against false teachers and deceivers:

• "Take heed that no one deceives you" (24:4).
• "For many will come in My name, saying, 'I am the Christ,' and will deceive many" (24:5).
• "Then many false prophets will rise up and deceive many" (24:11).
• "Then if anyone says to you, 'Look, here is the Christ!' or 'There!' do not believe it" (24:23).
• "For false christs and false prophets will rise and show great signs and wonders to deceive, if possible, even the elect" (24:24).

- "Therefore if they say to you, 'Look, He is in the desert!' do not go out; or 'Look, He is in the inner rooms!' do not believe it" (24:26).

Of course, there have always been false teachers, for that is Satan's way of distorting the truths of God. Jesus called him a "deceiver" and a "liar," declaring that he had been a liar from the very beginning. That is why we have so many cults, religions, and other *-isms* that claim a Christian basis for their beliefs. If Satan cannot get people to disbelieve or rebel against God altogether, he will get them hooked on some false doctrine to lead them astray. There is nothing new about that.

Yet who can deny that everywhere we look today, we find deception growing stronger and more prevalent? Hardly a week goes by that someone doesn't write to us in an attempt to convince us of some new teaching that either is unrelated to Scripture or twists Scripture out of its original meaning.

Dr. M. R. DeHaan, a popular Bible teacher in the fifties and sixties, wrote:

> Never before in all history have there been such divisions in Christendom. There are today over 350 denominations, sects and cults in Protestantism in America alone. All of these claim that they are right and that all others are necessarily wrong.[1]

He then added, "It has been said that a new cult springs up at least once a month in the United States, and that no matter how fantastic and fanciful its teaching may be, or how wild its claims, there are always those who are willing to be deceived."[2]

And that was written over forty years ago! Think of what he would say today with all the occult and spiritualist activities that multiply each day. In the past few years we have all heard the tragic stories of several extremists whose bizarre false teachings ended up costing the lives of hundreds of people: Jim Jones's followers in Guyana, 1978; David Koresh and the Branch Davidians in Texas, 1993; the Heaven's Gate group in southern California, 1997.

But destroying lives is only one form of end-time deception. What about destroying biblical faith? As our Lord said, "Do not fear those who kill the body but cannot kill the soul. But rather fear Him who is able to destroy both soul and body in hell" (Matthew 10:28). As tragic as is the loss of life, it is worse to lose one's soul. False teachers, some of whom use drugs as an inducement to "open" their disciples' minds "to new thought," are today leading thousands of young people astray. And that doesn't even include the cultic UFO groups that are proliferating today.

A *Time* magazine reporter described this problem late in 1997:

> These are the waning years of the 20th century, and out on the margins of spiritual life there's a strange phosphorescence. As predicted, the approach of the year 2000 is coaxing all the crazed out of the woodwork. They bring with them a twitchy hybrid of spirituality and pop obsession, part Christian, part Asian mystic, part Gnostic, part X Files . . . we have seen the Beast of the Apocalypse. It's Bambi in a tunic.[3]

We expect deception to increase the closer we come to the next millennium—particularly if these really are the "last days" the prophets spoke so much about.

In 1982 I was speaking at a prophecy conference at Hume Lake Christian Camps in California. The manager of the camp bookstore sought me out to see what I thought about a full-page ad in the *Los Angeles Times* announcing the arrival of "the Christ Mytraya" of England. Like thousands before him, there was sound and fury and no small speculation, but nothing of substance. He has not brought in the world peace he promised.

The fact that deception and false teachings are increasing should not take us by surprise. Not only did our Lord predict them, but so did the apostle Paul. He warned, "The coming of the lawless one [Antichrist] is according to the working of Satan, with all power, signs, and *lying wonders,* and with all *unrighteous deception* among those who perish, because they did not receive the love of the truth, that they might be saved" (2 Thessalonians 2:9-10, emphasis added). The apostle John, in the book of Revelation, warned several times against false teachings, false religion, and even an official false prophet who leads people astray by the millions during the Tribulation.

The greatest time of deception the world has ever faced or ever will face is the seven-year Tribulation, when the contest between God and Satan for the souls of men will reach its greatest heights. Satan will go all out with deceiving spirits and signs and lying wonders potent enough almost to deceive even "the very elect." Although that period has not yet come, it is highly probable that false teachers and deceivers committed to Satan are already in the world, working their deceptive magic on the minds and emotions of people.

A well-known saying is appropriate here: "Future events cast their shadow before them." Deception will continue to increase as the end times approach. Consequently, it is imperative that God's people be well informed about what the future holds for this world so that they can avoid being deceived. We suggest the following six steps:

A. *Know your Bible!* Jesus said that "the truth shall make you free." The Bible is the truth of God, so the better you know the Scriptures, the better prepared you will be to withstand Satan's deceptive ways. The daily reading of the Scriptures, particularly the New Testament, is a must for every Christian who would know truth. Study biblical prophecy, both from the Scriptures and from those prophecy scholars you trust.

B. *Test the spirits! (1 John 4:1)* Everything comes down to whether a teaching agrees with the Scripture. That is why you should study the Bible regularly, so that you can test any new teaching by the Scripture. Another important question to ask is, What do you believe about Jesus? Most false teachers have a faulty view of Jesus. Some are blatantly false; the more dangerous ones will accept Him as a god but not God in human flesh. Never trust any teacher who does not believe in the virgin birth of Jesus, His sinless life, sacrificial death, bodily resurrection, and His promise to come again physically to this earth. Always ask, Does the message or teaching glorify Jesus? (See John 16:13-14.) Again, the place a teacher gives Jesus is key. The most dangerous teachers are those who speak well of Him but do not exalt Him by recognizing Him as our special object of worship, love, and service.

*C. Seek God's guidance in life and teaching! (Proverbs 3:6)* The Lord wants to guide and direct His children. If you are willing to be led by God, He will guide you to truth.

*D. Avoid immorality!* Nothing clouds the mind like lust and sin. They impair the reasoning of the mind on matters eternal.

*E. Share your faith aggressively with others!* This world has never been more religiously confused. As you witness to others about your faith, you strengthen your own convictions and help many of those to whom you reach out.

*F. Walk in the spirit! (Ephesians 5:17-21)* All Christians in every age should walk in the Spirit, for Paul says that is "the will of the Lord" (verse 17). As the Spirit fills and uses your life, He will make you sensitive to both truth and error.

Many false teachers are endowed with a natural charisma, which at first makes them seem tremendously spiritual and insightful. But by following the steps outlined above, the Holy Spirit within you will witness to your spirit about whether a teacher is dispensing truth or error. I've seen this at work in my own life.

Every month I receive a four-to-six-page "prophecy" from a woman who claims she is an "end-time prophetess." At first I read her letters to compare her teachings to those of Scripture. Finally, I concluded that she was a false prophetess because she so often contradicted the Scriptures. You can be sure of one thing: Since God authored the Bible, He will never inspire His true prophets to teach anything contrary to what He already inspired His prophets, His Son, or His apostles to write in the Old and New Testaments.

## 2. The "sign" of wars and rumors of wars

Did you know that there have been approximately fifteen thousand wars in recorded human history? Mankind has always been eager to settle his disputes or expand his borders through the carnage of war, but the twentieth century in particular has been far bloodier than any century that preceded it. Far more people have died in wars during the past hundred years than in all the centuries before. And the wars just keep proliferating.

Brutal ethnic confrontations have erupted around the globe—in Africa, in Asia, in Eastern Europe, in India, in the territories of the former Soviet Union, and elsewhere—and more of these simmering hot spots seem about to break out into open war.

Yet how did Jesus tell us to respond to such reports?

"See that you are not troubled," He said. And why should we not be troubled? Two reasons:

1. "All these things must come to pass"
2. "But the end is not yet." (Matthew 24:6)

Obviously, wars are not "the sign" of the end! The fact is, however, Christ *did* inject the subject of war into His answer to His disciples' question "What will be the sign of Your coming, and of the end of the age?" This can only mean that "the sign" had to be a special kind of war.

### THE FIRST IDIOM: A SPECIAL KIND OF WAR

Once more recall Jesus' words from Matthew 24:7-8 in response to His disciples' question about the end of the age:

For nation will rise against nation, and kingdom against kingdom. And there will be famines, pestilences, and earthquakes in various places. *All these are the beginning of sorrows.* (emphasis added)

Our Lord used two Hebrew idioms here that His Jewish friends would quickly recognize. The first, based on 2 Chronicles 15:1-7 and Isaiah 19:1-2, is "nation against nation, and kingdom against kingdom" (KJV). He was speaking of a war started by two nations, each combatant soon joined by the surrounding kingdoms until all the nations involved in the prophet's vision are included. In Matthew 24 our Lord had the world in view. So He is saying, "When you see a war started by two single nations that is soon joined by the kingdoms of the world—followed by unprecedented famines, pestilence, and multiple earthquakes at the same time—you have *the sign.*"

We submit that is exactly what occurred in June 1914 when the Archduke of Austria, prince Francis Ferdinand, was shot by a Serbian zealot in the very area of the world where in these days UN peacekeepers must be stationed to keep the Serbs and Croats from killing each other. One month later Austria declared war on Serbia, followed shortly by the other kingdoms of the world, until all but seven nations officially joined the conflict (and even the seven "neutral" countries sent mercenaries). At first historians officially called it "the Great War," for indeed, to that point it was the greatest war in human history. The war involved more men in uniform (estimates total 53 million, 13 million of whom were killed) than all the troops in all the wars before it. But it didn't end there, for an incalculable number of civilians on both sides were injured or killed in the bombings and skirmishes. Not many years later the war's original title was replaced by the even more descriptive title, World War I, thus fulfilling the first idiom our Lord used to describe "the sign."

If this were all that happened in 1914–1918, however, it would not be sufficient to fulfill all of our Lord's prophecy. Remember, He added, "There will be famines, pestilences . . . in various places." A look at history reveals that the flu epidemic of 1918 spread throughout Europe, Canada, and the United States and took more lives than were lost on the battlefields. In Europe, much of this vulnerability to disease was caused by malnutrition and famine as a result of the war. In fact, because of this acute lack of food due to the first World War, farmers were exempted from military service in World War II.

So three parts of the first sign Jesus gave His disciples—a special kind of war, famines, and plagues—were fulfilled at the beginning of the twentieth century. The fourth part, multiple earthquakes at the same time, is more difficult to pin down. However, as I stated in my 1972 book, *The Beginning of the End*:

> I have read statistics that certain earthquakes, like the one in Baluchistan, West Pakistan, on May 31, 1935, was the "most devastating earthquake in all history," but that record has been exceeded several times since then. Major earthquakes have occurred since World War I in such various places as Kansu Province, China; Tokyo, Japan; Persia; India; Peru; Taiwan; and southern California. The only known multiple earthquakes in history have been recorded since World War I. For example, during the Turkish

earthquakes similar reports came in from Africa, South America, South Carolina, and southern California. During a prolonged quake in Helena, Montana, there were similar reports in New York and Honduras.[4]

Because of their frightening intensity, earthquakes have always been considered a sign of God's judgment, at least since His destruction of Sodom and Gomorrah. Earthquakes have been God's way of getting man's attention. When things are going well and man feels secure, he rarely thinks of God. However, when his skyscrapers and "quakeproof" high-rises begin to sway, man looks for something bigger than himself. The shaking of terra firma terrifies him. And well it should!

One Christmas I spoke at the Rotary Club in San Diego at the invitation of Dr. Ron Jones, a dentist and recent convert to Christ. He had served as president for one year, and at his last meeting he wanted to "leave a testimony with the city fathers." At least seven hundred persons were gathered at that luncheon. Most seemed bored with my gospel presentation . . . until an earthquake hit. The dishes rattled, water sloshed in dinner glasses, and the chandeliers swung back and forth. The lights even dimmed momentarily. Everyone in southern California recognizes that feeling because we have occasional tremors. Suddenly I had everyone's rapt attention! Just as man's life looks different from a hospital bed, so he feels more insecure during an earthquake. We believe that is why the end times, both before the Tribulation and during it, will be highlighted by an increase of these frightening tremors.

Something unusual is transpiring with planet Earth!

One seismologist at the Scripps Research Center in La Jolla, California, said, "It is almost as though the earth's plates are gyrating in anticipation of the world's greatest earthquake." In the book of Revelation, the apostle John forewarned that the worst earthquakes ever to hit the planet will occur during the Tribulation. Whether the La Jolla seismologist was describing the earthquake in Revelation 6, 11, or 16 is yet to be determined. But who can doubt that we are seeing the earth being prepared for the coming judgments of God as foretold for the Tribulation?

When all four parts of this "sign" are considered together, we believe it is reasonable to conclude that our planet has already witnessed the beginning of the end.

## THE SECOND HEBREW IDIOM

The mistake many students of prophecy make in rejecting World War I (and its subsequent catastrophes) as the fulfillment of "the sign," mentioned in Matthew 24:3, concerns timing. Everyone realizes that "the Great War" did not usher in the time of the end, for only twenty-two years later the world was plunged into World War II. Jesus did not say the first sign would usher in the end, but said, "All these [the four parts of the one sign] are the beginning of sorrows" (Matthew 24:8). That is the second Hebrew idiom Jesus used. This term "beginning of sorrows" was used by four of the Hebrew prophets to describe a woman in labor and the pain Israel will endure at the end of the age.[5]

Unless a woman's labor is medically induced, her "sorrows . . . in childbirth" mirror those of mother Eve after her sin and expulsion from the Garden of Eden. Her first birth pain does not mean her baby will be born immediately; in fact, she may have thirty or fifty birth pains, some of which are days apart, before giving birth. In most cases, these pains follow a pattern: The first birth pain warns her that her nine months of waiting are nearly over. Still, in most cases she does not look for the birth of the child immediately; she looks for another birth pain. And when it comes, she looks for another. When at last they become more intense and regular—usually three minutes apart for a period of ten minutes—then she and her husband know the birth is near.

World War I did not signal that we should look for the immediate coming of Christ or "the end of the age." It signaled that we should look for more birth pains. And it is our thesis that many other signs, or birth pains, have arisen during these more than eighty years since that "Great War." Many of them grew out of that first "sign," until today the "birth pains" are very intense—and may even be in the last phase. If so, "the end" may be rapidly approaching. In fact, it may be as Jesus said: "Near, even at the doors" (Matthew 24:33, KJV).

# FIVE

## *Jerusalem and Israel:*
## *The Focus of World Attention*

HAS it ever seemed strange to you that almost every night on the evening news the eyes of the world focus on a little country of five million people in the Middle East? And only recently has China, a nation of 1.2 billion people, gained recognition on the international news airwaves. But seldom does Mexico City, one of the largest population centers in the world, draw international attention. Singapore is similarly out of the news, despite what a missionary in Singapore told me several years ago: "If you draw a two-thousand-mile circle around this island, you will encompass 50 percent of the world's population."

Those enormous centers of world population regularly stay out of the news—but when did a week last go by when Israel and Jerusalem did *not* fill the world's headlines? Why this remarkable focus on a little country in the Middle East?

The answer is simply that the Hebrew and Christian prophets had so much to say about Israel and Jerusalem in the end times. The valley of Megiddo is there, probably the most famous valley in the world, where two end-time battles will be fought. The Mediterranean and the Arab allies of Russia will do battle there, and Jerusalem—mentioned in prophecy more than any other city on earth—will be a pain in the neck to the rest of the world, just as it seems to be today.

We have visited that city, and although it is home to many sacred places—such as the traditional Mount Calvary and the garden tomb where it is believed Jesus rose from the dead—it really is not a beautiful place. It is crowded, smelly, and extremely noisy. It has been built and destroyed and rebuilt more than any other city, and today is thriving. Unlike the great cities of the world, it is not famous for any great river that flows through it, nor does it have a harbor to connect it to the great shipping routes of the world; in fact, it is many miles even from the nearest *airport*. It is not the headquarters of any world government body or banking institution—yet it remains at the center of world attention.

## JERUSALEM IS A "BURDENSOME STONE"
Through Zechariah the prophet, God predicted that at the time of the end:

> Behold, I will make Jerusalem a cup of drunkenness to all the surrounding peoples, when they lay siege against Judah and Jerusalem. And it shall happen in that day that I will make Jerusalem a very heavy stone for all peoples; all who would heave it away will surely be cut in pieces, though all nations of the earth are gathered against it. (Zechariah 12:2-3)

One of the biggest problems for the planners of the coming one-world order is what to do with Palestine. The five million Jews who live there are not about to surrender their sovereignty to the United Nations or the United States or anyone else; the smell of the Holocaust is still too fresh in their memories. The Jews have made their last move. They make that clear to anyone who will listen—and so does the God of prophecy.

The significance of Jerusalem's end-time prominence is not lost on Dr. John Walvoord, dean of all living prophecy experts. He writes, "The prophecies about Jerusalem make it clear that the Holy City will be in the center of world events in the end time. . . . The conflict between Israel and the Palestinian Arabs will focus more and more attention on Jerusalem. . . . In all of these situations Jerusalem is the city to watch, as the city of prophetic destiny prepares to act out her final role. The total world situation may be expected more and more to be cast into the mold that prophecy indicates. . . . It seems that the stage and the actors are ready for the final drama, in which Jerusalem will be the key."[1]

This fascination with Israel—at the geographical center of the world and at one point only nine miles wide—is not accidental. It was predicted long ago. Many ancient prophecies are unfolding before our eyes . . . but they could not be fulfilled until Israel was back in her land, as she is today.

## GOD'S TIME CLOCK

I call the regathering of five million Jews back to the Holy Land and their becoming a nation in our generation "the infallible sign" of the approach of the end times. To fully see its significance you must first understand that the regathering of the nation, exactly as the prophets foretold, can be understood only in light of the fact that the Jews exist at all. Never has a nation been able to maintain its national identity, even three to five hundred years after being removed from its homeland—until Israel.

Today you will look in vain for descendants of the Hittite nation, the Assyrian nation, and the Babylonian nation, although all were major powers in the ancient world. In fact, were it not for the Bible, the Hittites would never have been remembered by history, so far into the sands of time had they sunk. At one time scoffers used to ridicule the Bible for even mentioning the Hittites; it was thought they were fictional. But archaeologists in the nineteenth century eventually confirmed the accuracy of Scripture when they uncovered irrefutable evidence of the extensive Hittite Empire. Still, you won't find any Hittites today. Nor will you meet any Assyrians or Babylonians. All of these proud peoples have disappeared forever. They are extinct.

Not so the Jews! Although they were driven out of Israel by the Romans in A.D. 135 after the rebellion of Barchaba—the Roman government even issued a decree that any Jews found in Palestine could be killed on sight—they never ceased to be a people. Scattered throughout eastern Europe, Spain, and eventually to the Americas (where more than half of the world's Jews reside today), they maintained their national heritage through seventeen centuries of bloody exile.

Why have they continued to survive, when mighty Hittites and Assyrians and Babylonians have vanished? *Because God promised!* There are so many promises in the Scripture that God would eventually regather the children of Israel back into their land, that if none could be found in the twentieth century to be made into a nation, the Bible would have been revealed as a fraud.

## O LORD GOD, YOU KNOW

The following is just one example of the many promises that could be named regarding the regathering of Israel.[2] God showed the prophet Ezekiel the bones of the Hebrew nation and asked him if they could live. The godly prophet wisely replied, "O Lord God, You know" (Ezekiel 37:3). Then he writes:

> So I prophesied as I was commanded; and as I prophesied, there was a noise, and suddenly a rattling; and the bones came together, bone to bone. Indeed, as I looked, the sinews and the flesh came upon them, and the skin covered them over; but there was no breath in them. Also He said to me, "Prophesy to the breath, prophesy, son of man, and say to the breath, 'Thus says the Lord God: "Come from the four winds, O breath, and breathe on these slain, that they may live."'" So I prophesied as He commanded me, and breath came into them, and they lived, and stood upon their feet, an exceedingly great army. Then He said to me, "Son of man, these bones are the whole house of Israel. They indeed say, 'Our bones are dry, our hope is lost, and we ourselves are cut off!'"
>
> "Then say to them, 'Thus says the Lord God: "Surely I will take the children of Israel from among the nations, wherever they have gone, and will gather them from every side and bring them into

their own land; and I will make them one nation in the land, on the mountains of Israel; and one king shall be king over them all; they shall no longer be two nations, nor shall they ever be divided into two kingdoms again. They shall not defile themselves anymore with their idols, nor with their detestable things, nor with any of their transgressions; but I will deliver them from all their dwelling places in which they have sinned, and will cleanse them. Then they shall be My people, and I will be their God.'''" (Ezekiel 37:7-11; 21-23)

## HOW IT CAME ABOUT

The gradual growth of the Israeli nation from scattered skeleton to full body development is startling. As Ezekiel's prophecy indicates: "There was a noise, and . . . a shaking, and the bones came together, bone to his bone" (37:7, KJV). Following this, "the sinews and the flesh came up upon them, and the skin covered them above: but there was *no breath* in them" (37:8, KJV, emphasis added). From the sound of an earthshaking event (World War I), the seemingly dead nation of Israel was to *gradually* formulate a body, *after* which the spirit would be breathed into it. We submit that history records the birth of the nation of Israel exactly in this manner, beginning in 1917.

The late Bible scholar Dr. David L. Cooper used to tell how he clearly remembered the astonishing events whose roots can be traced to World War I. By 1916 the war was going adversely for England. German machine guns and other advanced weaponry were cutting down the flower of Europe's manhood. England was desperate to find a rapid method of manufacturing TNT and a smokeless gunpowder. A brilliant Jew named Chaim Weizmann invented such a formula that made possible the rapid production of these vital materials, thus changing the course of the war. In return, David Lloyd George, representing the British government, told Dr. Weizmann to name his price. Rejecting personal reward, Weizmann requested that Palestine be declared the international homeland for the Jewish people. Consequently the Balfour Declaration was drawn up and signed on November 2, 1917. A famous letter recounts what happened next:

Dear Lord Rothchild:

I have much pleasure in conveying to you, on behalf of his Majesty's Government, the following declaration of sympathy with Jewish Zionist aspirations, which has been submitted to, and approved by, the Cabinet. His Majesty's Government views with favor the establishment in Palestine of a national home for the Jewish people, and will use their best endeavors to facilitate the achievement of this object, it being clearly understood that nothing shall be done which may prejudice the civil and religious rights of existing non-Jewish communities in Palestine, or the rights and political status enjoyed by Jews in any other country.

I should be grateful if you would bring this declaration to the knowledge of the Zionist Federation.

Yours sincerely,
Arthur James Balfour[3]

Could it be mere coincidence of language that the impetus to officially start the regathering of Israel was prophesied as a "noise and shaking," and that the fulfillment took place during the loudest war—due to the prodigious amounts of TNT and gunpowder used—the world had ever yet known? I was stationed in Germany after World War II and heard enough TNT exploded to know that it always generates a great shaking. Fearing that our former Russian allies would sweep down into Germany and confiscate our stockpiles of P-51, P-47, and P-38 aircraft, the U.S. government ordered the planes destroyed. For two months our airbase was shaken by the detonation of TNT as those once-mighty fighters were blown to bits. It is not necessary to be dogmatic on this point, but the parallel between dynamite and a "noise" and a "shaking" does seem noteworthy.

The gathering of the Jews into Palestine after the signing of the Balfour Treaty was indeed a gradual development— "bone to his bone." In 1917 it is estimated that less than 25,000 Jews lived in the land. By 1922 there were 83,000; by 1932—180,000; by 1935—300,000; by 1937— 430,000; and by 1945, more than 500,000. Today the population is at 5 million and growing. In the same way the population has grown, so has the geographical size of the nation. In the early days the Jews purchased, with Zionist funds, 350,000 acres of land, primarily for agricultural purposes. Now it is a nation of about 7,992 square miles, with another approximately seven thousand square miles of occupied territory in the Golan Heights, in the West Bank, and in the Gaza Strip. Between 1917 and 1948, slowly but certainly, "bone came to [his] bone."

But while God blessed Israel, Britain reneged on her 1917 treaty. In 1939, after much deliberation over the growing conflicts between Arabs and Jews, Britain issued a white paper that favored Arab independence and control of the area. After failing to keep peace between the Arabs and Jews following World War II, the British withdrew from Palestine; shortly thereafter the National Council and the General Zionist Council proclaimed from Tel Aviv the establishment of the sovereign state of Israel. The date was May 14, 1948. David Ben Gurion was appointed Prime Minister, and Dr. Chaim Weizmann was elected president of a provisional council. Both the United States and Russia recognized the new nation which, after much debate, was accepted as a member nation of the United Nations by a vote of 37 to 12.

## THREE MIRACLES FOR ISRAEL

In Luke's version of the Olivet discourse (Matthew 24–25, the most important two chapters on prophecy in the Bible), Jesus prophesied that "Jerusalem will be trampled by Gentiles until the times of the Gentiles are fulfilled" (Luke 21:24). In the next four verses, the Lord Himself put a time frame on the "times of the Gentiles," which began with the Babylonian captivity in 606 B.C. and will continue to the end of the Tribulation and the coming of Christ.

How close are we to the end of "the times of the Gentiles"? Just a miracle away. That the Jews even exist today is a miracle, but it is just as miraculous that in 1967, for the first time since the Babylonian captivity, they took charge of Jerusalem. That has to be the most impressive fulfillment of Bible prophecy in twenty centuries!

In Israel's famous Six Day War, the war hero General Moshe Dayan did a strange thing. After planting the Israeli flag on the Muslim Dome of the Rock (which now occupies the place where the Jews must rebuild their temple), he decided to be conciliatory toward his Muslim captives. Instead of keeping this site, coveted by every orthodox Jew in the world, he decided to take down the flag and give the Muslims control over that sacred spot.

Why? Apparently this general, a secularist Jew, was trying to placate the Arab world. Even though his armies had won the war, he knew his Arab neighbors outnumbered him fifty or more to one. Thinking he would make friends of the Arabs, he succeeded only in making his friends angry. It may be that the general thought it was safer to let the Arabs keep their holy place than to permit the religious Jews to have it, for he knew they would immediately dismantle the mosque and rebuild their temple. This would, of course, have ignited a holy war.

Some religious Jews still have not forgiven Dayan for his actions. But in so doing he may well have been fulfilling prophecy. For today, although the Israelis control most of Jerusalem, they still do not control the Arab quarter and the much coveted temple site. And so the "times of the Gentiles" have not yet come to an end.

The fact that the last fifty years has seen a worldwide regathering and reestablishment of the nation of Israel—which is now poised in precisely the setting required for the revealing of the Antichrist and the start of the Tribulation—is God's grand indicator that many other current world developments are prophetically significant. Dr. John Walvoord says,

> Of the many peculiar phenomena which characterize the present generation, few events can claim equal significance as far as Biblical prophecy is

concerned with that of the return of Israel to their land. It constitutes a preparation for the end of the age, the setting for the coming of the Lord for His church, and the fulfillment of Israel's prophetic destiny. Israel, God's "super-sign" of the end times, is a clear indicator that time is growing short. God is preparing the world for the final events leading up to Israel's national regeneration.[4]

## ONLY A BREATH AWAY

All that is left for Ezekiel's vision to be fulfilled relates to the statement "but there was no breath in them" (Ezekiel 37:8). That expression is not difficult for Bible students to decipher, since "breath" or "wind" often refers to the Holy Spirit. That would indicate that, one of these days, Israel is going to have a fresh visitation of the Holy Spirit, when a mighty revival sweeps the land. This agrees with many passages that predict a great spiritual awakening when the Jews call upon the Messiah they rejected in A.D. 30 (see Joel 2:18-32; Zechariah 12:10–13:2; Romans 11:26-27; Revelation 7:1-10).

It is important to note that this revival is the *only* part of this prophecy that has not yet been fulfilled. Over five decades have passed since Israel became a nation, and it still rejects Christ as Messiah. That is the reason the prophet challenged them to "hear the word of the Lord!" (Ezekiel 37:4). If the nation were to genuinely "hear" the scriptural testimony to the true identity of the Messiah, it would be forced to recognize Christ as the Lord.

## RENEWED SPIRITUAL INTEREST

The last time I was in Israel, our Jewish guide, a college professor and major in the Israeli army, told me that many Jews are examining the messianic prophecies of the Old Testament as never before. The religious Jews are so concerned about this that they are themselves trying to learn the qualifications to expect of the Messiah. They are convinced that the time of Messiah's revelation to the nation is near.

In my book *Jesus, Who Is He?*, I tell of one of the few rabbis in America who is expert in both the Old and New Testaments. He admitted on television that Jesus fulfilled so many messianic prophecies during His lifetime that He was the Messiah for the Gentiles—but the Jewish Messiah has yet to come. Some Jews are beginning to recognize that their Messiah will be just like Jesus Christ! That is how close the nation is to the "breath" stage. Israel is just "a breath away" from turning to her Messiah.

## THE GENERATION THAT SEES ISRAEL REEMERGE

It is time now to learn a "parable from the fig tree":

> Now learn this parable from the fig tree: When its branch has already become tender and puts forth leaves, you know that summer is near. So you also, when you see all these things, know that it is near, at the doors. Assuredly, I say to you, this generation will by no means pass away till all these things are fulfilled. (Matthew 24:32-34)

Many prophecy students interpret this passage to mean that when we see the rise of Israel as a nation (as we did in 1948), we will know that the time of the end is "near—at the doors." They reason that when a fig tree is used symbolically in Scripture, it usually refers to the nation Israel. If that is a valid assumption (and we believe it is), then when Israel officially became a nation in 1948, that was the "sign" of Matthew 24:1-8, the beginning "birth pains"—it meant that the "end of the age" is "near." It was as if the tree were planted in 1914–1918 when the first "birth pain" was felt, but it did not grow into a full-blown tree capable of budding until 1948 when Israel was granted statehood, thus fulfilling Ezekiel 37:1-8.

If indeed this is what our Lord had in mind when He spoke of the fig tree in Matthew 24:32, then we can assume we are "in the season" of our Lord's coming. For He said: "So you also, when you see all these things, know that it is near, at the doors" (Matthew 24:33). In other words, when all the signs mentioned appear—World War I, famines, pestilence, earthquakes, and Israel becoming a nation—you know that Jesus' return is close at hand.

## TWO SETS OF "THESE THINGS"

There are two sets of "these things" in Matthew 24:33-34. If you fail to distinguish between them, you will not understand what our Lord said. They are definitely *not* the same. The first "these things" in verse 33 refers to the tumultuous events begun by verses 7 and 8. The second "these things" refers to the prophetic future, including the Tribulation and the glorious appearing of Christ.

Therefore our Lord means in verses 32 and 33 that just as a budding tree indicates summer is coming, so the first "things" means the Lord's coming is near, even "at the very doors." We can thus know the season of His return.

Great care should be taken not to set dates in this connection! Jesus said, "But of that day and hour no one knows, no, not even the angels of heaven, but My Father only" (Matthew 24:36). The study of prophecy has probably suffered more from date setters than from anything else. On the other hand, this passage clearly indicates we *can* know the season. It is our belief that we are not only in the season but in the latter portion of it. We must not, however, make our interpretation any more specific than the Lord made His prophecy. As we shall see, He indicated the season could last as long as a "generation."

## THE KEY GENERATION

Now we are ready to examine the key to the timing of this whole passage and answer the disciples' question of Matthew 24:3, "When will these things be?" The key is found in verse 34. Jesus said, "This generation will by no means pass away till all these things [the second "things"] are fulfilled." The crucial issue concerns the meaning of "this generation," for whatever generation He had in mind would not pass away until the Second Coming occurred.

In Greek, the demonstrative pronoun *haute* (this) always refers to the person or thing mentioned immediately before it. The thing mentioned just before "generation" involves those who see the sign of Israel as she either becomes a recognized nation or when she takes possession of most of Jerusalem. There seem to be only four generations from which to choose:

1. *The disciples' generation.* But nothing like this happened historically during their lifetime. Their generation has passed, and the Lord has not yet come, so it doesn't seem possible He had the disciples' generation in mind.

2. *The generation that saw World War I.* It was thought by many fine Bible teachers to be a possibility. That scenario becomes increasingly unlikely today because most of that generation has already passed away. Still, the unlikely possibility that "this generation" means the generation that saw World War I should not be ruled out completely for another five years or so.

3. *The generation that saw Israel officially become a nation in 1948.* That generation was old enough to "see" the United Nations officially recognize Israel as a nation. Assuming this generation includes children ten years of age or older in 1948, it probably means the generation born around 1938—give or take five or ten years.

4. *The generation that lived through the Six Day War of 1967.* That war took place when the Israeli army marched into Jerusalem and raised its flag over the city. This would mean the generation born around 1957.

One thing is for sure: It's dangerous to be dogmatic! Which is why we prefer to say we believe "this generation" refers to those alive in 1948. It may, however, mean those alive in 1967 or those alive during some yet future war when the Jews will once again gain total control of their holy city.

## HOW LONG IS A GENERATION?

The second major interpretive issue regarding this prophecy is the meaning of "generation." How long is a biblical generation?

Shortly after Israel was recognized as a nation in 1948, many prophecy teachers predicted that Christ would return by 1988. They reasoned that since a generation was forty years, then all these things would be completed by

1988, including the return of Christ. Obviously they were mistaken! They earnestly wanted to promote the imminent coming of Christ, but instead their unscriptural speculation dulled interest in His return. One man wrote a book titled *Eighty-Eight Reasons Christ Will Return in 1988*. Even though he was wrong, he sold three hundred thousand copies of his book. When 1988 came and went, instead of admitting he was wrong, he refigured his calculations and decided he had erred by one year. So he rushed back into print to say Christ would return in 1989. I have been told there are thirty thousand unsold copies of that book in a warehouse somewhere. And that is where they belong! Such speculations bring only harm and disillusionment to the body of Christ.

This man erred in many ways, but particularly by assuming that a generation in the Bible is exactly forty years. It is not a safe assumption. The fact that Israel wandered in the wilderness for forty years, or that David and Solomon reigned in Israel for forty years, does not mean four decades is the biblical length of a generation. As my friend and prophecy scholar Dr. Arnold Fruchtenbaum has written, "The Bible nowhere limits the period of a generation simply to forty years. The one place where the term *generation* is given a specific time length, it is reckoned to be 100 years (Genesis 15:13–16). Actually, the term generation can mean 20, 40, 70, 80, or 100 years."[5]

Psalm 90:10 tells us, "The days of our years are threescore years and ten; and if by reason of strength they be fourscore years, yet is their strength labour and sorrow" (KJV). Moses here suggests that a generation is seventy to eighty years. This does not mean that a generation is limited to seventy or eighty years; he is merely acquainting us with the general length of a generation.

We should weigh the Lord's words very carefully here. He said, "This generation will by no means pass away till all these things are fulfilled" (Matthew 24:34). How many people make up a generation? No particular number—even one person who comprehended the significant events of 1948 would qualify to represent the "generation." However, we should not expect the entire generation to pass away before Jesus returns! Jesus was aware that the last generation before His coming would be marked by longevity—we are acquainted with several ninety-year-old men and women—so "this generation" is *not* limited to eighty years.

Therefore, if we use either the 1948 or the 1967 date, apply the span of a person's lifetime (give or take ten years for a person to "see" and comprehend the events), then subtract seven or more years for the Tribulation and an interim period between the Rapture and the signing of the covenant with Israel, we come to the same time period for the return of our Lord that many others have suggested: sometime between the turn of the century and the first quarter of the twenty-first century. In other words, *our generation.*

While we cannot be certain that ours is the last generation before our Lord returns, we are certain of one thing: our generation has more reason to believe He *could* return during our lifetime than any generation preceding us.

## ISRAEL, GOD'S KEY TO THE FUTURE

For many years Israel has been called "God's timepiece" or "God's time clock" by Bible prophecy teachers. Confirmation that these are indeed the end times is seen almost every night on the evening news as Israel's five million Jews occupy our attention. The miraculous return of the Jews to their homeland after seventeen hundred years in exile may well be the most significant of the end-time signs, even the "super sign." Significantly, this return happened in our generation—more weighty evidence that we are indeed living in the end times.

That should remind us not only that God keeps His promises, but that God's time clock has begun winding down to the midnight hour of this age. Something of enormous proportions is about to happen, just as Jesus and the prophets predicted.

Consider this: The nation of Israel, for its size, is one of the most militarily prepared nations on earth. It has the atom bomb and is suspected to possess the neutron bomb. It has a much improved antimissile defense system since the U.S.–made Patriot missiles did such a poor job of protecting the nation from Saddam Hussein's SCUD missiles during the Gulf War. It has the latest weapons delivery systems and could wipe out any army or country that attacked it, a fact its Arab neighbors well understand. Frankly, we believe that is the only human reason the Arab countries do not attack; they know they are no match for Israel.

One of my longtime friends is a Navy reserve pilot, current in all F-16 and F-18 fighters. Through the years he has befriended many Israeli air force pilots, some of whom have risen to the highest rank. The last time my friend was in Israel, he and a general friend flew F-18s on a training mission. Afterward he told me that the Israelis have taken our best fighters and latest equipment and improved on them. Their planes, which are on constant alert, can probably perform better than our own and can deliver their bombs more accurately.

The Jews have their backs to the wall and will use any means necessary to defend their homeland against any aggressor. On the opposite side of the fence is an intense Arab hatred. Israel's several Muslim neighbors are backed and armed by oil-rich countries who share their faith and their hatred of Israel. The Arabs will not rest until Israel is driven from the land—and Israel will not be driven from the land.

America lies in the middle. Sixty-five percent of our nation's oil comes from the Israel-hating nations of the Middle East. You have doubtless noted a sea change in the political attitude of federal officials who want Israel to surrender its land in the name of "negotiations." That is madness—hostilities are doomed to erupt sooner or later.

The point is that Israel and her Arab neighbors, who comprise only one one-thousandth of the world's population, are at the center of the world's stage—just as the Bible said they would be in the end times.

# PART TWO

# *Events*

## SIX

## *The Great Apostasy*

**Apostasy**
**2 Timothy 4:1-4**

TO SAY arbitrarily, Pontifex Maximus Peter wrote in an official Enigma Babylon declaration, *that the Jewish and Protestant Bible, containing only the Old and New Testaments, is the final authority for faith and practice, represents the height of intolerance and disunity. It flies in the face of all we have accomplished, and adherents to that false doctrine are hereby considered heretics.*

*TRIBULATION FORCE, 401*

Readers of our Left Behind series have been introduced to an oily character we named Peter Mathews, who after the Rapture becomes the head of an apostate one-world religion. Mathews doesn't believe that Jesus rose physically from the dead, or that He was born of a virgin, that the Bible is any more inspired than any other religious sourcebook, or that Christianity offers the only way to God. Mathews, of course, is entirely a work of fiction.

Or is he?

What would you think of an Episcopal bishop who loudly championed the views that:

- the resurrection of Christ was not a real event but a legend
- there was no empty tomb, no angels, no appearances
- no reasonable person could believe in the literal interpretation of the Bible
- the virgin of a literal Bible—the virgin of annunciation, Bethlehem, and the manger—"will have to go"
- the church should actively endorse and even celebrate homosexual behavior, as well as heterosexual liaisons outside of marriage

John Shelby Spong, the Episcopal bishop of Newark, New Jersey, has enthusiastically promoted all of those heretical views in his many controversial books. In his latest work, *Why Christianity Must Change or Die*—which he says is the summation of his life's work—he insists that the first-century ideas that shaped the New Testament are hopelessly outdated and provincial and must be discarded if Christianity is to survive in the modern world. He calls himself a "believer in exile."

One reviewer of this book wrote, "Oddly enough, Spong's views do not seem particularly new. In fact, his views seem very much in keeping with the religious humanist variety of Unitarianism. What is remarkable is not the beliefs themselves, but that an Episcopal bishop would be the one to embrace them."[1]

Remarkable, yes—but certainly not unforeseen.

## THE GREAT DEPARTING

The apostle Paul predicted that a time would come when men and women would turn away from the faith "once for all delivered to the saints" (Jude 1:3) and instead embrace heresy. He wrote to the young Thessalonian church:

> Concerning the coming of our Lord Jesus Christ and our being gathered to him, we ask you, brothers, not to become easily unsettled or alarmed by some prophecy, report or letter supposed to have come from us, saying that the day of the Lord has already come. Don't let anyone deceive you in any way, for that day will not come *until the rebellion occurs.*
> (2 Thessalonians 2:1-3, NIV, emphasis added)

The apostle is saying that before the day of the Lord and the revelation of the man of sin, there will first be a "rebellion" or a "departing." The Greek word translated "rebellion" is *apostasia,* the source word for our English term "apostasy." It means a defection from the truth or a departure from that which was given at the first. The plain meaning of this prophecy is that before Christ returns, many who once were entrusted with the truth will depart from it.

Robert L. Thomas, writing in *The Expositor's Bible Commentary,* explains that the word *apostasia* "points to a deliberate abandonment of a former professed position. . . . After the catching away of those in Christ (1 Thess. 4:17), all who are truly in him will be gone. Conditions will be ripe for people, especially those who call themselves Christian but are not really such, to turn their backs on God in what they do as well as in what they already have in thought. Then their insincerity will demonstrate itself outwardly. This worldwide anti-God move-ment will be so universal as to earn for itself a special des-ignation: '*the* apostasy'—i.e., the climax of the increasing apostate tendencies evident before the rapture of the church."[2]

This isn't the only biblical passage that speaks of this "departing." In 1 Timothy 4:1-2 Paul adds these addi-tional details:

> Now the Spirit expressly says that in latter times
> some will depart from the faith, giving heed to
> deceiving spirits and doctrines of demons, speaking
> lies in hypocrisy, having their own conscience seared
> with a hot iron.

The word translated "depart" means "to withdraw, be-come apostate." Commentator Ralph Earle writes, "In-stead of being led by the Holy Spirit, these apostates give their attention to deceiving spirits and the teaching of 'demons.' Since this last word occurs only here in the pas-toral Epistles, we might pause to look at it. KJV has 'dev-ils,' and British scholars still use this term (cf. *New English Bible*). But in the Greek there is a clear distinction between *daimonion* ('demon,' often in the pl.), and *diabolos* ('devil,' regularly in the sing.) The New Testament clearly teaches that there are many 'demons' but only one 'devil.' The plural of *diabolos* occurs only in the Pastorals (1 Tim. 3:11; 2 Tim. 3:3; Titus 2:3), where it is used for human 'slanderers.'"[3] And *The New Bible Commentary* says sim-ply, "Over against the Spirit and the mystery of godliness stand misleading spirits and their false teaching."[4]

This time of "departing," says Paul, will be led by human "devils" who slander God and His work. Their teaching may drip with honey, but it is produced, packaged, and distributed by the demons of hell.

So much for the apostate teachers. But an apostasy can't really get going unless the false teachers behind it are able to attract some loyal followers. So Paul also tells us about them:

> For the time will come when men will not put up with sound doctrine. Instead, to suit their own desires, they will gather around them a great number of teachers to say what their itching ears want to hear. They will turn their ears away from the truth and turn aside to myths. (2 Timothy 4:3-4, NIV)

False teachers rarely exist in a spiritual vacuum. They start appearing because people want to hear and act on their flesh-stroking doctrines. In many ways, spirituality is as much a commodity as is electronics or beef and is subject to similar laws of supply and demand. In this passage Paul says carnal people "gather around them a great number of teachers to say what their itching ears want to hear." In other words, the people demand to hear ungodly fables, and soon false teachers start appearing to supply the demand—like flies to a garbage dump.

Paul instructed his young protégé, Timothy, that his primary responsibility as a pastor in Ephesus was to defend and proclaim sound doctrine. Why? Because the time would come when people would not listen to the truth but would heap to themselves false teachers eager to say whatever their patrons' itching ears wanted to hear—ears that one commentator said "were always pricking with an uneasy desire for what would gratify the taste of a carnal, self-willed heart."[5]

We get another sobering picture of this end-time departing when we study the Savior's words about the church at Laodicea in Revelation 3. As I explain in my commentary *Revelation Illustrated and Made Plain,* the seven churches profiled in Revelation 2–3 furnish us with a picture of the church throughout history. Each of the seven churches represents a different era in church history. Laodicea, the final church in the series, illustrates what the church will be like just before the Rapture occurs. Here is what our Lord says about that apostate church:

> I know your deeds, that you are neither cold nor hot. I wish you were either one or the other! So, because you are lukewarm—neither hot nor cold—I am about to spit you out of my mouth. You say, "I am rich; I have acquired wealth and do not need a thing." But you do not realize that you are wretched, pitiful, poor, blind and naked. I counsel you to buy from me gold refined in the fire, so you can become rich; and white clothes to wear, so you can cover your shameful nakedness; and salve to put on your eyes, so you can see. (Revelation 3:15-18, NIV)

Laodicea was a rich inland city located about forty miles from Ephesus. Greek to the core in both culture and learning, its industries made it a thriving center of commerce. We know that the church there must have been wealthy, since three church buildings dating to the early days of Christianity have been discovered among the city's ruins.

Unlike the church at Ephesus, which is well known for its evangelistic outreaches, Laodicea left no record of any gospel preaching in its area. Laodicea is the only church among the seven profiled in Revelation 2–3 about which the Lord had nothing good to say.

This church of the last days was neither zealous for good works nor lifeless. Instead it was indifferent. It claimed to represent Jesus Christ but never saw a soul transformed from darkness to life.

You tell me: Does today's church look and smell like the church at Laodicea? Certainly the church of today is rich. Her church buildings are the best. She has wondrous architecture, multimillion-dollar buildings, and a large but unregenerate church membership.

I believe the church at large today is in the same plight as those religionists described by Jesus in Matthew 7:22-23: "Many will say to me on that day, 'Lord, Lord, did we not prophesy in your name, and in your name drive out demons and perform many miracles?' Then I will tell them plainly, 'I never knew you. Away from me, you evildoers!'" (NIV).

## THE DRIFT TOWARD APOSTASY

Of course, the true church of Jesus Christ has always been plagued by apostasy—but nothing like at present. The devil has a fiendishly clever way of sowing tares among the wheat (the church), just as our Lord predicted in His kingdom of heaven parables in Matthew 13. The Bible makes it clear that doctrinal confusion will rise to a crescendo in the latter days, leading many to depart from the faith as they eagerly follow deceiving spirits and willingly adopt doctrines of demons.

It has been well established that many of the false religions and cults of history have grown out of deceptions or "apostate" branches of Christianity. Through the centuries whenever the church permitted theological error to creep in, God raised up reformers to call His people back to the foundational doctrines of Scripture. Or He raised up others who led movements to separate themselves according to the Scriptures; that is how many of our present denominations were formed.

In the middle of the nineteenth century, almost all U.S. denominations had one branch, all of which were basically fundamental; they adhered to the orthodox doctrines of the founders of their group. The Civil War caused several of these denominations to split along geographical lines, but the issues were social, not theological. Little changed by the turn of the century. The church was still basking in the afterglow of the Charles A. Finney evangelistic crusades, followed by those of D. L. Moody and others.

At that time certain individuals educated in Europe and influenced by German rationalism began teaching in denominational seminaries. The devil knew the best way to inject his apostate doctrine into the churches was to infiltrate the seminaries, indoctrinate young ministers, and send them into the churches to spread his false concepts across the land. The degree of faithfulness to the Word of God found in these denominations today directly reflects the success of denominational leaders in keeping heretics out of their seminaries two generations ago. It is a constant fight! Some who won the battle during the first half of this century seem to be losing it now.

One illustration of the effectiveness of this devilish method is a now-deceased seminary professor. For more than twenty-five years he occupied "the chair of Christian ethics" in what was the largest seminary in the nation. He helped to orient the thinking of thousands of present-generation ministers. Several years ago this man was identified under oath as a member of the Communist party. Is it any wonder that his denomination is the most radical and unbelieving in Christendom? It wouldn't take many such men, working consistently through the years, to turn an entire denomination away from the faith of the Bible.

This man's forerunners must have been at work prior to and during World War I, because modernism became increasingly powerful shortly after 1920 and openly challenged fundamentalists for control of the seminaries and the denominations. Sad to say, in many cases they won.

Since those days fragmentation has been the result. Many churches and groups broke with their parent denominations to start their own; later some of these splintered again. Today there are hundreds of Protestant groups and denominations. One hundred and twenty years ago, the group of which I am a member had only one denomination in this country; at last count there were twenty-nine.

In some big denominations, local congregations have little to say about the calling of a minister, and power is centralized in the hands of a few. Under these conditions, aggressive apostates have gained much influence. Millions of members have faced the decision whether to stay in the denomination or pull out and start a new church. Most of those who have "stayed with the ship" have been unable to stop the continual drift toward apostasy.

## THE DEADENING EFFECTS OF APOSTASY

Liberal churchmen organized the Federal Council of Churches in the 1940s, but it became so ultraliberal and pro-Communist that laymen abandoned it in droves. It was dissolved, and the National Council of Churches of Christ in America became the spokesman for cultural Christianity. Although the structure was changed slightly, a close look at the people in charge revealed a game of musical chairs; many of the former leaders of the Federal Council directed the new National Council.

This religious organization has accelerated the church's departure from the Bible and sent it deeper into apostasy. Through neglecting and rejecting Bible teachings, this group has been bringing in practices and programs that border on blasphemy.

The modernism of the first part of the century was too radical for many people and even some leaders, so a new group of theologians introduced neo-orthodoxy in the thirties. In this approach, leaders use some of the language of the fundamentalists but mean something quite different. This subterfuge has deceived many. Some in this apostate movement degenerated to the point that a number of its seminary professors launched the "God is dead" movement. They claim to be "Christian atheists," whatever that means (probably something akin to "believer in exile").

Relationships between socialistic politics and theological apostasy have been consistent. The early modernists rejected the basic teachings of Christianity, such as the virgin birth of Christ, His deity, His sinlessness, and many other essential doctrines. Since that left them no spiritual message for the people, they came up with the social gospel. This has been the one consistent chord of the apostate movement in America and has thrust its adherents into the forefront of the social revolution.

Today most liberal denominations are aligned with liberal social causes, while theological conservatives tend to align themselves with conservative government policy. In fact, today's vicious attack on moral absolutes has not been led merely by secular humanists but has been advocated by liberal ministers of many mainline denominations and leaders of the National Council of Churches. Some of the religious leaders who are most aggressively pushing homosexuality are apostates on the doctrines of the Virgin Birth, the deity of Christ, and the inerrancy of Scripture. An apostate in theology will hardly adhere to the moral directives of the Scriptures!

Apostasy ruins whole denominations. The Methodist church could be seen as an illustration. When I started out in the ministry, Methodists outnumbered all other Protestant denominations, a carryover from the days of the holiness movement of the nineteenth century. Then apostates began taking over schools such as Union Theological Seminary and produced a generation of apostate ministers, who in turn went into Methodist and Presbyterian churches and seminaries, where they apostatized many of the churches. As a consequence, both of these denominations have suffered a serious drop in church attendance and membership; whole groups have split off and started new groups based on the Scriptures. Many members became so disillusioned with this liberal heresy that they quit attending church altogether.

Not only does apostasy kill Christian doctrine and practice, but God also gives up apostates to their reprobate minds, and they begin to die. Today these "mainline" churches, as they like to call themselves, have lost touch with mainline Christian doctrine. The liberal news media still contacts them when seeking comment from the Christian community, not because they stand for Christ, but because they share the same moral agenda as the media. However, these churches have lost enormous influence with the men and women in the pews.

## HOW CLOSE ARE WE?

The story of how God overruled during this century of apostasy is too lengthy to detail here, but it is a thrilling story. Toward the end of the nineteenth century and throughout the twentieth century, D. L. Moody and others were burdened to start Bible institutes, Christian training centers, and Christian colleges, which have prepared an army of ministers who hold tenaciously to the Scriptures. This and other movements of the Spirit caused phenomenal growth among conservative churches until a recent Gallup poll indicated that 41 percent of the American population claims to be "born again," a doctrine seldom or never mentioned by the apostate denominations.

Were it not for the moving of the Holy Spirit and the obedience of millions of Christians to the plain teaching of Scripture, America would today be a totally secularized nation, thus destroying the greatest source of world missions in history. Instead, even in this day of denominational apostasy, the Holy Spirit is working in the hearts of enormous numbers of true believers. It has intrigued me that those churches that teach the Bible, depend upon the ministry of the Holy Spirit, and do the work of evangelism are growing, dynamic congregations. At the same time, apostate churches are dying by the thousands—another sign of the end times.

# SEVEN

## *Blooming in the Desert*

THE humble man called himself a botanist, but he
was in truth a chemical engineer who had concocted
a synthetic fertilizer that caused the desert sands of
Israel to bloom like a greenhouse.

"Irrigation has not been a problem for decades,"
the old man said. "But all that did was make the
sand wet. My formula, added to the water, fertilizes
the sand."

Buck was not a scientist, but he knew enough to
shake his head at that simple statement. Rosenzweig's
formula was fast making Israel the richest nation on
earth, far more profitable than its oil-laden neighbors.
Every inch of ground blossomed with flowers and
grains, including produce never before conceivable in
Israel. The Holy Land became an export capital, the
envy of the world, with virtually zero unemployment.
Everyone prospered.

*LEFT BEHIND, 8*

While most of the major events depicted in our Left Behind series are based directly on specific biblical prophecies about the Tribulation and the end times, a few significant plot elements depend less on careful prophetic interpretation than on pure imagination. One such imaginative element in the first novel was the development by an Israeli scientist (Chaim Rosenzweig) of a secret chemical compound that could make the desert bloom and its inventors rich—and by consequence, its neighbors envious and angry.

While the invention of such a chemical compound has no basis in Scripture, as a literary device it did enable us to develop two plot lines with definite prophetic bloodlines:

1. The extraordinary blessing of God on the physical land of Israel;
2. A plausible "trigger" for the surprise attack of Russia and her allies against Israel (see chapter 8).

That God intends to shower His remarkable blessing upon the land of Israel in the future is made obvious in several passages from the prophet Isaiah:

> The desert and the parched land will be glad; the wilderness will rejoice and blossom. Like the crocus, it will burst into bloom; it will rejoice greatly and shout for joy. . . . Water will gush forth in the wilderness and streams in the desert. The burning sand will become a pool, the thirsty ground bubbling springs. In the haunts where jackals once lay, grass and reeds and papyrus will grow. (Isaiah 35:1-2, 6-7, NIV)

I will make rivers flow on barren heights, and
springs within the valleys. I will turn the desert
into pools of water, and the parched ground into
springs. I will put in the desert the cedar and the
acacia, the myrtle and the olive. I will set pines in
the wasteland, the fir and the cypress together, so
that people may see and know, may consider and
understand, that the hand of the Lord has done this,
that the Holy One of Israel has created it. (Isaiah
41:18-20, NIV)

See, I am doing a new thing! Now it springs up; do
you not perceive it? I am making a way in the desert
and streams in the wasteland. (Isaiah 43:19, NIV)

God is determined to show the world that He has not
forgotten about Israel, nor has He taken His eye off the
land of promise. In our time we have seen several areas of
the world turn from fertile grassland and productive farm-
land into barren, scorched wilderness; the Sahara Desert in
northern Africa, for example, continues year by year to
swallow ever more acreage. But when was the last time we
saw a desert turn into a lush garden? That, however, is exactly what God has promised to do in the land of Israel!

While we believe God will accomplish this great feat during the reign of the millennial kingdom, already we see hints
of what He has in mind. In the years since Israel became a
nation, rainfall has increased remarkably throughout Palestine. As a consequence, the nation has produced crops of as-
tounding proportions. In fact, when we were in Israel some
time ago, we saw fruit and vegetables larger than those
grown in the famed Imperial Valley of California!

One thing is for sure: The Israeli desert certainly appears ready to be "glad," to "rejoice" and "blossom," and to "burst into bloom" like the crocus. How could it be otherwise? For when the hand of God caresses a blessed piece of land, the earth has no choice but to explode into a breathtaking display of life.

# EIGHT

## *A Disastrous Sneak Attack*

THE radio was alive with reports from Israeli pilots.
They had not been able to get airborne in time to do
anything but watch as the entire Russian air offensive seemed to destroy itself.

Miraculously, not one casualty was reported in all
of Israel. Otherwise Buck might have believed some
mysterious malfunction had caused missile and
plane to destroy each other. But witnesses reported
that it had been a firestorm, along with rain and
hail and an earthquake, that consumed the entire
offensive effort.

Had it been a divinely appointed meteor shower?
Perhaps. But what accounted for hundreds and
thousands of chunks of burning, twisted, molten
steel smashing to the ground in Haifa, Jerusalem,
Tel Aviv, Jericho, even Bethlehem—leveling ancient
walls but not so much as scratching one living creature? Daylight revealed the carnage and exposed

Russia's secret alliance with Middle Eastern nations, primarily Ethiopia and Libya.

Among the ruins, the Israelis found combustible material that would serve as fuel and preserve their natural resources for more than six years. Special task forces competed with buzzards and vultures for the flesh of the enemy dead, trying to bury them before their bones were picked clean and disease threatened the nation.

*LEFT BEHIND, 13–14*

The Hebrew prophet Ezekiel was given a detailed prophecy twenty-five hundred years ago foretelling that Russia would become a dominant player on the world scene in the last days (Ezekiel 38–39). He even predicted that her allies would march with her against the mountains of Israel. Their objective would be to finish what Adolph Hitler had been unable to accomplish, the destruction of the Jews from the face of the earth.

Yet these invaders will be even less successful than the Nazis, for Ezekiel also predicted that God would supernaturally destroy the attacking armies of Russia in order to show His omnipotent power to the world and to demonstrate that He has unfinished plans for the nation of Israel.

## WHEN AND WHO?

These two prophecies in Ezekiel are among the most specific and easy to understand in the prophetic word. They not only pinpoint the time of their fulfillment by immediately following chapter 37—a description of the gradual regathering of Israel—but the prophet also states expressly that the events will occur "after many days . . . in the latter years" (Ezekiel 38:8). Few if any prophecy scholars question that the potential fulfillment of this text comes in the end times and that Russia and her allies will go down to the little nation of Israel "to take a spoil" (Ezekiel 38:13, KJV).

Now the word of the Lord came to me, saying, "Son of man, set your face against Gog, of the land of Magog, the prince of Rosh, Meshech, and Tubal, and prophesy against him, and say, 'Thus says the Lord God: "Behold, I am against you, O Gog, the prince of Rosh, Meshech, and Tubal. I will turn you around, put hooks into your jaws, and lead you out, with all your army, horses, and horsemen, all splendidly clothed, a great company with bucklers and shields, all of them handling swords. "Persia, Ethiopia, and Libya are with them, all of them with shield and helmet; Gomer and all its troops; the house of Togarmah from the far north and all its troops—many people are with you.

"Prepare yourself and be ready, you and all your companies that are gathered about you; and be a guard for them. After many days you will be visited. In the latter years you will come into the land of those brought back from the sword and gathered from many people on the mountains of Israel, which had long been desolate; they were brought out of the nations, and now all of them dwell safely. You will ascend, coming like a storm, covering the land like a cloud, you and all your troops and many peoples with you. . . .

"Then you will come from your place out of the

far north, you and many peoples with you, all of them riding on horses, a great company and a mighty army. You will come up against My people Israel like a cloud, to cover the land. It will be in the latter days that I will bring you against My land, so that the nations may know Me, when I am hallowed in you, O Gog, before their eyes. . . .

"And it will come to pass at the same time, when Gog comes against the land of Israel," says the Lord God, "that My fury will show in My face. For in My jealousy and in the fire of My wrath I have spoken: 'Surely in that day there shall be a great earthquake in the land of Israel. . . . I will call for a sword against Gog throughout all My mountains,' says the Lord God. "Every man's sword will be against his brother. And I will bring him to judgment with pestilence and bloodshed; I will rain down on him, on his troops, and on the many peoples who are with him, flooding rain, great hailstones, fire, and brimstone. Thus I will magnify Myself and sanctify Myself, and I will be known in the eyes of many nations. Then they shall know that I am the Lord.""" (Ezekiel 38:1-9, 15-16, 18-19, 21-23)

Etymologically, the Gog and Magog of Ezekiel 38 and 39 can only mean modern-day Russia. "Magog was the second son of Japheth who, according to Josephus, the great historian, settled north of the Black Sea. Tubal and Meshech were the fifth and sixth sons of Japheth, whose descendants settled south of the Black Sea."[1] These tribes intermarried and became known as Magog. Several historians (Pliny, Josephus, Herodotus, and others) point out they were also known as the Scythians and referred to them as "a barbarous people."[2]

We are not dependent solely on the study of etymology for proof of Gog's identity. In Ezekiel 39:2 God says to Gog, "I will turn you around and lead you on, bringing you up from the far north, and bring you against the mountains of Israel." All Bible directions are given in relation to Israel. "North" means north of Israel, "south" means south of Israel, etc. Any map will show that Russia is indeed north of Israel. The text reaffirms this by referring to the attacking nation as from "the far north" (38:15).

We have, then, both internal and external evidence for believing that Russia indeed is the nation that will fulfill the prophet Ezekiel's warning for the last days.

What is even more remarkable is that Gog's allies—Persia, Libya, Gomer [thought to be Turkey], Ethiopia, and Togarmah—are all Arab Muslim countries today and they "just happen" to be Russia's faithful allies. Their binding, overriding, passionate, and common hatred is Israel. Indeed, 55 million of Russia's own 250 million people are *Arabs,* most of whom hate Israel. For centuries prophetic scholars have been convinced that Russia and those who control her will lead the march of the Arab world down to the mountains of Israel, where God will show Himself powerful to all the world by destroying their armies.

## BODIES, BODIES EVERYWHERE

And you, son of man, prophesy against Gog, and say, "Thus says the Lord God: 'Behold, I am against you, O Gog, the prince of Rosh, Meshech, and Tubal; and I will turn you around and lead you on, bringing you up from the far north, and bring you against the mountains of Israel. Then I will knock the bow out of your left hand, and cause the arrows to fall out of your right hand. You shall fall upon the mountains of Israel, you and all your troops and the peoples who are with you; I will give you to birds of prey of every sort and to the beasts of the field to be devoured. . . .

"Then those who dwell in the cities of Israel will go out and set on fire and burn the weapons, both the shields and bucklers, the bows and arrows, the javelins and spears; and they will make fires with them for seven years. . . . It will come to pass in that day that I will give Gog a burial place there in Israel, the valley of those who pass by east of the sea; and it will obstruct travelers, because there they will bury Gog and all his multitude. Therefore they will call it the Valley of Hamon Gog. For seven months the house of Israel will be burying them, in order to cleanse the land." (Ezekiel 39:1-4, 9, 11-12)

God's judgment on these invading hordes will be sure and swift. While Israel's friends apparently see the attack coming, all they do is send a delegation to ask about Russia's intentions: "Sheba, Dedan, the merchants of Tarshish, and all their young lions will say to you, 'Have you come to take plunder? Have you gathered your army to take booty, to carry away silver and gold, to take away livestock and goods, to take great plunder?'" (Ezekiel 38:13). But that is the extent of their response. They offer no help, no aid to Israel—and then God steps in.

The Lord Almighty sends an earthquake and a mighty

shaking so great that "mountains shall be thrown down" (Ezekiel 38:20). He rains on Gog great hailstones and fire and brimstone, along with flooding rain and pestilence. And when it's all over, none of the enemies of God are left standing. Instead their corpses lie on the ground, food for the birds of prey and the beasts of the field.

So great will be the carnage that the people of Israel will spend seven months finding and burying the dead troops. An enormous common grave will be dug in what will be called the Valley of Hamon Gog ("the hordes of Gog"). The implements of war left behind by the decimated armies also will be gathered up, not to be reused but to be burned. So many weapons will be recovered that to burn them all will take seven years.

This seven-year period prophesied for the burning of Russian weapons is the reason why in *Left Behind* we placed Russia's attack on Israel some three and a half years before the beginning of the Tribulation. Scripture teaches that in the second half of the seven-year Tribulation, Israel once more will be forced out of her homeland; therefore, if she is to spend seven years burning these weapons, the Russian invasion must take place at least three and a half years before that time.

Some readers of this prophecy have stumbled on the reference to burning weapons. While such an activity might have made sense in the days of wooden spears and arrows and chariots, they reason, it certainly does not in these days of steel tanks and planes and guns. How do you burn steel?

The answer is, you may not have to. For some years the Russians have been using Lignostone in the manufacture of many of their weapons of war. Lignostone, invented by a Dutchman in Ter Apel, is a special kind of wood used for "coke breakers." It is stronger than steel, is very elastic . . . and burns better than coal.[3]

## FROM THE ASH CAN OF HISTORY

Russian history goes back to the tenth chapter of Genesis, some two thousand or more years before Christ. For most of that time Russia amounted to little. At best she could be described by one historian as "a barbarous people, who dwelt in the Moschian Mountains." Otherwise the Russians received scant mention in history until Peter the Great in the eighteenth century tried unsuccessfully to pull the people together and make them a cohesive power. By European standards, the Russians were always a backward people. As late as 1905, so impotent was Russia that she could not even best the emerging Asian nation of Japan in the Russo-Japanese War.

Three years into the First World War, the Bolsheviks overthrew the czar and executed his family, putting an end to the monarchy forever. Since then the Soviet people suffered under seventy-plus years of the most inhumane repressions known to man. It is estimated that their successive communist dictators killed as many as 65 million people. During those years of suffering and want, the elitist Communists spent the country into virtual bankruptcy in a vain attempt to make the nation into a superpower equal to the United States.

It is interesting that Russia has little history of Christian evangelism until recently, when after World War II and the fall of the Soviet Empire, evangelistic efforts were made by shortwave radio. Since then millions have come to faith in Christ. Unfortunately, these new Christians represent the very group that Russian Premier Boris Yeltsin and the Communists who still control the country would like to eliminate, but it is the one group that, if given freedom, would best improve the life and culture of Russia.

Today Russia is allied with the Muslim nations, just as outlined by Ezekiel—and together they have the capabilities to do just what the prophet predicted. It is significant that all these capabilities can be traced to World War I and the Bolshevik Revolution that produced the Russian communist empire. Everything started as a result of the Russian government's involvement in World War I in 1917, the very year the Jews began migrating back to Israel.

## THE POTENTIAL COLLAPSE OF RUSSIA

Russia's current capability to do what Ezekiel predicted makes that nation a significant "sign" or "birth pain" of the return of Christ and the end of the age.

In the days of the so-called cold war between the superpowers, the U.S. and Russia, Israel was always a thorn in the Russian side. Soviet officials could not plot their tactics based solely on the U.S.; they always had to consider Israel, in some ways the third most powerful state in the world. As an ally of America, she was armed to the teeth. Russia could

**Rise of Russia**
Ezekiel 38–39

never consider attacking the U.S. without taking Israel into consideration. We believe the reason the Soviets spent billions of rubles (that she could ill afford) to arm the Arab world was to offset the power of the Jewish state.

The problem is that for the past ten years, ever since the fall of the Berlin Wall and the breakup of the Soviet Union,

Russia has been on shaky ground. The nation's leader, the charismatic Boris Yeltsin, has been rendered all but ineffective by his vice of alcoholism and his serious heart condition. The economy of the country is in shambles as officials have refused to adopt full-scale free enterprise; Russia has retained enough socialist policies to stultify its economy. The country is in worse shape today than when it first enjoyed freedom for the first time in seventy years. The unstable government makes it vulnerable to a takeover by hard-line Communists, who are waiting in the wings to regain control. At risk is the peace of the world, because Russia and her satellite countries still have more than thirty thousand nuclear missiles pointed at the West.

Our point is that Russia is in precarious straits. She could have a revolution, become a dictatorship, or simply collapse under her own bureaucratic weight and become a fifth-rate power. Her army is no longer the fearful monster it was once pictured to be; witness what happened in Afghanistan and the little independent country of Chechnya.

It does not seem as if time is on Russia's side. If she is going to be the major power that Ezekiel forecasts her to be, she had better make her move soon, or she won't be able to do so. If Russia is to attack Israel, she had better do it soon!

And indications are that Russia is getting ready to do just that. According to many reports coming out of that region of the world, Russia and her Muslim allies are doing everything they can to foment war in Israel. That millions of lives are in jeopardy is inconsequential to them; they want to stamp out Israel at any cost.

For years one of the most trusted sources of geopolitical intelligence, particularly about Europe and the Middle

East, has been the *Intelligence Digest.* In the September 19, 1997, issue titled "The Next, and Final, Arab-Israeli War," the editors published this incredible report:

> There is now evidence to support the view that the Middle East's moment of truth could come as early as the second half of 1998—and the reason for this is as dramatic as the news itself. There is every possibility that Moscow, for whatever reasons of its own, has taken a decision to precipitate an Arab-Israeli war, within that time frame. Arab-Israeli War Has Been Brought Considerably Closer By Recent Russian Actions. The next 18 months in the Middle East will be fraught with danger, and it will take state craft of the highest possible order on the part of the United States if a catastrophic war in the Middle East involving chemical, biological, and nuclear weapons is to be avoided. *An Arab-Israeli war could come as early as the second half of 1998.*
>
> There are reasons why we have previously argued that the next Arab-Israeli war is unlikely to occur before 2000. The first of these is that there is no logic in going to war before every possible concession has been wrung out of Israel by peaceful means, and for all their public opposition to the peace process, those in the Arab/Iranian war party have always understood that negotiating the return of the Gaza Strip, West Bank, and possibly even the Golan Heights made much more sense than fighting for them. So, we have argued, war was never likely to come before the end of 2000. Now, however, the feeling in the war camp is that most of the major

concessions have been gained. No one believes any longer that the Israeli army will come down off the West Bank watershed, abandon the Jordan Valley, or retreat from the Golan Heights—all or any of which would be worth waiting for.

There are now 40,000 armed Palestinians in the West Bank and Gaza. Recent intelligence has shown that Syria has far more SCUD C missiles (armed with advanced-type chemical warheads) than previously thought. Most important, the latest intelligence shows that Syria has an unusually high proportion of launchers to missiles. . . . This will enable Syria to launch a barrage of missiles at Israel in one go. With such capability, Syria might legitimately think that Israel would not dare use its nuclear arsenal.[4]

Of course, 1998 has come and gone, and this attack did not occur. But Russia still remains on the horns of a miserable dilemma. Either she strikes against Israel in the very near future or she falls into the economic trash bin of history, in which case she would no longer have the capability and the allies to do what the prophet Ezekiel predicted. How long does Russia have before her wretched economy destroys her from within? Based on her rate of decline since dismantling her empire, experts say five, ten, maybe twenty years. Warheads are known to have a seven-year shelf life; they will be dead in their silos before another decade passes, and Russia would no longer be able to fulfill prophecy.

Just one more reason for believing Christ could come in our generation.

# NINE

## *Snatched Away!*

LOCAL television stations from around the world reported bizarre occurrences, especially in time zones where the event had happened during the day or early evening. CNN showed via satellite the video of a groom disappearing while slipping the ring onto his bride's finger. A funeral home in Australia reported that nearly every mourner disappeared from one memorial service, including the corpse, while at another service at the same time, only a few disappeared and the corpse remained. Morgues also reported corpse disappearances. At a burial, three of six pallbearers stumbled and dropped a casket when the other three disappeared. When they picked up the casket, it too was empty.

*LEFT BEHIND, 47–48*

One of the most compelling prophetic events in the Bible is called the "rapture" of the church. It is taught clearly in

1 Thessalonians 4:13-18, where the apostle Paul provides us with most of the available details:

> But I do not want you to be ignorant, brethren, concerning those who have fallen asleep, lest you sorrow as others who have no hope. For if we believe that Jesus died and rose again, even so God will bring with Him those who sleep in Jesus. For this we say to you by the word of the Lord, that we who are alive and remain until the coming of the Lord will by no means precede those who are asleep. For the Lord Himself will descend from heaven with a shout, with the voice of an archangel, and with the trumpet of God. And the dead in Christ will rise first. Then we who are alive and remain shall be caught up together with them in the clouds to meet the Lord in the air. And thus we shall always be with the Lord. Therefore comfort one another with these words.

No one can argue that the rapture of the church as taught in this passage will consist of the following five events:

1. "The Lord Himself will descend from heaven with a shout, with the voice of an archangel, and with the trumpet of God."
2. "The dead in Christ will rise first."
3. "Then we who are alive and remain shall be caught up together with them in the clouds."
4. We shall "meet the Lord in the air."
5. "We shall always be with the Lord."

## A GREAT MYSTERY

The word *rapture* comes from a fourth century Latin vulgate translation of the Greek word *harpadzo* (occurring in 1 Thessalonians 4:17) and has been picked up by many as the best single word to express the event it describes. Some translators have rendered that word "caught up," which is a good term—but you can see how "rapture" is more appealing. A preacher friend of mine translates it "snatched," for Christians in that day will indeed be translated instantly from natural flesh to "incorruptible heavenly bodies" and "snatched" up to be with Christ. But the terms "snatched" or "caught up" are simply not as appealing as "raptured."[1]

In 1 Corinthians 15:51-52 Paul unveiled what he called a "mystery"—that Christians "shall all be changed [transformed] in a moment, in the twinkling of an eye." This mystery was revealed primarily by the apostle Paul; it is not mentioned either in the Old Testament or by Jesus in the Olivet discourse. Some think John alludes to it in Revelation 4:1-2.

Enoch in the Old Testament provides an illustration of this transforming experience. The Bible says "Enoch walked with God; then he was no more, because God took him away" (Genesis 5:24, NIV). A day is coming when all believers will be transformed like the godly Enoch, whose earthly body was suddenly made fit to be in heaven with God. In Paul's terms, this happens when "this corruptible [our bodies] has put on incorruption, and this mortal has put on immortality" (1 Corinthians 15:54).

The Rapture, then, is not only for those Christians who "are alive and remain" at the coming of Christ, but includes all believers from the day of Pentecost (when the church began) to the day Christ returns for His church.

The clear teaching of this text is that in a moment of time, in response to Christ's "shout," both the dead believers and the living saints will be taken up to meet their Lord. En route they will meet each other in the clouds.

## RAPTURE, THE BLESSED HOPE

We prefer to call this miraculous event "the blessed hope," the term Paul uses in Titus 2:13: "Looking for the blessed hope and glorious appearing of our great God and Savior Jesus Christ." That is exactly what the Rapture is, a blessed hope.

When the Bible uses the word "hope" here, it does not mean a nice thing we earnestly suspect might happen, but rather a certified fact of the future, promised by God's un-failing Word. In this case, "hope" means a present, confi-dent expectation of a certain future event. It is this hope that has characterized believers in Christ for two thousand years. When a loved one dies (or "sleeps in Jesus," to use the bibli-cal phraseology), he awaits this resurrection when the dead rise first and then those believers who are still alive are trans-formed to go to be with the Lord. And this is no temporary respite, a brief vacation from earthly difficulties! Paul adds, "so shall we *ever* be with the Lord." Now, *that's* hope!

## TWO PHASES TO CHRIST'S SECOND COMING

When the more than three hundred Bible references to the Second Coming are carefully examined, it becomes clear that there are two phases to His return. There are far too many conflicting activities connected with His return to be merged into a single coming. We are indebted to Dr. Thomas Ice, the executive director of the Pre-Trib Research Center, for designing two charts, one that lists the contrasting events and the other giving the Scripture texts that refer to each.

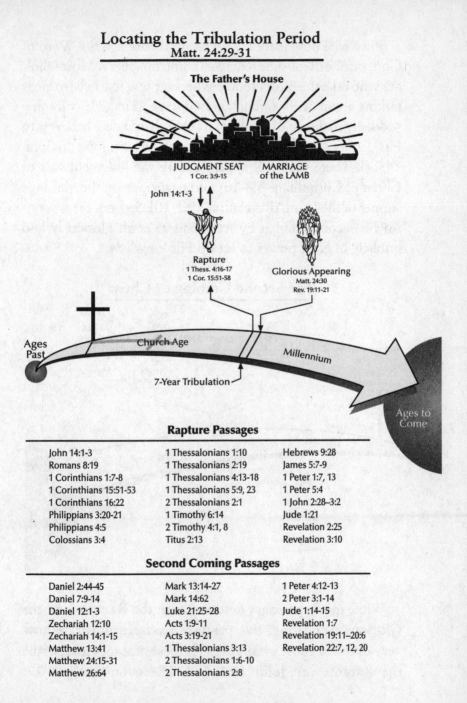

# Locating the Tribulation Period
### Matt. 24:29-31

**The Father's House**

JUDGMENT SEAT
1 Cor. 3:9-15

MARRIAGE
of the LAMB

John 14:1-3

Rapture
1 Thess. 4:16-17
1 Cor. 15:51-58

Glorious Appearing
Matt. 24:30
Rev. 19:11-21

Ages
Past

Church Age

Millennium

7-Year Tribulation

Ages to
Come

## Rapture Passages

| | | |
|---|---|---|
| John 14:1-3 | 1 Thessalonians 1:10 | Hebrews 9:28 |
| Romans 8:19 | 1 Thessalonians 2:19 | James 5:7-9 |
| 1 Corinthians 1:7-8 | 1 Thessalonians 4:13-18 | 1 Peter 1:7, 13 |
| 1 Corinthians 15:51-53 | 1 Thessalonians 5:9, 23 | 1 Peter 5:4 |
| 1 Corinthians 16:22 | 2 Thessalonians 2:1 | 1 John 2:28–3:2 |
| Philippians 3:20-21 | 1 Timothy 6:14 | Jude 1:21 |
| Philippians 4:5 | 2 Timothy 4:1, 8 | Revelation 2:25 |
| Colossians 3:4 | Titus 2:13 | Revelation 3:10 |

## Second Coming Passages

| | | |
|---|---|---|
| Daniel 2:44-45 | Mark 13:14-27 | 1 Peter 4:12-13 |
| Daniel 7:9-14 | Mark 14:62 | 2 Peter 3:1-14 |
| Daniel 12:1-3 | Luke 21:25-28 | Jude 1:14-15 |
| Zechariah 12:10 | Acts 1:9-11 | Revelation 1:7 |
| Zechariah 14:1-15 | Acts 3:19-21 | Revelation 19:11–20:6 |
| Matthew 13:41 | 1 Thessalonians 3:13 | Revelation 22:7, 12, 20 |
| Matthew 24:15-31 | 2 Thessalonians 1:6-10 | |
| Matthew 26:64 | 2 Thessalonians 2:8 | |

Since we know there are no contradictions in the Word of God, our Lord must be telling us something here. Most scholars who take the Bible literally wherever possible believe He is talking about one "coming" in two stages. First, He will come suddenly in the air to rapture His church and take believers to His Father's house, in fulfillment of His promise in John 14:1-3. There they will appear before the judgment seat of Christ (2 Corinthians 5:8-10) and participate in the marriage supper of the Lamb (Revelation 19:1-10). Second, He will finish his second coming by returning to earth gloriously and publicly in great power to set up His kingdom.

## The Second Coming of Christ

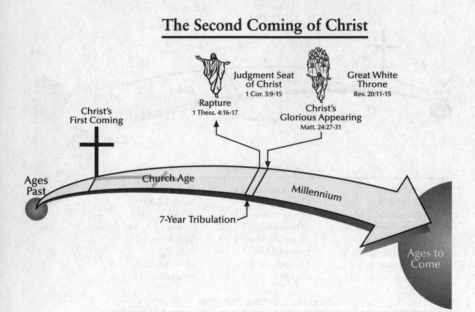

Judgment Seat of Christ
1 Cor. 3:9-15

Great White Throne
Rev. 20:11-15

Rapture
1 Thess. 4:16-17

Christ's First Coming

Christ's Glorious Appearing
Matt. 24:27-31

Ages Past

Church Age

Millennium

7-Year Tribulation

Ages to Come

While many passages describe both the Rapture and the Glorious Appearing, five primary passages illustrate how very different those events are. The best passages to describe the Rapture are John 14:1-3; 1 Thessalonians 4:16-17;

and 1 Corinthians 15:50-58. The best that detail our Lord's glorious appearing are Jesus' own description of His coming in Matthew 24:27-31 and the one given in Revelation 19:11–20:6. Note the details carefully!

### Events of the Rapture

1. The Lord Himself will descend from His Father's house, where He is preparing a place for us (John 14:1-3 and 1 Thessalonians 4:16).
2. He will come again to receive us to Himself (John 14:1-3).
3. He resurrects those who have fallen asleep in Him (deceased believers whom we will not precede; 1 Thessalonians 4:14-15).
4. The Lord shouts as He descends ("loud command," 1 Thessalonians 4:16, NIV). All this takes place in the "twinkling of an eye" (1 Corinthians 15:52).
5. We will hear the voice of the archangel (perhaps to lead Israel during the seven years of Tribulation as he did in the Old Testament; 1 Thessalonians 4:16).
6. We will also hear the trumpet call of God (1 Thessalonians 4:16), His last trumpet for the church. (Don't confuse this with the seventh trumpet of judgment on the world during the Tribulation in Revelation 11:15).
7. The dead in Christ will rise first. (The corruptible ashes of their dead bodies are made incorruptible and joined together with their spirit, which Jesus brings with Him; 1 Thessalonians 4:16-17).
8. Then we who are alive and remain shall be changed (made incorruptible by having our bodies made "immortal"; 1 Corinthians 15:51, 53).

9. Then we shall be caught up [raptured] together (1 Thessalonians 4:17).
10. With them in the clouds (where dead and living believers will have a monumental reunion; 1 Thessalonians 4:17)
11. To meet the Lord in the air (1 Thessalonians 4:17)
12. To "receive you to Myself." Jesus takes us to the Father's house "that where I am, there you may be also" (John 14:3).
13. "And thus we shall always be with the Lord" (1 Thessalonians 4:17).
14. The judgment seat of Christ (2 Corinthians 5:10). At the call of Christ for believers, He will judge all things. Christians will stand before the judgment seat of Christ (Romans 14:10; 2 Corinthians 5:10), described in detail in 1 Corinthians 3:11-15. This judgment prepares Christians for . . .
15. The marriage supper of the Lamb. Just prior to His coming to earth in power and great glory, Christ will meet His Bride, the church, and the marriage supper will take place. In the meantime, after the church is raptured, the world will suffer the unprecedented time of the wrath of God which our Lord called the great tribulation (Matthew 24:21).

(Note: Only the pre-Tribulation position allows sufficient time for the judgment seat of Christ and the marriage supper of the Lamb.)

### Events of the Glorious Appearing
1. Immediately after the Tribulation (Matthew 24:29)
2. Cosmic phenomena in sun, moon, and stars (Matthew 24:29)

3. Heaven opens, Christ appears on white horse (Revelation 19:11)
4. Followed by armies of heaven (Revelation 19:14)
5. Sign of Son of Man in heaven, seen by everyone (Matthew 24:30)
6. Coming in power and great glory (Matthew 24:30)
7. Unbelievers will mourn, for they are not ready (Matthew 24:30)
8. Beast (Antichrist) and his armies confront Christ (Revelation 19:19)
9. Christ casts Beast and false prophet into the lake of fire (Revelation 19:20)
10. Christ's rejecters killed (Revelation 19:21)
11. Satan cast into bottomless pit for a thousand years (Revelation 20:1-3)
12. Resurrection of Old Testament and Tribulation saints (Matthew 24:31; Revelation 20:4)
13. Christ judges nations and establishes His kingdom (Matthew 25)

Even a casual reading of these two lists reveals they describe two totally different events. One is a select coming for His church, a great source of comfort for those involved; the other is a public appearance when every eye shall see Him, a great source of regret and mourning for those whose Day of Judgment has come. Study the next chart and imagine, if you can, that these events are simultaneous; we think you will see there *must* be a period of time between them. Seven years would allow sufficient time for all these things and the Tribulation to take place.

The coming of Christ *must* occur in two installments because they are for two different groups of people and fulfill two different purposes. The first is the Rapture, when all living and dead Christians will be snatched up to be with Christ in the Father's house. The second is for all the people of the world, who will be judged for rejecting Christ. The first is secret, for a special group; the second is public, for everyone left on the earth. They are entirely distinct events!

Dr. David L. Cooper often compared the Second Coming to a two-act play separated by a seven-year intermission (the Tribulation). The apostle Paul distinguished these two events in Titus 2:13 by designating them "the blessed hope and glorious appearing."

"The blessed hope" could very well refer uniquely to the snatching up of believers just prior to the beginning of the Tribulation. On the other hand, it could also refer to the Resurrection when all believers will be raised to live with God for eternity, where they will be with their loved ones who share their faith in Christ. Or it could be both, for they are both a "blessed hope" to Christians and are designed by God to "comfort" His children (1 Thessalonians 4:18). This doctrine brings comfort and hope both when we lose our loved ones to death, and as we examine the signs of the times and conclude that the Tribulation could be rapidly approaching.

### THE TIMING OF THE RAPTURE

For almost two hundred years there has grown a much too bitter controversy over the timing of the Rapture. Sometimes the debate has become acrimonious—a most regrettable circumstance, since all these teachers (whatever their interpretations) love the Lord and long for His return. In fact, we have several friends with whom we agree on most other Bible doctrines, yet on this point we differ.

# Contrasting Second Coming Events

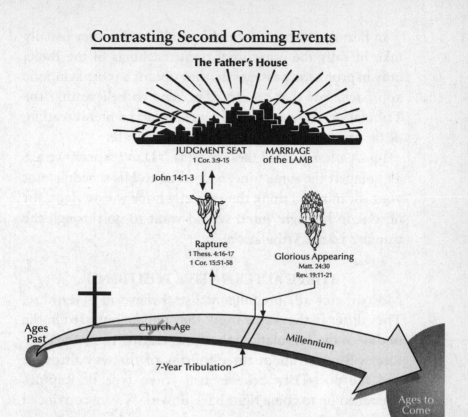

**The Father's House**

JUDGMENT SEAT
1 Cor. 3:9-15

MARRIAGE
of the LAMB

John 14:1-3

Rapture
1 Thess. 4:16-17
1 Cor. 15:51-58

Glorious Appearing
Matt. 24:30
Rev. 19:11-21

Ages
Past

Church Age

Millennium

7-Year Tribulation

Ages to
Come

## Rapture/Blessed Hope

1. Christ comes in air for His own
2. Rapture of all Christians
3. Christians taken to the Father's House
4. No judgment on earth at Rapture
5. Church taken to heaven at Rapture
6. Rapture imminent—could happen any moment
7. No signs for Rapture
8. For believers only
9. Time of joy
10. Before the "day of wrath" (Tribulation)
11. No mention of Satan
12. The Judgment Seat of Christ
13. Marriage of the Lamb
14. Only His own see Him
15. Tribulation begins

## Glorious Appearing

1. Christ comes with His own to earth
2. No one raptured
3. Resurrected saints do not see Father's house
4. Christ judges inhabitants of earth
5. Christ sets up his kingdom on earth
6. Glorious Appearing cannot occur for at least 7 years
7. Many signs for Christ's physical coming
8. Affects all humanity
9. Time of mourning
10. Immediately after Tribulation (Matthew 24)
11. Satan bound in Abyss for 1,000 years
12. No time or place for Judgment Seat
13. His bride descends with Him
14. Every eye will see him
15. 1,000-year kingdom of Christ begins

In fairness to them, I should point out that they usually take literally the other important teachings of the Bible; only in prophetic passages do they opt for a more symbolic approach. For that reason, they tend to believe that the Tribulation is not going to be as severe as a literal reading of the many passages on the subject indicate.

I have often kidded these friends, "Don't worry, we are all going at the same time, according to His schedule, not yours or mine." I think they secretly hope we are right, for no one in his right mind would want to go through the traumas of the Tribulation.

## THREE ALTERNATIVE POSITIONS

Most (if not all) premillennialists believe in a Rapture. They differ in that some think they will be raptured in the middle of the Tribulation; the "pre-wraths" think the Rapture will occur about three-fourths of the way through; and the post-Tribs believe in a yo-yo type of Rapture (snatched up to come right back down). We are convinced that the only view that takes into consideration all the Scriptures on the Blessed Hope and the Glorious Appearing is that Christ will rapture His church before the Tribulation. What is at stake here is whether the church will go through any, part, or all of the Tribulation.

The following chart graphically reveals where in the time line most prophecy teachers place the Rapture and the Glorious Appearing. You will notice only seven years separate the two events; consequently, from the standpoint of the human time line, they are not terribly far apart. However, because the Tribulation is such a traumatic time of trouble, the like of which has never existed before or ever will again, it becomes extremely important for those left behind to locate the exact time of the Rapture. Whether the church misses the entire Tribulation or goes through half of it, millions of people living at that time will be distinctly affected.

## WHY THE RAPTURE MUST BE PRE-TRIBULATION
So when will the Lord come back for His church, before, in the middle, or at the end of the Tribulation? When properly understood, the Scriptures are quite clear on this subject. I believe they teach that the Rapture will occur before the Tribulation begins. Consider four reasons why this is so:

### Three Views of the Rapture

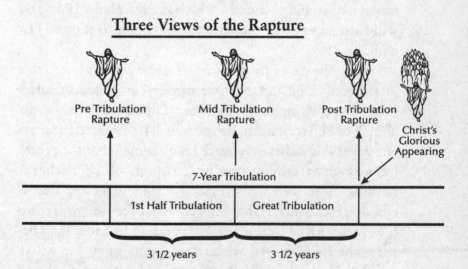

Pre Tribulation Rapture

Mid Tribulation Rapture

Post Tribulation Rapture

Christ's Glorious Appearing

7-Year Tribulation

1st Half Tribulation | Great Tribulation

3 1/2 years     3 1/2 years

## 1. The Lord Himself promised to deliver us.
One of the best promises guaranteeing the church's rapture before the Tribulation is found in Revelation 3:10: "Because you have kept My command to persevere, I also will keep you from the hour of trial which shall come upon the whole world, *to test those who dwell on the earth*"

(emphasis added). This verse is Christ's own promise to one of His seven churches, the church of Philadelphia.

The seven churches of Asia Minor were selected out of the hundreds of young churches at the time because they were types of the seven church ages that would exist from the first century to the present. The message of Revelation 2 and 3 is to the churches (plural), not just the seven churches of Asia Minor. Otherwise, the majority would have been excluded. The message of Christ to the church at Philadelphia was not only for that little church but also to the "open door" church—that is, the evangelistic, missionary-minded church, which started about 1750 and will exist right up to the time Christ comes to rapture His church.

During the past fifty years or so, some opposition to this interpretation has arisen. One of our Left Behind readers even wrote to question that our Lord's promise to the church of Philadelphia in Revelation 3:10 included the present-day, Bible-believing church. She claimed that the promise was given only to the little church of Philadelphia, nothing more. We wrote her back and suggested that it *couldn't* mean merely that little church, because it was completely destroyed by the Turkish invasion in 1382, long before "the hour of trial which shall come upon the whole world"! That period still has not come! It is the same period our Lord calls the "great tribulation, such as has not been since the beginning of the world until this time, no, nor ever shall be" (Matthew 24:21). He predicted that it would be such a horrible time that if God didn't shorten it, "no flesh would be saved" (Matthew 24:22). Obviously the church of Philadelphia has end-time significance, for it is referred to as "alive" during the last days.

Adherents to the mid- and post-Trib positions suggest God will keep us on earth *through* the Tribulation. This is difficult to reconcile, however, with other passages that teach that few, if any, believers will populate the earth when He comes "with power and great glory" at the end of the Tribulation. Instead, the saints who have been kept from wrath are with Him as He descends to this earth.

The word "from" (Greek, *ek*) in Revelation 3:10 literally means "out of." God is saying, "I will keep you *out of* the wrath to come." The editor of *Our Hope Magazine* wrote in August, 1959:

> *Ek* is rendered "out of" hundreds of times, as for example: "Out of Egypt have I called my Son" (Matthew 2:15, KJV); "First cast out the beam out of thine own eye" (Matthew 7:5, KJV); "For out of the heart proceed evil thoughts" (Matthew 15:19, KJV); "And [many bodies of the saints] came out of the graves after his resurrection" (Matthew 27:53, KJV); "I will spew thee out of my mouth" (Revelation 3:16, KJV); etc.[2]

This verse teaches that the faithful church of the open door, which will not deny His name but will practice good works, evangelism, and missions, will be kept "out of" the hour of trial (the Great Tribulation) that shall try the whole earth. The guarantee of Rapture before Tribulation could hardly be more powerful. No wonder one writer labeled it "a cardinal Scripture."[3]

Failure to recognize this truth has Christians believing

they are going into the Tribulation, contrary to our Lord's promise.

## 2. The church is to be delivered from the wrath to come.

The promise in 1 Thessalonians 1:10 ("Jesus . . . delivers us from the wrath to come") was given by the Holy Spirit through the apostle Paul to a young church planted on his second missionary journey. He had only three weeks to ground this church in the Word of God before being driven out of town. Many of his teachings during that brief period evidently pertained to Bible prophecy and end-time events, since this letter—one of the first books of the New Testament to be written—emphasizes the Second Coming, the imminent return of Christ, the Rapture, the Tribulation, and other end-time subjects. These topics may indicate what subjects Paul considered essential for new converts.

Paul wrote this epistle upon the death of some of the church's loved ones. Since the apostle had predicted that believers would be raptured, the Thessalonians wondered about loved ones already buried. Evidently they wrote Paul a letter of inquiry, and in answer he extended his commentary to prophetic questions for the saints of all ages.

Paul mentions the Second Coming in every chapter, so there is no doubt about the main subject of his letter. After complimenting his readers on their faith and testimony, he commends them for turning "to God from idols to serve the living and true God, and to wait for His Son from heaven, whom He raised from the dead, even *Jesus who delivers us from the wrath to come*" (1 Thessalonians 1:9-10, emphasis added).

The context of this passage is the Rapture, for Christians are not waiting for the Glorious Appearing (see chapter 15). Paul tells them in 2 Thessalonians 2:1-12 that the latter will not occur until Antichrist (or "lawless one," see chapter 21) is revealed (verse 8). No, the Christians in Thessalonica were awaiting the coming of Christ for His church—that is, the Rapture. They already knew the Tribulation (or "wrath to come") would follow the Rapture, and that is the part that God has promised to keep the Christians "out of."[4]

### 3. Christians are not appointed to wrath.

According to 1 Thessalonians 5:9, "God did not appoint us to wrath, but to obtain salvation through our Lord Jesus Christ." Again, this passage, which follows the strongest passage on the Rapture in the Bible, must be considered in light of its context.

After teaching the Rapture, Paul takes his readers to "times and . . . seasons" of "the Day of the Lord." Some suggest this refers to the single day on which Christ returns to this earth to set up His kingdom, but that is not consistent with other biblical references to "the Day of the Lord." Sometimes this phrase does refer to the Glorious Appearing, but on other occasions it encompasses the Rapture, the Tribulation, and the Glorious Appearing (see chapter 2).

For our purpose here, 1 Thessalonians 5:9 makes it clear that God did not "appoint us to wrath" (the Tribulation) but to "obtain salvation," or deliverance from it. Since so many saints will be martyred during the Tribulation, there will be few (if any) alive at the Glorious Appearing of Christ. This promise cannot mean, then, that He will deliver believers *during* the time of wrath, for the saints mentioned there (the Tribulation saints) will *not* be delivered; in fact, most will be martyred. To be delivered out of it, the church will have to be raptured before it begins.[5]

Since the Tribulation is *especially* the time of God's wrath, and since Christians are not appointed to wrath, then it follows that the church will be raptured *before* the Tribulation. In short, the Rapture occurs before the Tribulation, while the Glorious Appearing occurs after it.

### 4. The church is absent in Revelation 4–18.

The church is mentioned seventeen times in the first three chapters of Revelation, but after John (a member of the church) is called up to heaven in chapter 4, he looks down on the events of the Tribulation—and the church is not mentioned or seen again until chapter 19, when she returns to the earth with her bridegroom at His glorious appearing. Why? The answer is obvious: *She isn't in the Tribulation.* She is raptured to be with her Lord before it begins!

There are many other reasons besides these four for believing that the Rapture occurs prior to the Tribulation. I have cited many of these in an earlier book, *Rapture under Attack.*

### IS THE PRE-TRIB VIEW A RECENT THEORY?

For several years opponents of the pre-Trib position have argued that it was invented by John Darby in the mid-1800s and was never mentioned before that. Quite simply, this argument is false—a fact that cost one post-Trib writer a bundle of cash. This author offered five hundred dollars to anyone who could prove that the pre-Trib Rapture theory was known before John Darby began to popularize it in the 1840s. When it was discovered that the Reverend Morgan Edwards saw it back in 1742, the writer had to pay off his costly challenge. He has since had to admit his error and withdraw his offer.

The Reverend Morgan Edwards was a Baptist pastor in Philadelphia who described a pre-Trib return of Christ for His church in his 1788 book *Millennium, Last Days Novelties*. Although he saw only a three-and-a-half year Tribulation, he definitely saw the Rapture occur before that Tribulation. What is even more interesting is that he claimed he had preached and written the same thing as early as 1742. He may have been influenced by John Gill before him or by others whose writings or teachings were available at that time but have not been preserved.

What is known is that the Protestant Reformation resulted in a proliferation of Bibles being translated, printed, and made available to common people for the first time in seventeen hundred years. As believers began reading the Scriptures, they were impressed with the many prophetic teachings it contained. I have a copy of a commentary of the book of Revelation written by Sir Isaac Newton in the mid-seventeenth century. He was an avid Bible scholar (as well as one of the greatest scientists in history) and was obviously influenced by others before him. So the gradual development of prophetic understanding through history is understandable—it progressed along with the availability and study of the Bible.

By the nineteenth century, the Bible was available and being read by millions in the English-speaking world. It is said that "prophecy was in the air," particularly at Trinity College of Dublin, Ireland, where John Darby and other prophecy scholars attended between 1800 and 1830. Doubtless some of the Bible teachers on the faculty had a strong influence on Darby's thinking, as perhaps did S. R. Maitland, who developed the case for futurism (the position that most of the Bible is yet future). Maitland wrote his first book on that subject in 1826.

Darby claimed he got the inspiration for his understanding of a pre-Trib rapture in 1828 after he saw the distinction between Israel and the church in his study of the book of Ephesians. Few scholars who do not make that distinction see a pre-Trib rapture of the church. In fact, separating Israel and the church is one of the major keys to rightly understanding Bible prophecy. Second is taking the prophetic Scriptures literally whenever possible.

Grant Jeffrey, a current prophecy scholar and speaker, has done extensive research into the writings of many prophecy teachers prior to the eighteenth century. In his book *Apocalypse,* he quotes many who had a definite understanding of the difference between the two phases of our Lord's coming, particularly His coming for His people prior to the Tribulation and the revealing of the "man of sin."

Jeffrey's most important contribution was his electrifying discovery of a statement in an apocalyptic sermon from the fourth century. Designated Pseudo-Ephraim, there is some question that it was really written by Ephraim of Nisibis, (A.D. 306–373), a prolific Syrian church father. Some prefer a later date for this homily, called "Sermon on the End of the World," and suggest it may not have been written until A.D. 565–627. For our purpose, the real date is immaterial, for allowing its composition as late as the seventh century proves that even at this early date (eleven hundred years before John Darby), some Christians saw the Rapture occurring *before* the Tribulation. In challenging Christians to holy living (always a result of Rapture teaching), the ancient author wrote:

> Why therefore do we not reject every care of earthly actions and prepare ourselves for the meeting of the Lord Christ, so that he may draw us from the confusion, which overwhelms all the world? . . . *All the saints and elect of God are gathering together before the tribulation, which is to come, and are taken to the Lord,* in order that they may not see at any time the confusion which overwhelms the world because of our sins.[6]

There can be no doubt that this fourth- (or at the latest, seventh-) century Bible scholar saw the saints gathered *before* the Tribulation. His statement has all the marks of a pre-Trib rapture of the saints distinct from the Glorious Appearing. While Ephraim (or whoever the true author was) saw the Tribulation lasting only three and a half years, the fact remains that he saw a *pre-Trib* rapture of the church long before that view became popular in the nineteenth century. Considering that less than 10 percent of ancient Christian documents have been preserved, we have no doubt there must have been other Bible students who also discovered the teaching of the Blessed Hope.

## HOW LONG BEFORE THE TRIBULATION?

Since the Scriptures teach that the Rapture occurs prior to the Tribulation, it is reasonable to ask, How long before the Tribulation? The answer is simple: *No one knows!*

One of the greatest misconceptions about the pre-Trib rapture is that it starts the Tribulation. It does not. Daniel 9:27 is clear: The signing of the covenant between the Antichrist and Israel begins the seven-year Tribulation, *not* the Rapture. The Rapture could happen a day, a week, or several years prior to the signing of that covenant.

In *Left Behind* we arbitrarily put the Rapture two weeks prior to that signing. We must confess, we just assumed that would give Nicolae Carpathia (the name we gave to the Antichrist) time to organize his takeover of the One World Government. In actuality, it may take two months or two or more years.

## THE RAPTURE IS IMMINENT

One of the chief characteristics of the Rapture of the church is that it will be sudden, unexpected, and will catch people by surprise. Some students of Scripture will anticipate "the season" or general period, but as our Lord said, "No man knows the day or the hour." Which is why we should so live as to "be ready, for the Son of Man is coming at an hour when you do not expect Him" (Matthew 24:44). Only the pre-Tribulation rapture preserves that at-any-moment expectation of His coming.

God, in His wise providence, has designed Bible prophecy in such a manner that the Rapture has appeared imminent to Christians of every generation. Nothing is a better motivator than to believe Jesus could come at any moment! An imminent Rapture moves us to greater consecration, to holy living in an unholy age, and to evangelism and missions (both giving and going). Frankly, that is why two hundred and fifty prophecy scholars, authors, and teachers joined me in founding the Pre-Trib Research Center seven years ago, to help popularize the biblical teaching that Christ could come at any time. We do not see any of the other Rapture theories having such an effect on the body of Christ.

While we do not assert that our brethren who are looking for the Savior after the Tribulation are deceived by the devil, we do not think their positions do anything to motivate the body of Christ to heed the Savior's words, "occupy till I come" (Luke 19:13, KJV).

## THE GREAT LIE

Scripture teaches that a great lie will be published and believed by the masses left behind after the Rapture. The apostle Paul describes it like this:

> The coming of the lawless one [the Antichrist] is according to the working of Satan, with all power, signs, and lying wonders, and with all unrighteous deception among those who perish, because they did not receive the love of the truth, that they might be saved. And for this reason God will send them strong delusion, that they should believe the lie, that they all may be condemned who did not believe the truth but had pleasure in unrighteousness. (2 Thessalonians 2:9-12)

This passage teaches that the people left behind on earth after the Rapture will believe "the lie," a gargantuan, bald-faced untruth presented to the public with "all unrighteous deception among those who perish, because they did not receive the love of the truth, that they might be saved."

No one knows for sure what this "lie" will be, but in *Tribulation Force* we imagined that it would be a carefully designed fabrication created to "explain away" the Rapture. We imagined that the religious-minded would be given an "explanation" like this:

> Those who opposed the orthodox teaching of the Mother Church were winnowed out from among us. The Scripture says that in the last days it will be as in the days of Noah. And you'll recall that in the days of Noah, the good people remained and the evils ones were washed away.[7]

For the more secular and irreligious crowd, we created another "explanation": some confluence of electromagnetism in the atmosphere, combined with an unknown atomic ionization process generated by the world's nuclear power and weaponry stockpiles, was triggered by some natural cause such as lightning, resulting in the instantaneous disappearance of millions of persons worldwide.

The actual lie that will be perpetrated is unknown to us, but we do know its purpose: to discount and discredit the work of God in the world and to allow men and women to follow their own evil lusts. Whatever the lie is, that's what it does.

## ARE YOU READY?

This "blessed hope" of ours contrasts sharply with the "no hope" of the unbelievers referred to in 1 Thessalonians 4:13. What a vast gulf stretches between that "blessed hope" of Christians and the "no hope" of non-Christians!

And the gulf can be bridged only by a true salvation experience.

This "no hope" lifestyle is unnecessary to anyone reading this book. For as the apostle said, "If we believe that Jesus died and rose again, even so God will bring with Him those who sleep in Jesus" (1 Thessalonians 4:14). And what is it that all must do to have this blessed hope? Believe in the death of Christ for our sins and His resurrection! If you do not believe that, we urge you to confess your sins directly to Christ and invite Him into your life to become your Lord and Savior. If you would like to receive Christ by faith but are not sure how, we suggest you pray the following prayer or one like it:

> Dear Heavenly Father, I believe you sent your Son Jesus to die on the cross for my sins and the sins of the world. I also believe you raised Him from the dead and that He is soon coming again to set up His kingdom. Therefore, today I confess my sin of rebellion to you and invite Jesus into my heart to become my Lord and Savior. The best I know how, I give myself to Him and declare that I would like to serve Him as long as I live. Amen.

This matter is of such great importance that we urge you to examine your heart to make sure you have invited Him into your life. If you have any doubt about ever having done so, erase it today by calling on the name of the Lord, and receive His salvation. Accepting Christ's offer of salvation helps you avoid the traumas of the Tribulation on earth even as it allows you to enjoy eternity with Christ.

If you already are a Christian, may we suggest that in

light of what you have just read, you surrender your life to Him and cooperate with Him in making you holy. As the apostle Peter looked ahead to the coming of the Lord, he gave the following advice to all Christians:

> Therefore, since all these things will be dissolved, what manner of persons ought you to be in holy conduct and godliness, looking for and hastening the coming of the day of God, because of which the heavens will be dissolved, being on fire, and the elements will melt with fervent heat? Nevertheless we, according to His promise, look for new heavens and a new earth in which righteousness dwells. Therefore, beloved, looking forward to these things, be diligent to be found by Him in peace, without spot and blameless; . . . but grow in the grace and knowledge of our Lord and Savior Jesus Christ. To Him be the glory both now and forever. Amen. (2 Peter 3:11-14, 18)

# TEN

## *The Temple Rebuilt*

"WHO but Messiah could ask devout Muslims to move the shrine that in their religion is second in importance only to Mecca, the birthplace of Mohammed? But you see, the Temple Mount, the Dome of the Rock, is built right over Mount Moriah, where we believe Abraham expressed his willingness to God to sacrifice his son Isaac. Of course we do not believe Mohammed to be divine, so as long as a Muslim mosque occupies the Temple Mount, we believe our holy place is being defiled."

"So this is a great day for Israel."

"A great day! Since the birth of our nation, we have collected millions from around the world for the rebuilding of the temple. Work has begun. Many prefabricated walls are finished and will be shipped in. I will live to see the reconstruction of the temple, and it will be even more spectacular than in the days of Solomon!"

*TRIBULATION FORCE, 295*

All prophecy teachers who interpret the Scriptures literally agree that the Jewish temple in Israel will be rebuilt.

The first temple, built by Solomon, was destroyed by the Babylonians in 586 B.C. The second temple—begun in 535 B.C. and completed in 516 B.C., then lavishly renovated by Herod the Great starting in 19 B.C.—was destroyed by the Romans in A.D. 70. That there will be a third temple is predicted by the prophet Daniel, the apostles Paul and John, and none other than the Lord Jesus Himself. They all taught that Israel's third temple will be rebuilt either before the Tribulation begins or soon thereafter, for it is seen in complete operation by the middle of the Tribulation, when it will be desecrated. Obviously, since Israel does not now have a temple, the third temple must be rebuilt for such an event to occur.

## THE SCRIPTURE SPEAKS

In the Olivet discourse, Jesus said, "Therefore when you see the 'abomination of desolation,' spoken of by Daniel the prophet, standing in the holy place" (Matthew 24:15).

Our Lord had in mind the passage in Daniel where it is written: "Then he [Antichrist] shall confirm a covenant with many for one week [in this context, a seven-year period]; but in the middle of the week he shall bring an end to sacrifice and offering. And on the wing of abominations shall be one who makes desolate" (Daniel 9:27). And a little later, "and forces shall be mustered by him, and they shall defile the sanctuary fortress; then they shall take away the daily sacrifices, and place there the abomination of desolation" (Daniel 11:31).

The apostle Paul said it this way: "Let no one deceive you by any means; for that Day will not come unless the falling away comes first, and the man of sin is revealed, the son of perdition, who opposes and exalts himself above all that is called God or that is worshiped, so that he sits as God in the temple of God, showing himself that he is God" (2 Thessalonians 2:3-4).

And the apostle John wrote this: "Then I was given a reed like a measuring rod. And the angel stood, saying, 'Rise and measure the temple of God, the altar, and those who worship there. But leave out the court which is outside the temple, and do not measure it, for it has been given to the Gentiles. And they will tread the holy city underfoot for forty-two months'" (Revelation 11:1-2).

Both Daniel and John place this awful event in the middle of the Tribulation, at the start of what our Lord called "Great Tribulation." Clearly, if the temple is to be desecrated at that point, it must be built earlier. When the Antichrist commits the ultimate blasphemy by appearing in the temple to declare that he is God, the real Lord of heaven responds by inflicting on the Antichrist's earth the worst judgments in history—the Great Tribulation.

### WHEN WILL THE TEMPLE BE REBUILT?

Anyone interested in end-time events has his eyes on the temple project. Ever since the Jews took temporary possession of the temple site after the Six Day War in 1967, there have been rumors that various groups have been working clandestinely to prepare all the materials it needs—from the robes of the priests to the tapestry in the temple. I have even heard reports that all the elaborate worship utensils have been prefabricated in preparation for the day that permission is granted to begin construction of the third temple. There have been reports that a detailed model of the temple has been traveling throughout the United States to raise money for the project. That would make sense, for almost 50 percent of world Jewry lives in America, and doubtless the richest Jews in the world reside in this country. American Jews have a long history of providing generous donations to the needs and causes of fellow Jews, particularly those in Israel.

One of the most active individuals gathering materials for the Tribulation temple has been Gershom Salomon of the Temple Mount Faithful, who uses activist measures in an attempt to motivate fellow countrymen to rebuild the temple. Salomon's group has been given much American press, particularly about its tour of the United States to advance such a project. During that tour Salomon was a guest on Pat Robertson's *700 Club* and was interviewed on many Christian radio stations throughout the country.

Salomon has also received some bad press in Israel and throughout the world for his efforts to organize prayer meetings on the site of the first two temples. On one occasion he even tried to lay a four-and-a-half ton cornerstone upon the Temple Mount, but he was halted by the Israeli government. Officials know that the Middle East is a tinder box waiting for a spark to thrust the nation into another war; and nothing would start it sooner and protract it longer than to desecrate this Muslim holy site.

In their excellent pocket book series *The Truth about the Last Days Temple,* researchers Thomas Ice and Timothy Demy wrote, "Many plans are being made for a rebuilt Temple and many diverse groups in Israel are preparing for it."[1] One of the groups they mention is Salomon's Temple Mount Faithful. Salomon is quoted as saying:

In the right day—I believe it is very soon—this stone will be put on the Temple Mount, and be worked and polished . . . and will be the first stone for the Third Temple. Just now this stone lies not far from the Temple Mount, very close to the walls of the Old City of Jerusalem, near the Shechem Gate . . . and this stone watches over the Temple Mount. But the day is not far that this stone will be in the right place—it can be today . . . or tomorrow, we are very close to the right time.[2]

Another group Ice and Demy cite is the Temple Institute, led by Israel Ariel. This organization has made almost all the 102 utensils needed for temple worship according to biblical and rabbinic standards. These are on display for tourists to see at the Temple Institute tourist center in the Old City in Jerusalem. The Ateret Cohanim has established a *yeshiva* (religious school) for the education and training of temple priests. Their task is to research regulations, gather qualified Levites, and train them for a future priesthood. Many yeshivas have arisen throughout Jerusalem to prepare for the eventuality of a rebuilt, fully functioning temple service. Clothing is being made, and some rabbis are deciding what modern innovations can be adopted into a new temple. Also, an effort is well underway to secure kosher animals for sacrifice, including red heifers. And some people continue to see daily prayer upon the Temple Mount to help prepare the way.[3]

One of the ingredients necessary for reactivating Old Testament-style temple worship is the ashes of a red heifer. Early in 1997 the press of the Western world showed pictures of a rare red heifer in Israel. Efforts are being made to breed such animals. We would not be surprised to find that cloning experiments are currently being conducted, for to have an operational temple, workers would need several such animals.

Ice and Demy conclude by saying, "Many other preparations are currently underway for Israel's return to all aspects of Temple worship."[4] There is little doubt that faithful Jews all over the world are preparing all the necessary materials so that they will be ready to begin construction at the first opportunity. It is doubtful they have already cut the yellow limestone rock for the temple, for it would be impossible to hide such a huge number of such stones in Israel. But who is to say that agents have not already prepared such stones in various parts of the world, ready to be shipped at a moment's notice?

The point is that with thorough preparations and modern shipping and building equipment, the temple could be rebuilt in nine months to one year—fully functional and performing the daily sacrifices before the Antichrist desecrates it near the middle of the Tribulation.

## POSSIBLE SCENARIOS FOR TEMPLE REBUILDING

Some observers see an insoluble problem to the rebuilding of the temple because the Muslim Dome of the Rock is yet located on the only possible site. But careful students of the prophetic Scriptures see several possible solutions. Consider these suggestions:

### 1. The temple could be rebuilt sometime between Russia's attack on Israel (Ezekiel 38–39) and the beginning of the Tribulation.

Precisely when Russia and her Muslim allies will attack Israel is not possible to determine. It could happen prior to

God's last soul harvest just before the Rapture. Or it could come after the Rapture and before the Tribulation. Keep in mind, there could be a period of days to several years between the Rapture and the beginning of the Tribulation. Since the Jews will burn the remains of the war—described in Ezekiel 38–39—for seven winters (39:9) and because they will be driven out of the Holy Land by the Antichrist during the last three and a half years of the Tribulation (Revelation 12:6, 14), it would seem logical that the destruction of Russia and her allies will occur at least three and a half years prior to the Tribulation. If that deduction is correct, there will be ample time for the Jews to rebuild their temple. In one moment God will have broken the back of the Muslim hordes who hate Israel so intensely, freeing Israel to rebuild her temple. This would be a drawing card to Jews around the world to return to the Holy Land to worship in their third temple.

### 2. The Antichrist could negotiate an agreement between Israel and the remnants of the Arab world to relocate them to other countries.

Since the Antichrist will come on the world scene after the strength of Russia and her Arab allies has been broken, he could talk the Muslim survivors into moving their sacred mosque somewhere else.

### 3. One provision of the covenant between the Antichrist and Israel might permit the Jews to rebuild their temple.

The Tribulation officially begins when the Antichrist signs a seven-year covenant with Israel (Daniel 9:27). He will not fully honor that covenant but will break it in the middle of the seven years, desecrate the new temple, then launch the most anti-Semitic crusade in history.

No one knows exactly what is in the covenant. In our Left Behind series we imagined that as part of the covenant he promises to dismantle and move the Dome of the Rock to his new capital in Babylon, where the mosque will be set up as a Muslim holy place. That would solve the tension between the Jews and Arabs over the Temple Mount and allow the Jews to rebuild their temple.

Which of these scenarios (if any) is the real one, no one knows. As Ice and Demy acknowledge:

> From a Christian perspective, there is nothing bibli-
> cally that prohibits or teaches that the Temple cannot
> be rebuilt prior to the Rapture or in our own day,
> even though all biblical references to the Tribulation
> Temple occur during the future seven-year period
> known as the Tribulation. The Temple may be rebuilt
> prior to the Rapture and Tribulation—like the way
> Israel, in our own day, returned to the land before
> events of the Tribulation have begun.
>
> The fact that there are many movements and organi-
> zations in Israel today that are planning and preparing
> for the third Temple only heightens our expectation that
> problems will soon be resolved and construction may
> soon begin. The only biblical requirement is that the
> Temple has to be rebuilt and functioning by the mid-
> point of the seven-year tribulation.[5]

## HOW CLOSE ARE WE?

Israel's temple plays an important role in several end-time prophecies of the Tribulation. The Antichrist is going to desecrate that temple halfway through the Tribulation—but to do so, it must first be rebuilt.

Fifty years ago we would not have been discussing the possibility of reconstructing the Jewish temple. It was impossible. Today that is no longer true. For the first time since the destruction of the second temple in A.D. 70, we are on the verge of seeing a third temple built in fulfillment of prophecy—another powerful evidence that we have more reason to believe Christ could return in our lifetime than any generation before us!

# ELEVEN

## *The Rise and Fall of Babylon*

"THE logistics alone are incredible, the cost, the . . . everything."

"What?"

"He wants to move the U.N."

"Move it?"

Steve nodded.

"Where?"

"It sounds stupid."

"Everything sounds stupid these days," Bailey said.

"He wants to move it to Babylon."

"You're not serious."

"*He* is."

"I hear they've been renovating that city for years. Millions of dollars invested in making it, what, New Babylon?"

"Billions."

*LEFT BEHIND, 352*

Long before Saddam Hussein became a household name, he was busy fulfilling Bible prophecy. As early as 1971, he was given 30 million dollars by an oil-rich citizen of Iraq to commence the rebuilding of the ancient city of Babylon. The donor was probably a sun worshiper, for the first building constructed was a temple to the sun god. Since then Hussein has spent untold millions more to rebuild the twenty-one-square-mile ancient city that historically was one of the oldest and certainly one of the most important cities in history.

## THE IMPORTANCE OF BABYLON

Babylon is mentioned 280 times in the Bible—more than any city except Jerusalem. It is easily the most important pagan city that ever existed, for there is hardly any city in the world that it has not in some way influenced—whether religiously, governmentally, or commercially. Her influence spread not only west to Rome, where it shaped all the developing nation states and most cities during the next two and a half millennia, but also to the east and south. Long before the word for it had been coined, socialism had been a Babylonian philosophy for the conduct of government, commerce, and religion. Most of the governments that followed it adopted many of its policies—a form of organized living independent of God.

Babylon is where Satan located his headquarters and began his centuries-old battle against God for the conquest of the souls of men. It was there that the seeds were planted for all the major religions of the world. There, government had its earliest beginnings, eventually producing Nebuchadnezzar, considered by some to have been the most autocratic dictator in history. According to both Daniel the prophet and secular history, all world governments from that time on have been inferior to Babylon.

Since the demise of Rome fifteen hundred years ago, no other world government has arisen—just as the prophet foretold (Daniel 2, 7). Not that many haven't tried! But they all failed, for God revealed that there would be only four world governments. Then at the "time of the end," the world would unite once more under ten kings who would loan their authority to one man—a Nebuchadnezzar-type, if you will—who would do as he pleased, even "changing the times and seasons" . . . for a very short time.

> And in the days of these kings the God of heaven will set up a kingdom which shall never be destroyed; and the kingdom shall not be left to other people; it shall break in pieces and consume all these kingdoms, and it shall stand forever. (Daniel 2:44)

These great events will occur when God puts an end to the conflict that has been raging for millennia between Him and Satan for the allegiance of human hearts. God woos us through His Word and His Spirit to walk by faith; Satan woos us through government, commerce, and religious idolatry to walk by sight.

When Christ comes to set up His kingdom, He will destroy the city of Babylon, as well as Babylonian religion, commerce, and government. Then He will rule the world forever (Revelation 17–18). But first . . .

## THE CITY OF BABYLON MUST BE REBUILT!
Once Satan moved his religious, commercial, and governmental capital to the city of Rome (in the first century be-

fore Christ), he lost interest in the original site of Babylon, located in the present country of Iraq. The city was abandoned many years later and was gradually covered by the winds and sands of time.

Around the turn of the twentieth century, some Bible teachers began to popularize the idea that the abandoned ruins of the city fulfilled prophecy. To support their position they quoted some of the prophecies relating to the eventual destruction of the city, particularly those that predict that it will never again be built. It made for colorful preaching, but as we shall see, Babylon was never destroyed as the Bible says it would be, in a single day as God destroyed Sodom and Gomorrah.

The failure to take literally these prophecies about Babylon has led otherwise good men to make some fanciful attempts to identify the Babylonian cities of Revelation 17 and 18. I well recall hearing a noted prophecy teacher expound on those texts, predicting that New York City was the new Babylon of the twentieth century and would soon be destroyed. Again, it made for colorful preaching . . . but it was wrong.

Many of us who take a literal approach to Bible prophecy have felt for years that the city of Babylon must be restored before the Second Coming. In fact, when I wrote my commentary on the book of Revelation thirty years ago, I predicted that Babylon would be rebuilt. Little did I realize that Saddam Hussein, one of the cruelest dictators of our time, was launching such an undertaking as a monument to himself!

## WHY MUST BABYLON BE REBUILT?

The main reason for believing that Babylon must be rebuilt depends on some unfulfilled prophecies concerning the city's destruction. Let's briefly consider five sets of these prophecies.

## 1. Isaiah 13 and 14 and Jeremiah 50 and 51 describe the destruction of Babylon at "the day of the Lord."

A careful reading of these four chapters will reveal that the prophecies concerning the destruction of Babylon use the law of double reference; that is, they refer to two overthrows of Babylon. The first occurred in the seventieth year of Israel's captivity. The second will occur on the day of Yahweh, that is, the seven-year Tribulation. At that time Babylon will be the headquarters of the world's governmental, commercial, and religious systems—in opposition to the will of God. And at that time it will be utterly destroyed, never to rise again.

## 2. The ruins of Babylon have been used to build other cities, contrary to Jeremiah 51:26.

Jeremiah predicted of Babylon, "They shall not take from you a stone for a corner nor a stone for a foundation, but you shall be desolate forever." It is reliably reported that at least six cities bear the marks of ancient Babylon in their buildings: Seleucia, built by the Greeks; Ctesiphon, by the Parthians; Allmaiden, by the Persians; Kufa, by the Caliphs; Hillah, just a twenty-minute walk from ancient Babylon, built almost entirely from Babylon's ruins; and Baghdad, fifty miles north of Babylon, also used materials from the ancient city.

These facts alone demand the rebuilding of Babylon, because when God destroys it as recorded in Revelation 18, no part of it will ever be used to build another city.

### 3. The prophecies of Jeremiah and Isaiah indicate that Babylon will be suddenly and totally obliterated.

"Babylon is suddenly fallen and destroyed" says the prophet in Jeremiah 51:8 (KJV). And Isaiah 13:19 states, "And Babylon, the glory of kingdoms, the beauty of the Chaldeans' excellency, shall be as when God overthrew Sodom and Gomorrah" (KJV).

A look at history reveals the city was never destroyed in the way these Hebrew prophets predicted it would be, which guarantees it must be rebuilt. Babylon declined gradually, over hundreds of years, and never was devastated in anything like the sudden conflagration that consumed Sodom and Gomorrah. Through the centuries Babylon gradually lost influence and population as the seat of world government changed to the Medes, then the Greeks, and finally to the Romans, who already had established their capital in Rome. We know that Babylon existed during the time of Christ, for Peter wrote his epistles from there (1 Peter 5:13). As late as A.D. 917 it was a small village.

An interesting aspect to Isaiah's prophecy is that, like the city of Sodom, Babylon is built over vast supplies of bituminous asphalt and pitch. When my friend, prophecy preacher Dr. Charles Pak, led a tour to Babylon in 1975, he was told that the asphalt is only ten feet below the surface of the earth throughout the whole city. And while that may indicate there is oil underground, it is also an ideal condition to produce its ultimate destruction by fire and brimstone. A volcanic eruption could easily fulfill the destruction of the city as described in Revelation 18.

Taking all this into account, we see that Babylon must be rebuilt in order to be destroyed and made a desolation in the way the Bible predicts.

## 4. Isaiah 13:20 states that the ruins of Babylon are never to be inhabited.

The prophet declared of the devastated Babylon, "It will never be inhabited, nor will it be settled from generation to generation; nor will the Arabian pitch tents there, nor will the shepherds make their sheepfolds there."

But as we just saw, Babylon *was* inhabited for much of ancient history even after the Medes and Persians conquered the Babylonian Empire. In fact, one writer records that about A.D. 1100, under the name of Hillah, Babylon was enlarged and fortified; in 1898 Hillah boasted ten thousand inhabitants.

And certainly it has never been true that "nor will the Arabian pitch tents there, nor will the shepherds make their sheepfolds there." Both still occur to this day. Neither can it be said of Babylon, "Her cities are a desolation, a dry land and a wilderness, a land where no one dwells, through which no son of man passes" (Jeremiah 51:43). Throughout history the site has been surrounded by fertile lands, with abundant date groves stretching along the banks of the Euphrates River. And these days, visitors pass through there on a regular basis.

No, in order for this prophecy to be fulfilled, Babylon must be rebuilt, then destroyed in a mighty display of God's righteous power.

## 5. An ancient rabbinic rule of interpretation says that when the Bible mentions an event twice, it means the event will happen twice.

If this rabbinic guideline is correct, then we can be assured that Babylon will be rebuilt, for both Isaiah and the apostle John use the same double verbs to describe its destruction:

> Babylon is fallen, is fallen! And all the carved images of her gods He has broken to the ground! (Isaiah 21:9)

> Babylon is fallen, is fallen, that great city, because she has made all nations drink of the wine of the wrath of her fornication. (Revelation 14:8)

> Babylon the great is fallen, is fallen, and has become a dwelling place of demons, a prison for every foul spirit, and a cage for every unclean and hated bird! (Revelation 18:2)

Since the word "fallen" is used twice in each of these passages, the rabbinic rule demands that the city fall twice. But if it is to fall again, it must first be rebuilt.

## BABYLON ALREADY LIVES

During the early eighties I began hearing stories of rebuilding in Babylon. Several times I tried to inquire how to make a visit there so I could see for myself. My friend Dr. Joe Chambers was invited in 1989 to make an official visit to the rebuilt city as a guest of the Iraqi government. When he returned, he wrote a book titled *A Palace for the Antichrist,* complete with pictures of the walls, the magnificent gate of Ishtar (the female goddess whose history dates to the mother of Nimrod, the worship of whom is growing in the Western world), the palace of Nebuchadnezzar, and three pagan temples.

On June 28, 1990, Diane Sawyer and Sam Donaldson took the nation to this incredible city of Babylon via their television program *Prime Time Live*. They pointed out that Saddam Hussein had spent over a billion dollars of his oil wealth rebuilding the city as a monument to himself. During the program Sawyer said:

> Now, Saddam Hussein dreams of rebuilding the grandeur, reclaiming the vision. This is Babylon, twenty-five hundred years ago, the dazzling center of a rich civilization. There were the hanging gardens, the palaces, all built by a man who managed to unite the country and rule with an iron hand. In fact, right over here there are bricks that bear an ancient stamp. It says, "I am King Nebuchadnezzar, King of Babylon, king of everything from sea to far sea." But there are new bricks here too, imprinted with a different stamp. This one says [the camera pointing at a brick with Arabic inscriptions], "I am Saddam Hussein, president of the Republic of Iraq."[1]

The very fact that Saddam would mix bricks with his name in the foundation of the rebuilt city that once ruled the world confirms that he envisions becoming the modern counterpart to his lifetime hero, King Nebuchadnezzar. However preposterous it may appear to Westerners, there seems little doubt that the man dreams of becoming the next leader of the Arab world.

## SADDAM, THE SERVANT OF SATAN

It is difficult to explain the bizarre behavior of Saddam Hussein without thinking him quite possibly demon-possessed. Before he ever declared the eight-year-long war on his closest neighbor, Iran—a conflict that cost both countries over a million men and crippled countless thousands of others for life—he already had earned the title "butcher of Baghdad" for killing his own people. Even today, if it were not for the United Nations and U.S. presence in northern Iraq, he would exterminate the Kurds living in his country.

Many Westerners still don't understand what Hussein was doing when he invaded Kuwait and triggered the Gulf War. He had his eyes set not on little Kuwait alone but on the United Arab Emirates, Saudi Arabia, Syria, and Jordan—all the enemies of Israel and the very countries who own 70 percent of the world's oil. Most non-oil-producing nations like Japan would drop into chaos if the oil of the Mideast were halted for even thirty days. We are an oil-dependent world, and the megalomaniac of Iraq sees oil as his ticket to restoring "the glory of the Chaldeans' excellency," the days when Babylon ruled the world. He planned to control that oil, thus enabling him to rule the world and make Babylon his capital. He thought his friend Russia would neutralize the West and permit him to carry out his plans. He showed his ruthlessness by using SCUD missiles and perhaps the world's largest supply of poisonous gas and chemical weapons. In so doing, he underestimated the West and the fact that the major oil companies were not about to let him control the world through oil.

Religiously, Saddam may give lip service to Muhammad and act like a devoted Muslim, but there is strong indication that he is actually a Satanist. A key is found in Dr. Charles Pak's report of his 1975 visit to Babylon to witness firsthand the rebuilding of that ancient city. There, for the first time in his life, Dr. Pak witnessed the worship of the devil at a reconstructed temple to the sun. When you recall that Hussein is known to micromanage everything in his country, including that entire rebuilding project, you can be sure that a temple to Satan would not be there without his approval.

Certainly Hussein is not reported to be "normal." What normal man would take his revolver and blow the brains out of one of his own generals merely for asking to be excused from a staff meeting (where Hussein was rambling on and on) because his wife had just called to say she had to go to the hospital to deliver their child? Or what normal man would promise safety for his sons-in-law (who defected to a friendly country) if they came home with his daughters, only to murder them when they returned?

Dr. Charles Dyer, another author who has been to Babylon, said in his book *The Rise of Babylon* that Hussein's utter ruthlessness and disregard for his own people is not news; it was standard procedure for him by 1978 when he assumed the position of president, a move made possible by his friends and followers in the Baath Party. So it was no surprise when:

A few weeks after becoming president of Iraq in 1979, Saddam Hussein executed some of his closest friends and fellow members of the ruling Baath Party. Videotapes of the meeting at which the "traitors" were named show Hussein reading their names from a list, pausing to puff on a cigar while members of his audience squirmed in their seats. Once their names were called, the supposed conspirators were marched off and killed. Saddam Hussein had begun his pattern of rule by force.[2]

Hussein's bizarre behavior was again seen in late 1997 and early 1998 when he refused to comply with the Gulf War agreements, once more defying the United Nations by refusing to permit UN inspectors access to his munitions plants and warehouses. He even threatened to shoot down the U-2 spy planes of the United States.

Saddam Hussein's abnormal hatred for the Jews, Jesus Christ, His followers, and anyone else who would stand in the way of his goal to conquer the world, might best be understood by demonic possession—a virtual foretaste of the Antichrist to follow, who will be indwelt by Satan himself.

In any event, there is little doubt that Saddam Hussein sees himself as the replacement for Nebuchadnezzar, as the man whose destiny it is to rule the world. Of course, he is not fit for such an exalted position; in fact, he is little more than a cheap imitation of Nebuchadnezzar. He could well be, however, the forerunner of the one who we believe is soon going to emerge on the world scene to take control of the United Nations (or its successor), move the commercial and governmental headquarters of his world government to Babylon, and rule the world from what we call in our Left Behind novels "New Babylon." That city will be more than a replica of an ancient wonder of the world and the capital of the last satanic world empire; it will be the most technologically advanced, earthquake-proof city in the modern world.

## AS SURE AS GOD KEEPS HIS WORD

As sure as there is a God in heaven who keeps His word, Babylon will live again as "the seat of Satan." You can be sure that any city mentioned seven times in two chapters, as is Babylon in Revelation 17 and 18, will be a literal city. And since it is seen there as an enormously influential city, perhaps even the capital of government, commerce, and religion, it must yet be rebuilt.

Babylon will again become Satan's headquarters for a short time, serving as the governmental and commercial capital of the world during the first half of the Tribulation. Then, after the kings of the earth destroy religious Babylon near the middle of the Tribulation, Satan will move his religious headquarters from Rome to Babylon, setting the stage for the second three-and-one-half-year period, called "the Great Tribulation."

Even now, in our lifetime, Babylon is being prepared for its final appearance on the stage of human history. The ancient prophecies about Babylon are unfolding before us—just like so many other prophecies of the end times.

# TWELVE

## *The Tribulation: An Overview*

BRUCE pulled up the first blank sheet on a flip chart and showed a time line he had drawn. "I'll take the time to carefully teach you this over the next several weeks, but it looks to me, and to many of the experts who came before us, that this period of history we're in right now will last for seven years. The first twenty-one months encompass what the Bible calls the seven Seal Judgments, or the Judgments of the Seven-Sealed Scroll. Then comes another twenty-one-month period in which we will see the seven Trumpet Judgments. In the last forty-two months of this seven years of tribulation, if we have survived, we will endure the most severe tests, the seven Vial Judgments. That last half of the seven years is called the Great Tribulation."

*LEFT BEHIND, 309*

Jesus warned His disciples that in the last days just prior to His second coming, there would be "great tribulation, such as has not been since the beginning of the world until this time, no, nor ever shall be" (Matthew 24:21). Our Lord was referring to the shortest—but most traumatic—of the prophetic events scheduled for human history.

## A THORN BY ANY OTHER NAME

The disciples were not unfamiliar with this prophesied time of anguish, for many of the Hebrew prophets had warned Israel that a period of intense national suffering was coming because the nation had refused to obey God's commands. Jeremiah the prophet had called it "the time of Jacob's trouble" (Jeremiah 30:7; the *New American Standard Bible* calls it "the time of Jacob's distress"). It will certainly be far worse than the Spanish Inquisition of the sixteenth century or even the Holocaust of Adolph Hitler in the twentieth century. Other prophets called it "the day of His wrath" or "the day of Yahweh's wrath," and on one occasion Isaiah referred to it as "the day of vengeance of our God" (Isaiah 61:2). Interestingly, when Jesus quoted from Isaiah 61, He stopped reading right before He came to this phrase. Here is Luke's account:

> He went to Nazareth, where he had been brought up, and on the Sabbath day he went into the synagogue, as was his custom. And he stood up to read. The scroll of the prophet Isaiah was handed to him. Unrolling it, he found the place where it is written: "The Spirit of the Lord is on me, because he has anointed me to preach good news to the poor. He has sent me to proclaim freedom for the prisoners

and recovery of sight for the blind, to release the oppressed, to proclaim the year of the Lord's favor." Then he rolled up the scroll, gave it back to the attendant and sat down. (Luke 4:16-20, NIV)

The passage in Isaiah actually reads, "to proclaim the year of the Lord's favor *and the day of vengeance of our God*" (Isaiah 61:2, NIV, emphasis added). Why did Jesus stop with "the year of the Lord's favor"? Why did He not mention "the day of vengeance"? Because the day of grace had come; the day of vengeance was yet future.

Dr. Arnold Fruchtenbaum, a Hebrew scholar, has this to say of the Tribulation:

In every passage of the Scriptures that the term the "Day of Jehovah" or the "Day of the Lord" is found, it is always and without exception a reference to the tribulation period. This is the most common name for this period in the Old Testament, and it is also found in various passages of the New Testament.

But there are a number of other names or designations for this time period found in the Old Testament. Following the 1901 American Standard Version of the Bible, these names include:

The Time of Jacob's Trouble—Jeremiah 30:7
The Seventieth Week of Daniel—Daniel 9:27
Jehovah's Strange Work—Isaiah 28:21
Jehovah's Strange Act—Isaiah 28:21
The Day of Israel's Calamity—Deuteronomy 32:35; Obadiah 1:12-14

The Tribulation—Deuteronomy 4:30

The Indignation—Isaiah 26:20; Daniel 11:36

The Overflowing Scourge—Isaiah 28:15, 18

The Day of Vengeance—Isaiah 34:8; 35:4; 61:2

The Year of Recompence—Isaiah 34:8

The Time of Trouble—Daniel 12:1; Zephaniah 1:15

The Day of Wrath—Zephaniah 1:15

The Day of Distress—Zephaniah 1:15

The Day of Wasteness—Zephaniah 1:15

The Day of Desolation—Zephaniah 1:15

The Day of Darkness—Zephaniah 1:15; Amos 5:18, 20; Joel 2:2

The Day of Gloominess—Zephaniah 1:15; Joel 2:2

The Day of Clouds—Zephaniah 1:15; Joel 2:2

The Day of Thick Darkness—Zephaniah 1:15; Joel 2:2

The Day of the Trumpet—Zephaniah 1:16

The Day of Alarm—Zephaniah 1:16

The New Testament names and designations include:

The Day of the Lord—1 Thessalonians 5:2

The Wrath of God—Revelation 15:1, 7; 14:10, 19; 16:1

The Hour of Trial—Revelation 3:10

The Great Day of the Wrath of the Lamb of God—Revelation 6:16-17

The Wrath to Come—1 Thessalonians 1:10

The Wrath—1 Thessalonians 5:9; Revelation 11:18

The Great Tribulation—Matthew 24:21; Revelation 2:22; 7:14

The Tribulation—Matthew 24:29

The Hour of Judgment—Revelation 14:7[1]

The prophet Daniel specified a time frame for this "day of vengeance," as did John in the book of Revelation. Daniel 9:24-27 says it will last a "seven." In this context, years are the subject, which indicates the Tribulation will last seven years. Verse 27 tells us that the evil prince that shall come (Antichrist) will "make a covenant" with Israel to begin that seven-year period, then break it in the middle of the seven years by desecrating the rebuilt temple in Jerusalem. John divided those same seven years into two three-and-a-half-year periods, neatly paralleling the distinction our Lord made in the Olivet discourse between "tribulation" and "Great Tribulation" (Matthew 24:15-21).

No one wants to think of a future period—even a short one of seven years—that will be the greatest time of suffering and terror in all of human history. But the Bible is clear on the traumas of this period. Those Christians who believe in a mid-Tribulation, post-Tribulation, or pre-Wrath view of the end times do not realize how much suffering will be packed into those entire seven years. It is unrealistic to spiritualize away the devastations God is going to unleash on this world during the Tribulation. While that period may be short, the judgments will seem endless to those caught in them. Get out your Bible and read the following Scriptures that describe the judgments God plans to send upon the earth at that time:

- Seal Judgments: Revelation 6
- Trumpet Judgments: Revelation 8–9
- Vial (KJV; also called Bowl) Judgments: Revelation 16

The following chart is taken from Tim's book *Rapture Under Attack: Why Christians Will Escape All the Tribulation* and is based on the three series of judgments outlined in Revelation 6–16. Since these judgments follow each other as shown in the chart, it is plain that the whole seven years constitute "tribulation," with the last three and a half years even worse than the first three and a half. Even a casual examination of this chart and reading of the Scripture text should convince you it will be what Jesus predicted: "great Tribulation, such as has not been since the beginning of the world until this time, no, nor ever shall be" (Matthew 24:21).

## The Tribulation Period

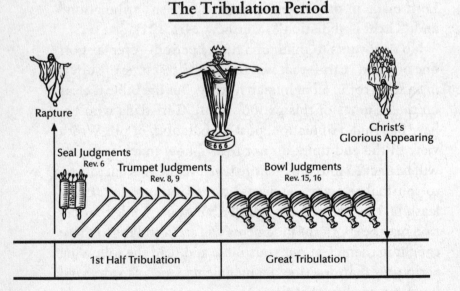

Rapture

Christ's Glorious Appearing

Seal Judgments
Rev. 6

Trumpet Judgments
Rev. 8, 9

Bowl Judgments
Rev. 15, 16

1st Half Tribulation

Great Tribulation

## ONE ASTONISHING EVENT AFTER ANOTHER

No other event in the Bible, except perhaps the Second Coming itself, is mentioned more frequently than the Tribulation. It is so important that we cannot cover it all, even in the twelve books of the Left Behind series. There is no end of astonishing events from this awful period. Consider the following that are clearly described in Scripture:

1. The four horsemen of the Apocalypse (including a world war that wipes out 25 percent of the world's population)
2. The two witnesses who have the power to stop the rain and call down fire from heaven
3. The 144,000 servants of God who preach the gospel
4. A soul harvest which no one can number
5. Unprecedented martyrdom
6. Another world war that kills one-third of the world's remaining population
7. Uncounted assassinations and murders
8. Supernatural activities beyond description

No wonder Jesus said the Tribulation was unique from anything that has ever happened or would happen again!

## WHY A SEVEN-YEAR TRIBULATION?

All of this horror prompts the question "What is the purpose of the Tribulation?" The prophet Daniel does not leave us guessing:

> Seventy 'sevens' are decreed for your people and your holy city to finish transgression, to put an end to sin, to atone for wickedness, to bring in everlast-

ing righteousness, to seal up vision and prophecy and to anoint the most holy. (Daniel 9:24, NIV)

Daniel was told that the special "seventy 'sevens' [or 7 x 70 = 490 years]" were decreed for "your people [Israel] and your holy city." This period was designed to:

1. finish transgression and to put an end to sin
2. atone for wickedness (the first coming and death of Christ will culminate in His second coming)
3. bring in everlasting righteousness (establish Christ's kingdom)
4. seal up vision and prophecy (complete all prophecy)
5. anoint the Most Holy—the second coming of Messiah (forcing billions of people to choose between Christ or Antichrist, a decision with eternal consequences)

And what are we to make of the 490 years prophesied to accomplish all these things? Gleason Archer writes:

> Verse 25 is crucial: "From the issuing of the decree to restore and rebuild Jerusalem until the Anointed One [*masiah*], the ruler, comes, there will be seven 'sevens' and sixty-two 'sevens.'" It should be observed that only sixty-nine heptads are listed here, broken into two segments. The first segment of seven amounts to forty-nine years, during which the city of Jerusalem is to be "rebuilt with streets and a trench, but in times of trouble." [This probably occurred in 457 B.C. when Artaxerxes I authorized

Ezra the scribe to return to Jerusalem to reestablish temple worship.]

Verse 26 specifies the termination of the sixty-nine heptads: the cutting off of the Messiah. That is to say, *after* the appearance of Messiah as Ruler— 483 years after the sixty-nine weeks have begun—he will be cut off.[2]

In other words, 483 of the 490 years "decreed" for Daniel's people have already elapsed; the divine "counter" stopped just before the death of Jesus, with seven years still left to go. That remaining seven-year period is what we call the Tribulation.

From several other prophetic passages we are told that the Tribulation will be a time of:

1. judgment on men who reject the Savior
2. ending of the millennia-old rebellion of mankind against God by the establishment of Christ's kingdom of righteousness
3. decision in which men and women will be forced to make up their mind whom they will serve, Christ or Antichrist. If they choose Antichrist, they will be killed; if they choose God, they will be subject to martyrdom, except for a few who "endure to the end" and go into the Millennium.
4. chaotic, worldwide conditions designed by God to shake man's false sense of security and cause many to look to Him for deliverance. In short, it will be a seven-year conflict between God and Satan for the souls of men at a time of enormous world population.
5. ushering in a worldwide revival of unprecedented

proportions, resulting in the conversion of "a great multitude which no one could number, of all nations, tribes, peoples, and tongues" (Revelation 7:9). This will be known as the greatest soul harvest in all of human history.

## LOCATING THE TRIBULATION

The big question is: Where in time do we locate the Tribulation? Fortunately, we are able to pinpoint the exact spot from the words of Jesus Himself in the Olivet discourse: "Immediately after the tribulation of those days . . . the sign of the Son of Man will appear in heaven . . . and they will see the Son of Man coming on the clouds of heaven with power and great glory" (Matthew 24:29-31).

### Locating the Tribulation Period
#### Matt. 24:29-31

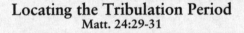

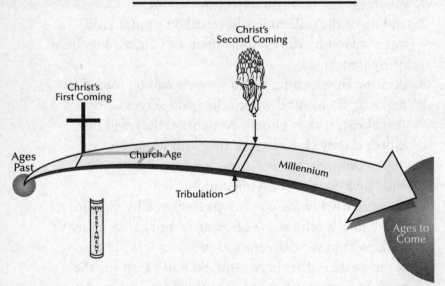

It is obvious the Tribulation must occur immediately *before* the glorious appearing of Christ. This location in time was confirmed by the apostle Paul in 2 Thessalonians 2:1-10, where he predicts that the coming of Christ to earth will not occur until the "man of sin . . . the son of perdition" is revealed, and that Christ will "consume [him] with the breath of His mouth and destroy [him] with the brightness of His coming."

We believe that the time for God's seven-year "clock" to start ticking again is drawing very near. Are you ready?

## JUDGMENT . . . AND MERCY

The Tribulation is a terrifying period of seven years in which God pours out His wrath on a rebellious and unbelieving mankind. It is also "the time of Jacob's trouble," in which the Lord will once again deal specifically with the nation of Israel, bringing the Jewish people to faith in Jesus Christ, the Messiah they rejected almost two thousand years ago.

Yet while this period is primarily a time of wrath and judgment, it also features a very strong note of mercy and grace—a note that too often gets overlooked. Sometimes we think God gets a "bad rap" when people focus exclusively on the judgments and terrors to come. They see the Lord as some kind of angry monster, heaping up catastrophes and pouring them on the heads of defenseless, innocent men and women, like an obnoxious child might pour gasoline down a teeming anthill with one hand while getting ready to drop a lit match with the other.

But this is all wrong! First, those who suffer the judgments of God in the Tribulation are *not* "innocent men and women." As we will see in chapter 26, the rebels alive at that time will not only reject God and His offer of salvation but will run greedily toward every vile sin known to man, including blasphemy of a kind beyond description. And second, despite their gross sin, God intends that these Tribulation judgments *might lead even these wicked sinners to faith in His Son, Jesus Christ!*

That is the reason we had one of our characters in the novel *Tribulation Force* say to a congregation of men and women about to enter the Tribulation,

> "These judgments, I believe, are handed down for the purposes of shaking us loose from whatever shred of security we might have left. If the Rapture didn't get your attention, the judgments will. And if the judgments don't, you're going to die apart from God. Horrible as these judgments will be, I urge you to see them as final warnings from a loving God who is not willing that any should perish."[3]

We believe with all our hearts that the Tribulation judgments of God serve a dual purpose: to punish hardened sinners *and* to move others to repentance and faith. The Tribulation will be God's ultimate illustration of the truth found in Romans 11:22: "Therefore consider the goodness and severity of God." It is true that the Tribulation will demonstrate God's severity, but it is equally true that it will showcase His goodness.

The Old Testament prophet Joel clearly saw these two aspects of God's nature working side by side in the Tribulation. In Joel 2:28-32 the Lord said through him,

> And it shall come to pass afterward that I will pour out My Spirit on all flesh; your sons and your

daughters shall prophesy, your old men shall dream dreams, your young men shall see visions. And also on My menservants and on My maidservants I will pour out My Spirit in those days. And I will show wonders in the heavens and in the earth: blood and fire and pillars of smoke. The sun shall be turned into darkness, and the moon into blood, before the coming of the great and terrible day of the Lord. And it shall come to pass that whoever calls on the name of the Lord shall be saved.

We believe these verses teach that there will be a great "soul harvest" during the Tribulation. Uncounted millions of men and women and girls and boys will recognize that, although they missed the Rapture and thus will have to endure the terrors of the Tribulation, yet God is still calling them, wooing them to His side. And through the ministry of the Holy Spirit, these individuals will respond in repentance and faith and will choose to forsake their rebellion and instead commit their lives and their futures into the hands of the Lord Jesus Christ. That is why the apostle John could write,

After these things I looked, and behold, a great multitude which no one could number, of all nations, tribes, peoples, and tongues, standing before the throne and before the Lamb, clothed with white robes, with palm branches in their hands. (Revelation 7:9)

We believe these "Tribulation saints" could well number into the billions. And do not forget: Every one of these new believers will have been left behind after the Rapture precisely because he or she had (to that point) rejected God's offer of salvation. Yet even then, the Lord will not give up on them! Even then, He will use whatever means necessary—fire, blood, earthquakes, plague, war, famine, persecution—to jolt them out of their spiritual slumber and into the waking enjoyment of His glorious light.

Far from being a stomach-turning display of divine meanness, the Tribulation demonstrates beyond all doubt that our holy God is also a God who loves beyond all human reckoning. No wonder the apostle Peter could write that the Lord is "not willing that any should perish but that all should come to repentance" (2 Peter 3:9)! No wonder the apostle Paul could write that "our great God and Savior Jesus Christ . . . gave Himself for us, that He might redeem us from every lawless deed and purify for Himself His own special people, zealous for good works" (Titus 2:13-14)! And no wonder Jesus Himself told us, "For even the Son of Man did not come to be served, but to serve, and to give His life a ransom for many" (Mark 10:45)!

Scripture teaches that a fantastically large number of those "many" Jesus came to ransom are what we call "Tribulation saints." Yes, the Tribulation is a time of fury and wrath and terrifying judgments, but it is also a time of long-suffering grace and mercy. Only God could hold both extremes in perfect balance.

And in the Tribulation, He does exactly that.

# THIRTEEN

## *The Tribulation: The First Half*

WITH handshakes, embraces, and kisses on both
cheeks all around, the treaty was inaugurated.

And the signers of the treaty—all except
one—were ignorant of its consequences, unaware
they had been party to an unholy alliance.

A covenant had been struck. God's chosen people, who planned to rebuild the temple and reinsti-
tute the system of sacrifices until the coming of their
Messiah, had signed a deal with the devil.

Only two men on the dais knew this pact signaled
the beginning of the end of time. One was mania-
cally hopeful; the other trembled at what was to
come.

At the famed Wall, the two witnesses wailed the
truth. At the tops of their voices, the sound carrying
to the far reaches of the Temple Mount and beyond,
they called out the news: *"Thus begins the terrible
week of the Lord!"*

The seven-year "week" had begun.
The Tribulation.
*TRIBULATION FORCE, 373–74*

Former president George Bush did not originate the idea of a "new world order" when he led the nations of the world in attacking Saddam Hussein and the Iraqi armed forces during the Gulf War. He merely popularized the phrase. Satan, the master conspirator, had just such a world government in mind centuries ago. God revealed that hellish plan to His servant-prophet Daniel more than five centuries before Christ was born—and history has unfolded exactly as predicted.

## DANIEL'S PROPHECY OF THE END

Daniel was the first prophet to write about the Antichrist's one-world government, and interestingly enough, the prophecy was given in a dream to the man whom historians consider the most absolute dictator in world history.

In his dream King Nebuchadnezzar saw a beautiful statue with four distinct parts, each part inferior to the section above it. Under pain of death, the king demanded that his astrologers and soothsayers tell him the vision and its interpretation—something they could not do. Daniel the Hebrew prophet, however, inquired of the living God, who revealed both the dream and its interpretation. Daniel prefaced his remarks to the king by saying, "There is a God in heaven who reveals secrets" (Daniel 2:28). He then predicted there would be four successive world governments, and in the last days just before the Messiah came to establish His kingdom, ten kings would form one final world government. This prophecy is so significant that it is worth your time to read both the vision and its interpretation.

You, O king, were watching; and behold, a great image! This great image, whose splendor was excellent, stood before you; and its form was awesome. This image's head was of fine gold, its chest and arms of silver, its belly and thighs of bronze, its legs of iron, its feet partly of iron and partly of clay. You watched while a stone was cut out without hands, which struck the image on its feet of iron and clay, and broke them in pieces. Then the iron, the clay, the bronze, the silver, and the gold were crushed together, and became like chaff from the summer threshing floors; the wind carried them away so that no trace of them was found. And the stone that struck the image became a great mountain and filled the whole earth. This is the dream.

Now we will tell the interpretation of it before the king. You, O king, are a king of kings. For the God of heaven has given you a kingdom, power, strength, and glory; and wherever the children of men dwell, or the beasts of the field and the birds of the heaven, He has given them into your hand, and has made you ruler over them all—you are this head of gold. But after you shall arise another kingdom inferior to yours; then another, a third kingdom of bronze, which shall rule over all the earth. And the fourth kingdom shall be as strong as iron, inasmuch as iron breaks in pieces and shatters all things; and like iron that crushes, that kingdom will break in pieces and crush all the others.

Whereas you saw the feet and toes, partly of potter's clay and partly of iron, the kingdom shall be
divided; yet the strength of the iron shall be in it,
just as you saw the iron mixed with ceramic clay.
And as the toes of the feet were partly of iron and
partly of clay, so the kingdom shall be partly strong
and partly fragile. As you saw iron mixed with
ceramic clay, they will mingle with the seed of men;
but they will not adhere to one another, just as iron
does not mix with clay.

And in the days of these kings the God of heaven
will set up a kingdom which shall never be destroyed; and the kingdom shall not be left to other
people; it shall break in pieces and consume all these
kingdoms, and it shall stand forever. Inasmuch as
you saw that the stone was cut out of the mountain
without hands, and that it broke in pieces the iron,
the bronze, the clay, the silver, and the gold—the
great God has made known to the king what will
come to pass after this. The dream is certain, and its
interpretation is sure. (Daniel 2:31-45)

## THE HISTORICAL ACCURACY OF DANIEL

Daniel wrote his book long before this prophecy came
to pass; yet here we are, twenty-five hundred years later,
and it has been fulfilled exactly as he predicted. In fact, his
prophecy was so specific that for many years it was fash-
ionable to suggest that an unknown author wrote it long
after the four world governments were in place. Skeptics
said the reason the prophecies were so accurate was that
the writer (whoever he was) was merely writing history,
not prophecy.

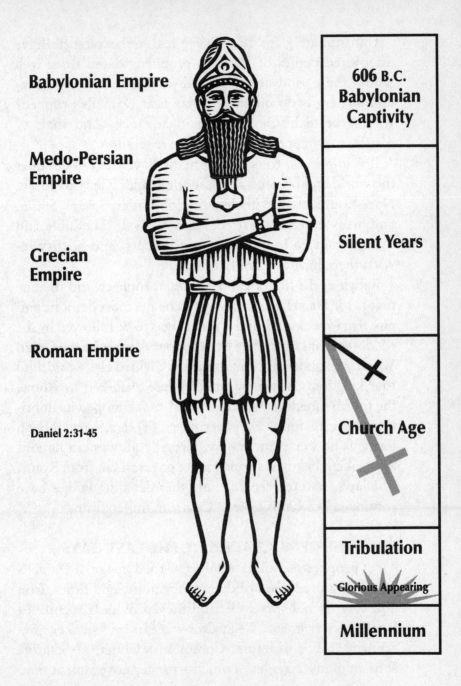

Babylonian Empire

Medo-Persian
Empire

Grecian
Empire

Roman Empire

Daniel 2:31-45

606 B.C.
Babylonian
Captivity

Silent Years

Church Age

Tribulation

Glorious Appearing

Millennium

Unfortunately for those skeptics, archaeologists have discovered copies of Daniel's prophecy dated from well within the period of the second (or Medo-Persian) kingdom. There is no question today that Daniel's prophecy was accurate history written in advance. And that, of course, can happen only by divine revelation.

It is important to note that many have tried to conquer the world and become a fifth world leader. Genghis Khan, Napoleon, Kaiser Wilhelm, Adolph Hitler, Joseph Stalin, and many others have tried, all to no avail. The Bible said there would be four world governments, and history reveals there have been only four.

Babylon, the first kingdom in the prophecy and the one that made Daniel a captive, was to be the most despotic empire that ever existed, and it was. It was to be followed by the Medo-Persians, then the Greeks under Alexander the Great. When Alexander died, his generals divided the world into four kingdoms, which eventually were absorbed by Rome, the fourth kingdom "made of iron" that stamped its imprimatur on all forms of government. Today, even though Rome is no longer an empire, virtually all western nations have taken their basic principles of government from Rome. The laws, statutes, senate, and other debating bodies have continued in what is called "Cesarean imperialism."

## THE DEMOCRACIES OF THE LAST DAYS

Most prophecy scholars see the ten-toed image of Daniel's vision as a prediction of democracy in the end times. Iron and clay do not mix well, and they provide a picture of weaker government. What do we mean by "weaker government"? For example, Communist China, a dictatorship, in many ways has a much stronger government than that of the United States. Its leaders do what they want to do, and no one opposes them. The U.S. government, on the other hand, changes from liberal to conservative depending on the mood of the voters, and politicians who want to ensure their election cannot focus on what is best for their country but on what will garner them the most votes. This does not lend itself to a strong, stable government.

In the thirteenth chapter of Revelation the apostle John describes Daniel's ten kings as "horns" on the seven heads of a "beast." Don't let this imagery confuse you; while Nebuchadnezzar saw the future governments of man as a beautiful image or statue, God (in parallel descriptions found in Daniel 7 and 8) saw them as beasts. This contrasts the human and divine views of government. Man sees government as beautiful and impressive and worships it, while God sees the governments of the world as beasts.

The seven heads John describes in Revelation (12:3; 13:1; 17:3, 7, 12-14, 16) probably refer to the seven stages of the Roman Empire, the embodiment of evil government. While Revelation 17:9 says they refer to "seven mountains" (possibly a reference to the seven hills on which Rome is said to be built), the next verse says they also refer to seven kings, of whom "five have fallen, one is, and the other has not yet come." I believe the five "fallen" kings were the five Roman emperors before John's time; the sixth ("one is") was Domitian, the emperor at the time John wrote; and the seventh, (who "has not yet come") will be the Antichrist himself—the evil genius who will inaugurate the Tribulation by signing a seven-year treaty with Israel (Daniel 9:27), only to break the accord after three and a half years when he desecrates the rebuilt temple by declaring himself to be God.

## THREE KINGS DEFEATED

Daniel reveals that the ten kings pictured in Nebuchadnezzar's dream will not always obey every whim of the Antichrist. In fact, three of them rebel against him—and are quickly crushed. Here is how he describes their rebellion and defeat:

> I was considering the horns, and there was another horn, a little one, coming up among them, before whom three of the first horns were plucked out by the roots. And there, in this horn, were eyes like the eyes of a man, and a mouth speaking pompous words. (Daniel 7:8)

> Then I wished to know the truth about the fourth beast, which was different from all the others, exceedingly dreadful, with its teeth of iron and its nails of bronze, which devoured, broke in pieces, and trampled the residue with its feet; and about the ten horns that were on its head, and about the other horn which came up, before which three fell, namely, that horn which had eyes and a mouth which spoke pompous words, whose appearance was greater than his fellows. (Daniel 7:19-20)

> The ten horns are ten kings who shall arise from this kingdom. And another shall rise after them; he shall be different from the first ones, and shall subdue three kings. (Daniel 7:24)

Daniel makes it plain that these ten kings will "arise" before the Antichrist makes his own rise to power. Three of them will not like his rapid ascent and will try to resist him, but they will quickly be defeated; Daniel says they will be "plucked out by the roots," "fall," and be "subdued" by the Antichrist, the horn with eyes and a pompous mouth, "whose appearance was greater than his fellows."

In *Tribulation Force* we imagined that one of these kings was the president of the United States; he was joined by the leaders of England and Egypt. Of course, all three were quickly defeated. "This was all part of the foretold future," we wrote. "The uprising against Antichrist would be crushed and would initiate World War III, from which would come worldwide famine, plagues, and the death of a quarter of the earth's population."[1]

## A TWENTIETH-CENTURY OBSESSION

We are rapidly approaching the time when the ten kings of Daniel and Revelation are to appear. How did we get to this point? Would it surprise you to learn that the stage was beginning to be set at the conclusion of World War I?

Like nothing before it, World War I prompted millions across the globe to clamor for "peace in our time." President Woodrow Wilson, who promised the American people he would keep the nation out of the war, soon led the nation into it. Not only did he break his promise, he also promised it would be "the war to end all wars"—a grand idea but one that obviously never took root.

Right after the war, Wilson and his most trusted advisor, Colonel Mandell House (an obsessed socialist), went to the Geneva Peace Conference and tried to set up the League of Nations, the first broadscale step toward a one-world government. But when they returned to the United States, their hopes were dashed by Senate conservatives, who in 1919 prevented America's involvement in the League. Still, House and his associates did not give up. In 1921, House and others founded the Council on Foreign Relations (CFR), probably the most influential organization in this century. It has consistently promoted a one-world government.

The council was the prime mover in establishing the United Nations in 1945, promising to halt man's ancient nemesis, war. Unfortunately, the UN's track record has been less than reassuring. In the past sixty years we have endured more wars and war-related deaths than during any other similar period in history. That, of course, does not deter the socialists, who are convinced that if they could just have more power, they would succeed.

Since then the Club of Rome Conference, featuring the elite leaders of the world, announced that a one-world government was the only hope for our planet. Its members are convinced that overpopulation is going to destroy the earth; thus they insist that humanity must change its attitude about children and the need to preserve the environment. They, of course, advocate population control through abortion, contraceptives, and government-directed "progress." They also insist that the rich nations of the world subsidize third world countries so that all become equal, thus removing greed as a motivation for war.

During the nineties a major change occurred in the CFR and other one-world advocates: They became more visible and open about their intentions. The Gulf War provided exhibit A of what could be done through world unity when a dictator like Saddam Hussein flexed his muscles. The master planners could not possibly permit him to continue his grab for the world's oil, so in the name of the

United Nations, the United States Army, Navy, and Air Force put on what may be one of its last demonstrations of power. At the rate America is disarming and the UN is increasing its stature and power, it is only a matter of time until the UN is capable of controlling the world.

## TEN KINGS ON THE DRAWING BOARD?

One idea from the Club of Rome suggested that a stepping stone to world government might be to divide the world into ten regions with a "head" appointed to lead each area, with representation at the UN. The Security Council could be expanded to ten; consequently, the world would be governed by what a major U.S. newspaper described as "ten wise men"!

**One World Government**
Daniel 2

Already there is almost universal acceptance among elite insiders that the governments of the world will relinquish their sovereignty to one head, an international world leader. This is clearly predicted in Revelation 13, Daniel 2, 2 Thessalonians 2, and other prophetic passages. Already many secret societies and organizations are working tirelessly to make that come to pass. During the past few years, shocking revelations have been confirmed that, for over two hundred years, many influential leaders of some of the most powerful countries of the world have been committed to ushering in a one-world government.

What is important about these organizations is that whenever their membership comes to light, it includes those who control government, banking, education, and media. Few Christians are ever found in such groups, which often display overt hostility to Judeo-Christian culture and values.

All these groups are working in one way or another for a world government. No doubt when Satan does prepare the world for uniting under one master controller, he will use a system of interlocking, secret organizations that seek to control the economy, the religion, and the media of the world. With this power he will be able to control all world leaders.

In the mid-nineties the world planners started talking about a "world tax," a "world court," a "world police force," a "world standard for nations," a "world economy," and even a "world religion." One suggested recently that since religion has proven to be so divisive, we have come to the point when we need a one-world religion that will "unite the people." We predict that will come about immediately after Christ raptures His church.

We are rapidly approaching—indeed, we are already on the brink of—a time when the world will be divided into ten regions whose leaders form a one-world government. This, in the name of world peace. Who could oppose that? Only Christians who know their Bible and know that this is the predicted world condition just before the Antichrist comes to power.

When will these things culminate? No one really knows. Some one-world optimists have suggested the year 2000, but we think they are premature. Others more realistically say it will come by the year 2010; others suggest 2025. We are convinced that unless God intervenes, the one-worlders will not give up until they make the United Nations the ruling force of the world by at least 2025—and maybe much sooner!

## ONE WORLD RELIGION

Before we briefly consider the judgments and plagues of the first half of the Tribulation, we would do well to understand something of the reason for the ferocity of God's Tribulation judgments. One of the major causes of His divine wrath is the corrupt one-world religion that will arise at that time.

Revelation 17 gives us a graphic picture of this global "church." John calls it "MYSTERY, BABYLON THE GREAT, THE MOTHER OF HARLOTS AND OF THE ABOMINATIONS OF THE EARTH" (verse 5). He says she committed fornication with the kings of the earth, clothed in purple and scarlet and adorned with gold and precious stones and pearls. She also held a golden cup full of "abominations and the filthiness of her fornication" (verse 4)—all symbols of her great wealth and corrupt influence. John tells us in verse 3 that she sits on a "scarlet beast"—the same beast identified in Revelation 13 as the Antichrist. And he adds this in verse 16:

And the ten horns which you saw on the beast, these will hate the harlot, make her desolate and naked, eat her flesh and burn her with fire.

These verses describe a one-world religion that, in the first half of the Tribulation, will exercise significant control over even the ten kings who rule the world under Antichrist. The fact that this "harlot" rides the beast indicates that even the Antichrist will not be free of her controlling influence—at least, not for the first three and a half years of the Tribulation. At that point, John tells us the harlot is finally and violently overthrown; she will be made "desolate and naked," and the ten kings who serve Antichrist will "eat her flesh and burn her with fire" (Revelation 17:16).

## MYSTERY BABYLON'S LONG HISTORY

Every false religion in the world can be traced back to Babylon. Even before its citizens tried to build the Tower of Babel, Satan had made that city his headquarters and introduced idolatry, the first secret societies, and many of the religious practices that continue to the present day. These eventually appeared as the foundational teachings for Hinduism, Buddhism, Taoism, Gaia worship, and a host of other cultic systems summed up in the Bible as "Mystery Babylon." These false religions consistently violate the first four commandments, those that concern man and his relationship to God ("You shall not worship other gods!" "Make no graven images, nor worship them or serve them!" "Do not take the name of the Lord in vain!" "Remember the Sabbath day to keep it holy!"; see Exodus 20). In short, all pagan religions depend on the worship of images, or as some call them, "aids to worship."

If Babylon is the mother of all false religions and Jerusalem is the mother of true faith (since Jesus Christ was crucified, buried, and resurrected there), then Rome is the mother of an unholy mixture of the two. One of the things that impresses tourists visiting that city is its incredible religious history. It existed long before the Romans rose to power and today displays the ruins of many pagan religions, all of them received from Babylon. By the time Paul and other Christians got to Rome, the city had become not only the capital of a world empire—thus the center of civilization and the most important city in the world—but also the center of pagan "Mystery Babylon" religion. Satan had moved his spiritual headquarters from Babylon to Rome even before the birth of Christ.

When Constantine made his "confession of faith" in the fourth century (if indeed that is what it was), he turned over to the Christian leaders the temples of the pagans that, according to the official tour books of Rome, included:

> The Greek divinities, Athena, that had become Minerva, Ares became Mars, Aphrodite became Venus. Apollo retained its Greek name, thus the Greek god of mythology became the Roman Olympus. The temple of Isis [straight from Babylon] was there, along with the Egyptian Campus Martius, many oriental divinities including Mithras, the Persian God of the Sun.[2]

The city of Rome around A.D. 320 was filled with temples, idols, and shrines to almost every god in the pantheon of pagan religions. Turning these temples over to the Christians proved to be the worst thing Constantine did and the worst thing to happen to the early church. It is said the church retained much of the statuary in the pagan temples; it simply rededicated them to Christianity, then chiseled off the names of the pagan deities and replaced them with the names of the apostles, Jesus, and Mary. Gradually the pagan practices and teachings of Babylon began to worm their way into Christianity. These included prayers for the dead, making the sign of the cross, worship of saints and angels, instituting the mass, and worship of Mary—which in the church of Rome was followed by prayers directed to Mary, leading to the 1950 doctrine of her assumption into heaven and in 1965 to the proclamation that Mary was the "Mother of the Church."[3]

As pagan teachings increased, biblical authority decreased. Just over one hundred years after Constantine, the brilliant Augustine came along with his brand of Greek humanism and introduced "man's wisdom" along with "God's wisdom," further paving the way for more pagan thought and practice. Although he did not intend it, his spiritualizing of Scripture eventually removed the Bible as the sole source of authority for correct doctrine. At the same time, the Scriptures were kept locked up in monasteries and museums, leaving Christians defenseless against the invasion of pagan and humanistic thought and practice. Consequently, the Dark Ages prevailed, and the Church of Rome became more pagan than Christian.

Had it not been for Wycliffe, Tyndale, and other valiant pre-Protestant heroes of the faith, Christianity would have been destroyed, and Satan's Babylonian mysticism would have prevailed, effectively destroying true Christianity. Instead, because of the courageous efforts of a few Christian scholars—some within the Catholic church itself, including many priests and bishops who disapproved of the infusion of pagan doctrine and practice, along with many splinter groups like the Moravians and Waldensians, who carefully adhered to the teachings of Scripture—the sixteenth century spawned the Protestant Reformation. Under intellectual and spiritual giants such as Luther, Calvin, and many others, the Reformers called Christianity back to the Bible and at the same time condemned many of Rome's pagan practices, including selling indulgences, teaching the doctrine of purgatory, and praying to Mary.

In the Middle Ages and in premodern times true believers were subjected to martyrdom on an incredible scale. It is estimated that as many as 40 million persons were killed during that period when Babylonian mysticism controlled the church.

France, the most advanced country of the seventeenth century, is an example of the effects of Babylon on the seven-hilled city of Rome. Consider how the pope and Catholic authorities worked with the Catholic kings of France to produce the St. Bartholomew Square massacre, in which forty thousand born-again Christians were killed in a single day. That was followed by other massacres that eliminated up to 4 million Huguenots, who would be called evangelical Christians if they were living today. Their destruction so angered skeptics like Voltaire and Rousseau that they became anti-Christian thinkers and began to propagate an atheistic socialism born out of French skepticism, which ultimately merged with German rationalism. Today their intellectual descendants champion a philosophy called "secular humanism."

To this day the Catholic church has never truly repented of those massacres perpetrated "in the name of Christ and His church." These tragic events make it difficult for many Christians to trust current efforts at reestablishing unity between Protestants and Catholics.

Our Lord and Savior, Jesus Christ, is the *only* dispenser of salvation, which can come only by personal faith in Him, never by works of righteousness. His work of redemption was finished for all time on the cross. True Christians will never "unite" for the sake of religious unity with those who will not acknowledge the supremacy of Jesus Christ. We take Peter's admonition very seriously:

"Nor is there salvation in any other, for there is no other name under heaven given among men by which we must be saved" (Acts 4:12).

## THE RELIGIONS OF THE WORLD UNITE

However much we may agree with Pope Paul II on his stand against abortion, homosexuality, and other aspects of morality, we must oppose his promotion of unity among Christ-denying religions of the world. In 1986 he convened a conference for 130 religious leaders of the world in Iccese, Italy, to "pray for world peace." In attendance were Muslims, Buddhists, Hindus, pantheists, the Dalai Lama, and a host of others who reject Jesus Christ. Who could they all pray to? They don't agree on who (or even *what*) God is or in whose name we should pray. Of one thing we are certain: You can't reject or ignore God's Son and still expect to have your prayers answered.

The idea that all religions point to the same god is blasphemy. So is the idea that there are many ways to God. Buddha, Mary, Gaia, Muhammad, and Christ are *not* in the same category. They do not all carry equal weight with the triune God of the Bible. Just one was God's "only begotten Son," and only He gives us access to God through prayer.

The present pope is on record as believing in the Trinity and may indeed pray in the name of Jesus Christ. However, his infatuation with the vision of Fatima and his reverence for Mary (whom he credits with saving his life from an assassin's bullet) concerns some who fear he could be setting up his church and the religions of the world for the fulfillment of Revelation 17, where "Mystery Babylon, the mother of harlots" unifies all the religions of the world during the first half of the Tribulation.

## HOW CLOSE ARE WE?

All it would take for the world's religions to unite under the leadership of Rome would be the Rapture of all true Christians. That would successfully strip the Catholic Church, the Orthodox church, liberal Protestantism, and the evangelical church of any true believers and would make religious unity without respect for doctrinal differences instantly possible. It was exactly this in our novel *Tribulation Force* that enabled the eventual leader of the one-world church to say:

**One World Church**
Revelation 17

> We are all, every one of us, in total unanimity. Our religions themselves have caused as much division and bloodshed around the world as any government, army, or weapon. From this day forward we will unite under the banner of the Global Community Faith. Our logo will contain sacred symbols from religions that represent all, and from here on will encompass all. Whether we believe God is a real person or merely a concept, God is in all and above all and around all. God is in us. God is us. We are God.[4]

Have you heard all the contemporary voices calling for religious unity on the basis of "tolerance"? They are merely a harbinger of what is predicted for the first half of the Tribulation. Given today's religious climate, that could come within days or at most a few weeks of the departure of half a billion or so true Christians in the Rapture.

What we find interesting is that the only religious group *not* tolerated today is Bible-believing Christians. They are seen as intolerant because they insist that "Jesus is the only way." Once we are removed by the Rapture, nothing on the religious horizon would impede the idolatrous worshipers of the world from uniting and becoming the Babylonian harlot that has for centuries been "drunk with the blood of the saints and with the blood of the martyrs of Jesus" (Revelation 17:6). It is clear from Revelation that these idolatrous religionists will continue to hate Jesus Christ and His followers right into the Tribulation. In fact, the enormous persecution and martyrdom of the Tribulation saints during that period (see chapter 25) will be instigated by the religious system labeled by the apostle John as "Mystery Babylon."

In our day the religions of the world are moving together rapidly—a significant indication that we are living in or very near the end times.

## THE SEAL JUDGMENTS: IT ALL BEGINS

One of the worst horrors of the Tribulation is the many plagues that will strike the world's people, particularly those who reject the Savior and refuse to have their name written in the Lamb's Book of Life. The Greek word translated "plague" appears eight times in the book of Revelation and is a part of the first "birth pain" mentioned by Jesus in His Olivet discourse. Most of these plagues are the result of man's inhumanity to man, like the plagues that usually follow wars.

The many plagues of the Tribulation will be so extensive that only a small percent of the world's population will remain by the time Christ returns. Considering together the Rapture, the four horsemen of the Apocalypse, the many judgments of God, and the martyrdom of the saints during the second half of the Tribulation, it is unlikely that half a billion people will still be living on the planet when Jesus Christ returns. Probably billions will die of the plagues. Others will die from wars, earthquakes, changes in nature, and the other judgments of God. Unsanitary conditions will be everywhere during that time, doubtlessly exacerbating the many infectious diseases that already will be out of control.

Let's now take a brief look at each of the judgments of God that are to strike the earth and its inhabitants in the first half of the Tribulation.

### 1. The first seal: A white horse (Revelation 6:1-2)

The first seal introduces the initial member of the famous "four horsemen of the Apocalypse." The rider is said to have a bow but no arrows, indicating that although he is militarily strong, in the beginning he does his conquering by diplomacy. Since he wears a crown, we know he is successful in his efforts. And who is this rider on a white horse? There can be no doubt that it is the Antichrist, who through deceit and clever maneuvering will bring a false peace to the world. But that peace will not last.

### 2. The second seal: A red horse (Revelation 6:3-4)

John writes of the second horseman, "It was granted to the one who sat on [the red horse] to take peace from the earth, and that people should kill one another; and there was given to him a great sword." We believe this seal represents a great conflagration we might call World War III. When Daniel's "three kings" oppose the Antichrist, he will respond in deadly fashion, swiftly crushing his enemies and bringing death to earth on a massive scale never before known.

It is easy for modern readers to imagine the reality behind this second seal. The ability of modern armies to inflict staggering casualties on their enemies is well known but almost beyond comprehension. Only since the advent of the atomic age has it been possible to bring this kind of unimaginable, swift destruction to bear on widely scattered portions of the globe.

Did you know that the Soviet Union at the time it collapsed had thirty thousand atomic or neutron warheads, many aimed at population centers? Since the breakup of that "evil empire," no one knows what has happened to all those weapons. Russia claimed it was too poor to dismantle the ones in Yugoslavia and other struggling republics, and the host countries could not afford to man them, dismantle them, or protect them from terrorists. So what did they do? These cash-poor countries began selling them to rogue nations like Iran, Iraq, China, India, and only God knows who else. Over *ten thousand* nuclear scientists from Russia are reported to have migrated with these warheads to other countries. A case could be made that the world is in a much more precarious condition today than when the Soviet Communists controlled all their weapons!

Former president Ronald Reagan was once quoted as saying, "We see around us today the marks of a terrible dilemma, predictions of doomsday. Those predictions carry weight because of the existence of nuclear weapons and the constant threat of global war . . . so much so that no president, no congress, no parliament can spend a day entirely free of this threat." Our leaders fear not only rogue nations but also world domination by another Joseph Stalin. In addition, there is always the threat of nuclear proliferation by some terrorist group that, if it acquired a delivery system, could blackmail cities or whole countries. And that possibility is not as far-fetched as some people might think.

General Alexander Lebed, national security advisor to Russian president Boris Yeltsin, shocked the world some time ago by announcing that one hundred suitcase-size nuclear bombs were *missing!* The bombs in question were one-kiloton weapons developed by the KGB for special forces operations during the cold war. Weighing between sixty and a hundred pounds, each is easily transported and could be set up and detonated by a single man in less than half an hour. Detonated in a city, a single bomb could kill up to 100,000 people. No one has any idea where they are; neither do they know if the bombs have been destroyed, stored, sold, or stolen.[5]

Reports coming out of the former Soviet Union indicate that since the fall of the empire, security measures have been so lax that as many as 250 such bombs are missing. It is only a matter of time before these KGB-manufactured bombs, or more sophisticated miniaturized bombs, fall into the hands of the wrong people.

Of course, nuclear weapons are not the only technological threat to mankind today. The late Dr. George Wald, Nobel prizewinning scientist and biology department head at Harvard University, was quoted as saying, "I think human life is threatened as never before in the history of this planet. Not by one peril, but by many. They are all working together, coming to a head about the same time.

And the time lies very close to the year 2000. I am one of those scientists who find it hard to see how the human race is to bring itself much past the year 2000." French biologist Dr. Jacques Monod is only slightly more optimistic: "I don't see how we can survive much later than 2050."

We are not suggesting that these doomsday prophecies will be fulfilled in our lifetime or even before Christ returns; in fact, they most assuredly will not. My point is that since Christ is going to return to a *populated* earth, He will have to return soon, or some man or nation will try to destroy all humankind. Such a holocaust is now conceivable for the first time in human history. Certainly this must point to a soon coming of Jesus Christ!

### 3. The third seal: A black horse (Revelation 6:5-6)

Rampant inflation—a common aftermath of war—is suggested by John's words, "A quart of wheat for a denarius, and three quarts of barley for a denarius; and do not harm the oil and the wine." Since in biblical days a denarius was a common wage for a day's work, and a quart of wheat or three quarts of barley are basically subsistence diets, John is indicating that a man will have to work all day just to get enough food to eat, with nothing left over for his family or the elderly. On the other hand, the call to not "harm the oil and the wine"—symbols of wealth—indicates that the rich will do just fine.

The third horseman of the Apocalypse, who rides out early in the Tribulation, will take a heavy toll in deaths and sickness. The black horse he rides is an obvious symbol of famine and disease, which often follow war.

Although we don't have medical descriptions of these Tribulation plagues, already today we have identified some diseases, such as the Ebola virus, AIDS, and STDs (sexually transmitted diseases), which have similar effects. Four decades ago, the medical profession thought it had eliminated sexually transmitted diseases. Yet today these scourges have returned with a vengeance. Penicillin and antibiotics worked for a time, but the diseases developed stronger strains, too powerful for the usual drugs to contain, and today they are worse than before.

AIDS is one of the most frightening diseases of our times, particularly for the sexually promiscuous. Once it is contracted, it is always fatal. It spreads like wildfire, and no cure seems to be on the horizon. In 1982 the United States reported its first case; since then cases have reached into the millions. Experts predict it will infect ten million people by the year 2000, and that is probably a low estimate. In Africa, the country most tragically hit by AIDS, this disease will soon reach 50 percent of the population unless a cure is found.

We mention AIDS, not because we believe it fulfills some prophecies in Revelation, but because it is similar to the plagues that Revelation describes. We already have Revelation-type plagues on our hands, and the most advanced scientific laboratories of our day have been able to do little or nothing to halt them.

Fifteen years ago a doctor alerted me to chlamydia, a genital disease I had never heard of. He explained that there were over one million cases at that time. Recently I read that the number now is 11 million—just fifteen years later!

And sexually transmitted diseases aren't the only ones spreading; there are many others. "In the last 15 years, diseases that seemed to be in decline, such as dengue [fever] and tuberculosis, or diseases that had disappeared, such as cholera, have once again begun to take a toll on the population," said Dr. George Alleyne, director of the Pan American Sanitary Bureau of the World Health Organization (WHO). Dengue fever is an infectious viral disease transmitted by mosquitoes and marked by severe pains in the joints. "Infectious diseases are the world's leading cause of death, killing at least 17 million people—most of them young children—every year. Diseases that seemed to be subdued, such as tuberculosis and malaria, are fighting back with renewed ferocity. . . . This world has not seen the end of new epidemics, because the bugs are smarter than we are."[6]

This official report, based on WHO studies, indicates that cholera, dysentery, and malaria are also returning with a vengeance, and the new strains are resistant to present medication. The golden day of medical cures for man's sins seems about over.

All that is needed for Tribulation plagues to sweep this earth, as Scripture teaches they will, is for Christ to rapture his church, the Antichrist to sign his covenant with Israel, and the four horsemen to begin their march to doomsday. Many of the Tribulation-type plagues are already here!

### 4. The fourth seal: A pale horse (Revelation 6:7-8)

Why is the fourth horse pale? Because its colorless appearance symbolizes death. John says the rider who sat on this horse "was Death, and Hades followed with him. And power was given to them over a fourth of the earth, to kill with sword, with hunger, with death, and by the beasts of the earth." One quarter of the earth's population—well over a billion people—will die as a result of World War III. That Hades follows Death shows that those slain are unbelievers, for upon death believers do not go to Hades but straight to the Savior's side.

One man who heard about these first four seals was so impressed with the possibility of the soon second coming of the Lord that he said, "I sometimes think I hear the hoofbeats of the four horsemen of the Apocalypse." I replied, "Don't listen for hoofbeats, because the shout of the Savior from heaven to call His church to be with Himself comes first!" It can't be far off!

### 5. The fifth seal: The martyrs (Revelation 6:9-11)

When the fifth seal is opened, John sees "under the altar the souls of those who had been slain for the word of God and for the testimony which they held." Shortly after the beginning of the Tribulation there will be a great "soul harvest" in which millions will come to faith in Christ, many as a result of the preaching of the 144,000 witnesses described in Revelation 7 (see chapter 24). Most of these Tribulation saints will be killed by the forces of Antichrist. These martyred souls will cry out for God to avenge their deaths, but they will be told to "rest a little while longer, until both the number of their fellow servants and their brethren, who would be killed as they were, was completed." Imagine! Despite the desperate evil of the Antichrist, despite the horrors of war and famine and pestilence and death, God is still so much in control of earthly events that even the number of believing martyrs has been fixed by divine decree. Astonishing!

### 6. The sixth seal: The great earthquake (Revelation 6:12-17)

The first four seals described judgments largely inflicted by man; the sixth seal describes a judgment clearly supernatural in origin. John tells of an earthquake so massive that "every mountain and island was moved out of its place." Probably he also has in mind enormous volcanic activity, for he says "the sun became black as sackcloth of hair, and the moon became like blood." Particulate matter scattered in the atmosphere after a volcanic eruption has often turned the sky black and made the moon seem to turn red; recall the 1980 eruption of Mount St. Helens in Washington State or the gigantic explosion of Krakatau on August 27, 1883. John also foresaw meteorites crashing into the earth (verse 13) and what may be huge mushroom clouds of undetermined origin (verse 14). The people of earth will recognize these phenomena as coming from the hand of God, for they are said to cry out to the mountains where they take cover, "Fall on us and hide us from the face of Him who sits on the throne and from the wrath of the Lamb! For the great day of His wrath has come, and who is able to stand?" (verses 16-17).

## 7. The seventh seal: The trumpet judgments (Revelation 8:1-2)

The seventh seal is different from all its predecessors in that it introduces the next series of divine judgments, the seven trumpet judgments. While five of the seal judgments feature devastations wrought by man, all of the trumpet judgments come directly from heaven. They are so severe that verse 1 says, "When He opened the seventh seal, there was silence in heaven for about half an hour." In the rest of Revelation heaven is seen to be a joyous and worshipful place, with choruses singing, trumpets blaring, celestial beings crying out—but suddenly there comes this ominous silence. As horrible as the seal judgments were, the trumpet judgments will be worse.

## THE TRUMPET JUDGMENTS:
## FROM BAD TO WORSE

While the seal judgments occur in roughly the first twenty-one months of the Tribulation, the trumpet judgments take place in the second twenty-one months. In the first period of the Tribulation the earth has known the wrath of the Antichrist; now it will begin to feel the wrath of God Almighty.

### 1. The first trumpet: Hail, fire, and blood
### (Revelation 8:7)

In this opening salvo, ice and fire rain from the sky, burning up a third of all the earth's trees and all of its grass. This is an ecological disaster without parallel to this point in the history of mankind; its results are incalculable. To make matters even worse, John also adds that "blood" arrives with the hail and fire, as the prophet Joel had predicted: "And I will show wonders in the heavens and in the earth: blood and fire and pillars of smoke" (Joel 2:30). And this is but the first trumpet!

### 2. The second trumpet: A mountain of fire
### (Revelation 8:8-9)

When the second trumpet is blown, John sees "something like a great mountain burning with fire"—likely an enormous meteorite crashing through the atmosphere— "thrown into the sea, and a third of the sea became blood." As a result, a third of everything living in the sea dies, and a third of the ships on the sea are destroyed.

The World Health Organization report just cited also says that "nearly half of the world's people are affected by diseases related to insufficient and contaminated water," which is why the WHO is trying to improve the water supplies of the world. We shudder to think of the plagues that will be spread when the water supply turns bitter, then to blood in that "great and terrible Day of the Lord."

### 3. The third trumpet: A star called Wormwood
### (Revelation 8:10-11)

When the third angel blows his trumpet, another meteorite crashes to earth, "burning like a torch." It does not fall on the sea but on a third of the earth's rivers and springs, turning them "bitter" and poisonous. As a result of this plague, "many men" die.

### 4. The fourth trumpet: Darkness descends
### (Revelation 8:12)

All life on this earth depends on the sun: If it were to explode, the earth would incinerate; if it were to go cold, the earth would freeze solid. Neither of those extremes is in view with the fourth trumpet judgment, but in some way God does reduce by a third the amount of radiant energy reaching earth from the sun and all other celestial bodies. John writes, "A third of the sun was struck, a third of the moon, and a third of the stars, so that a third of them were darkened; a third of the day did not shine, and likewise the night."

This naturally reminds us of the plague sent on Pharaoh as described in Exodus 10:21: "Darkness over the land of Egypt, darkness which may even be felt." And it gives detail to our Lord's prediction, "There shall be signs in the sun, and in the moon, and in the stars; and upon the earth distress of nations, with perplexity; the sea and the waves roaring; men's hearts failing them for fear, and for looking after those things which are coming on the earth: for the powers of heaven shall be shaken" (Luke 21:25-26, KJV).

## 5. The fifth trumpet: The locusts of Apollyon attack (Revelation 9:1-11)

The fifth trumpet judgment is also the first of three "woes" pronounced by the angel of Revelation 8:13—a frightening sign of the ferocity of the coming judgments. When this trumpet is sounded, an angel unlocks the "bottomless pit," and out of the pit belches smoke and "locusts" with the scorpion-like power to sting and torment unbelievers for five months. Their sting is never fatal—in fact, John says, "In those days men will seek death and will not find it; they will desire to die, and death will flee from them"—but the pain they cause will be unbearable. Victims of scorpion bites say the animal's venom seems to set one's veins and nervous system on fire, but the pain is gone after a few days; not so with these locusts. They are given power to torment "those men who do not have the seal of God on their foreheads" for five long months. Yet unlike normal locusts, these beasts attack only unregenerate human beings, never foliage.

The appearance of these locusts is both frightening and repulsive (verses 7-10), and they do not act in an unorganized way; in fact, John says, "They had as king over them the angel of the bottomless pit, whose name in Hebrew is Abaddon, but in Greek he has the name Apollyon" (verse 11). Both names mean "Destroyer."

This seems to be one of the plagues that God sends on the followers of Antichrist to hinder them from proselytizing among the uncommitted of the world. It may also give Tribulation saints some time to prepare themselves for the horrors of the soon-to-come Great Tribulation. In our novel *Apollyon* we used the attack of the locusts for just this purpose. A character named Mac writes to a fellow Tribulation saint:

> A few of us believers have been able to pretend we are simply recuperating more quickly, so we don't lie around the infirmary twenty-four hours a day listening to the agony. Carpathia has sent me on some missions of mercy, delivering aid to some of the worst-off rulers. What he doesn't know is that David has picked up clandestine shipments of literature, copies of Tsion's studies in different languages, and has jammed the cargo hold of the Condor 216 with them. Believers wherever I go unload and distribute them.[7]

## 6. The sixth trumpet: The four angels released (Revelation 9:13-19)

At the blowing of the sixth trumpet, the second "woe" is unleashed: the release of "the four angels who are bound at the great river Euphrates" (verse 14). These angels apparently lead an army of 200 million "horsemen" who kill a third of mankind through the plagues of fire and smoke and brimstone. When you combine this third with the quarter of humanity killed in the seal judgments, by this point in the Tribulation half of the world's population (after the Rapture) already has been destroyed.

Who are these 200 million horsemen? In the May 21, 1965, issue of *Time* magazine, the author of an article on China threw a hand grenade into the laps of prophecy preachers by stating that the Chinese had the potential of raising an army of "200 million troops."[8]

That this number of troops matches exactly the number found in Revelation 9:16 triggered an outbreak of speculation that caused some interpreters to suggest the 200 million would come with the kings of the east to do battle with Christ at the consummation of the end of this age, known as the Battle of Armageddon. But while there is no question that the armies of the Orient coming to that battle at the very end of the Tribulation will be enormous, due to the incredible population of those countries, they definitely are *not* the Revelation 9:16 army. Consider the following reasons:

- The 9:16 army goes out during the sixth trumpet, which occurs near the middle of the Tribulation; the 16:12 army goes out at the end of the Tribulation.
- The 200 million in 9:16 are not humans but demons, doing things men cannot do. These "horsemen" have a supernatural effect on the earth.
- The *Time* article included all the men and women under arms in China, including their local militias or defense forces. There is no way the communist government could risk committing *all* its military and armament to the Middle East, for they know their freedom-hungry citizens would revolt before they returned. Besides, the logistics of moving an army of 200 million from the Orient across the Euphrates and the Arabian Desert to the little land of Israel seems impossible. Such an army would consist of four times as many troops as were utilized in all of World War II—and that stretched from the South Pacific through Europe and into the Near East and lasted over five years. This battle is over in a matter of days.

For these and other reasons not mentioned, it is not realistic (and scripturally unnecessary) to assume that the armies of 16:12 are synonymous with those of 9:16.

The 200 million horsemen who come on the scene in this text will obviously be supernatural—creatures that are so awesome to look on, as we portrayed them in *Assassins,* that they actually frighten some people to death. And their sting "is in their mouth and their tails"—and with them they kill one-third of the world's population of those who reject Christ and commit themselves to Antichrist (9:4).

## 7. The seventh trumpet: Loud voices in heaven (Revelation 11:15-19)

The third "woe," the blowing of the seventh trumpet, is like the breaking of the seventh seal in that it introduces the next series of divine judgments. The seventh trumpet is not in itself a judgment but rather shows all heaven rejoicing at the soon-to-be consummated victory of Christ over the Antichrist. John records that "loud voices" in heaven shouted, "The kingdoms of this world have become the kingdoms of our Lord and of His Christ, and He shall reign forever and ever!" (verse 15). Great rejoicing and loud worship fill heaven, and on earth many lightnings, noises, thunderings, hail, and an earthquake announce the approaching end.

But first, the Great Tribulation.

# FOURTEEN

## *The Great Tribulation*

RAYFORD wanted to vomit. "So now you're some sort of deity?"

"That is not for me to say, though clearly, raising a dead man is a divine act. Mr. Fortunato believes I could be the Messiah."

Rayford raised his eyebrows. "If I were you, I'd be quick to deny that, unless I knew it to be true."

Carpathia softened. "It does not seem the time for me to make such a claim, but I am not so sure it is untrue."

*SOUL HARVEST, 86*

In the first half of the Tribulation, vicious plagues sweep the earth, flaming meteorites poison a third of its water, warring armies kill millions, demonic beings torture the unredeemed, darkness swallows a third of the sun, and half the world's post-Rapture population dies horribly.

And then it gets worse.

As it is the Antichrist who begins the terrors of the Tribulation by signing a godless seven-year treaty with Israel, so it is the Antichrist who starts the Great Tribulation by using the rebuilt temple in Jerusalem as the stage to proclaim his divinity. In so doing he breaks the treaty after three and a half years and brings upon his kingdom the terrible wrath of God. So unspeakably dreadful is the period he triggers that Jesus said of it, "Then there will be great tribulation, such as has not been since the beginning of the world until this time, no, nor ever shall be. And unless those days were shortened, no flesh would be saved; but for the elect's sake those days will be shortened" (Matthew 24:21-22).

## THE WRATH OF GOD

Chapter 15 of Revelation provides a fitting introduction to the Great Tribulation, which we might rightly call forty-two months of hell on earth. The chapter begins and ends with the wrath of God, a holy wrath so intense and hot that verses 7-8 tell us, "one of the four living creatures gave to the seven angels seven golden bowls full of the wrath of God who lives forever and ever. The temple was filled with smoke from the glory of God and from His power, and no one was able to enter the temple till the seven plagues of the seven angels were completed."

Imagine! The rebellion and arrogance of the Antichrist and his followers has reached such staggering proportions that neither angel nor man can enter the temple in heaven until God's wrath is poured out in full strength.

While it is the "abomination of desolation" (the defiling of the temple by Antichrist) that triggers the Great Tribulation, it is not this vile event alone that merits the divine judgments to come. The sins of the "man of sin" have been piling high ever since his appearance on the world scene a few years before.

## THE RISE OF COMMERCIAL BABYLON

All the Antichrist's sins find their source in a single ultimate wickedness: the desire to live independently of God and even supplant Him. This supreme iniquity is reflected even in the economic system set up by the Antichrist. Commercial Babylon, as I call it, is every bit as much opposed to God in the realm of daily life as is religious Babylon in the realm of spiritual life—and it will be judged just as severely.

During these days of Tribulation, New York, London, and Brussels will no longer be the commercial hubs of the universe. Instead, the elite and superrich movers and shakers of the world will have offices and villas in Babylon, from which they will direct their worldwide commercial empires. The Antichrist will move the world's commercial center to the headquarters of his new world empire, New Babylon. This will happen sometime during the transition period between the Rapture and the Tribulation.

It is very clear from studying Revelation 13, 17, and 18 that the Antichrist will have total control of the world's economy during the last three years of the Tribulation. His primary tool will be absolute domination of the money supply. And how will he accomplish this great feat? Through a famous means commonly known as "the mark of the beast."

## THE MARK OF THE BEAST

One of the best known prophecies of the Tribulation is that the "Beast," or Antichrist, will have the ability to put his mark "666" on the forehead or hand of the world's people. According to Revelation 13:17, during the second half of the Tribulation, Antichrist will have such total control of the earth "that no one may buy or sell except one who has the mark . . . or the number of his name." There can be no greater human control than total control of the supply and flow of money. Whoever has the power to decide who can work, buy, or sell—has absolute power.

Revelation 13:13-18 teaches that after the midpoint of the Tribulation, all men and women will be ordered to bow down before the image of the Beast and worship him. Those who do will receive "a mark . . . on their foreheads" that is "the name of the beast, or the number of his name"—later identified as 666. This will identify them as worshipers of the Beast. All those without that mark will be killed.

Scripture makes it clear that receiving the mark of the Beast is no accident but the result of a deliberate choice made during the Tribulation. That choice involves rejecting the teaching of the two witnesses, the 144,000 Jewish witnesses, the outpouring of the Holy Spirit (Joel 2:28-32), and the angel with the everlasting gospel (Revelation 14:6-7). Twice in chapter 14 an angel warns that "if anyone worships the beast and his image, and receives his mark on his forehead or on his hand, he himself shall also drink of the wine of the wrath of God." Those who accept the mark will be cast into hell "and shall be tormented with fire and brimstone. . . . And the smoke of their torment ascends forever and ever; and they have no rest day or night, [those] who worship the beast and his image, and whoever receives the mark of his name" (verses 9-11).

Concerned believers sometimes worry that they might

somehow inadvertently receive this devilish mark. But this is impossible. First, we should remember that our God is loving and merciful; He proved that forever in the gift of His Son. We should see Him as our heavenly Father who stands at the gate of heaven, letting men and women *into* His paradise, not trying to keep them *out*. It would be totally out of character for Him to send someone to hell for accidentally standing in the wrong line and getting the mark of the Beast, when he really wanted the mark of the Father. Second, the aforementioned verses show that the mark is obtained only by those who sell their soul to the Beast and the devil who gives him his power. This involves a willful rejection of God—something a true Christian could never do.

A couple of years ago a *Los Angeles Times* reporter called me when an Air Force captain stationed in Hawaii refused to accept a government-mandated identification tag, for fear he would be taking the "mark of the beast" of Revelation 13. We can give the good captain an A+ for dedication to his Lord and his desire to serve Him, even if it meant the loss of his military career. But we must give him a D- on a proper understanding of the prophetic Scriptures. For the Bible is quite clear that a person *cannot* take the mark of the Beast accidentally. In fact, it will become the external sign of a deliberate decision to give one's self to the devil. Also, since the mark of the Beast does not appear until the middle of the Tribulation—which is at least three and a half years after the Rapture, and maybe even ten or more years after that world-shaking event—no Christian alive need worry about inadvertently taking the mark and becoming a follower of the Beast and the devil.

The only people who should be concerned are those

who miss the Rapture and are left behind to go through the Tribulation. For if they live into the Tribulation, they had better be prepared to make a choice. But they should understand this: Once the choice is made, it is eternal!

## TAKING THE MARK—IRREVERSIBLE

I have one word of caution for any reader who may not yet know the Lord. It seems quite clear that once the decision is made to worship the Antichrist and receive his mark or his name, it is an irreversible decision. It appears that receiving the mark of the Beast is an unpardonable sin—which is why we should warn the unsaved never to consider taking that mark or worshiping the Antichrist. During the Tribulation the Holy Spirit will convict men and warn them of sin and of their need to receive the gospel. You can be sure He will be there to protect anyone from making an inadvertent mistake!

The important thing, however, is that no one reading this portion of the book ever has to make such a decision. By accepting Jesus Christ by faith as your Lord and Savior, you can keep yourself from ever being put into this terrible situation. That's what the Bible means when it says, *"Now is the accepted time; . . . [today] is the day of salvation"* (2 Corinthians 6:2, emphasis added).

## THE CASHLESS SOCIETY

Thinking people who read Revelation 13 have long wondered how the Antichrist could exercise such total control over billions of people. How could it be possible that they could not buy or sell without his mark?

For the first time in two thousand years, it is now technologically possible to enforce such a system. Microchips have already been invented that can be placed in the fatty tissue behind the ear or in other places of the body to enable others to track that individual. (Such systems are already in place to track family pets.) We are all familiar with the scanner at the checkout counter of most stores. All it would take is a computer program that required the "666" number on people's accounts (or hands or foreheads) in order for them to "buy or sell." Mark-of-the-Beast technology is already here!

Still, technology by itself is nearly powerless. It will finally become prophetically potent in the coming worldwide move to a cashless society.

For years, many have taught that we were moving to a single world currency. Some time ago plans were laid to divide the world into three currencies: the Japanese yen for the Orient; the German mark for Europe; and the U.S. dollar for the Americas. Today those plans are obsolete! The one-world planners are on a fast track toward a cashless society.

Officials of the world already have begun using both natural and man-made catastrophes as a basis to call for a cashless society. For example, they know it would help solve the burgeoning crime problem. Last night on the evening news I heard how a local robber held up five 7-Eleven stores and picked up nine thousand dollars for his trouble. That would be impossible in a cashless society! All it would take is for you to agree to have your paycheck automatically deposited (over 25 percent of Americans already do); then you would use a "smart card" to purchase everything you buy, from bread to gas. You alone could use that card; microchips the size of a single hair would be encoded with your fingerprints and secret number. Such a card would solve the alarming rate of crime, for there would be no cash in banks or shops to steal. It would put an end to counterfeiting, racketeering, or anything that involves the flow of cash.

When my wife got me an ATM card, she canceled my old checkbook because it was "obsolete." With that card I am never very far from cash, even in primitive countries. But that card is already out-of-date. Now we talk of debit cards, electronic transfers, bar codes, credit cards, microchips, and the availability of a single smart card that will last for life. It will contain your identification, history, health records, financial status, and more things than we could have imagined just ten years ago.

Grant Jeffrey, a cutting-edge prophecy writer and speaker, was a financial consultant in Canada before dedicating his life to teaching prophecy. He believes that international bankers introduced the credit and ATM cards not just for speeding up transactions but to condition the public for a cashless society in which everything will be bought or sold by a smart card; even deposits and withdrawals will be made through a machine and a card.

Terry Cook, a careful investigator and expert on modern technology, suggests the following:

> The New World Order economists are not ignorant of the importance of cash and its ability to inhibit their total control of the world. They are aware that in order to completely control, track, and monitor the global population, they first must eliminate the use of cash. With cash, there is no way to know how people are using their finances, whether for or against the government and its agenda. Because con-

trol of one's finances in essence means control of one's entire life, advocates of world government have for decades been promoting a move toward cashless transactions via a myriad of banking plans, ATM machines, credit cards, point-of-sale machines, credit data—all funneled through massive computer systems. Eventually, the goal is control of all these computers by the economic leaders of the New World Order.[1]

Do governments want this technology to be compulsory? Absolutely! In America alone, millions of people are doing business under the table on a cash-only basis in order to bypass the enormous tax rate. Eliminating this possibility could net the United States treasury an estimated 200 billion to a trillion additional dollars a year. Just think how fast the national debt could be paid with an increase of close to a trillion a year in currently unpaid taxes! Or just think of the bureaucracies that could be set up to provide more control over the American people. Look soon for the government to begin calling for legislation that will do away with cash. This may well be a dominant feature in the presidential elections of 2000 or 2004.

The serious drawbacks to such a system, of course, will not be mentioned. The chief loss will be the death of freedom. Once the government has mandated a cashless society, it will have total control of purchasing, labor, wages, and everything else. Financial control of the people translates to total control. In addition, "Big Brother" will know everything about you. And national "Big Brother" is just one step away from "International Big Brother"—the number of his name is 666!

## THE TECHNOLOGY IS ALREADY HERE

The most frightening part of all this is that there is no need to wait for the emergence of new technologies to make possible a one-world commercial system. In fact, it already exists. What needs to change is not technology but public opinion and appropriate government legislation. And there is plenty of time, prophetically, to accomplish that! Right after the Rapture, liberals and socialists will unite and elect their leaders—the commercial, governmental, and eventually the religious leaders of the world.

Since the world already possesses the necessary technology to make this a reality, all it would take is an economic crash to spur its implementation—and the aftermath of the Rapture could well provide just such a worldwide crisis. Such a program could be implemented in three to five years or less.

## THE STAGE IS SET

On October 27, 1997, the U.S. stock market fell more than five hundred points in a single day. Wall Street almost pan-

**Capital and Labor Conflict**
James 5:1-6

icked because it feared its greatest nightmare had returned—a 1929-type crash followed by a 1930s-type depression. Fortunately, that didn't happen; the market rebounded over three hundred points the next day. In the meantime, however, the market in Hong Kong dropped drastically, then likewise rebounded.

This incident proves that we already have a global economy so interdependent that if Wall Street gets a cold, Japan, Hong Kong, London, Frankfort, and other key markets start to sneeze. That should not be surprising, for the Bildeberg, the Trilateral Commission, the CFR, and other secret and semisecret organizations have been working for years to set up an interdependent world economy. Two motivations spur them to action:

1. It is far more profitable to have the world as your market than one nation or even one region. This is what is behind the foolhardy investment of western capital to improve the economies of socialist China, Russia, and other failing countries.
2. The one-hundred-year-old (or older) idea that economic interdependence would make it economically impossible for nations to go to war with one another.

The recent passage in the United States of GATT, NAFTA, and other fast-track trading agreements proves we have reached the point of no return. This world is going to have world trade because the insiders who control our media, banking, government, and trade agreements want it that way.

They probably don't realize it, but they are greasing the skids that will usher in the most charismatic, slick politician the world has ever known. The Antichrist will take the reigns of world leadership and make it "work" commercially. The threat of bankruptcy or the loss of oil is all it would take to bring the most rebellious nation into line. Prophecy scholars have predicted for many years that this world of very independent nations would move toward commercial interdependence. Some have been surprised at the lightning pace and new technology that makes this possible, but many of us have expected it.

All this means that there is nothing from an economic or technological standpoint to hinder the Rapture from occurring at any time. What is exciting to Christians who are ready for the Rapture (and scary for those who are not) is that the world already has the technology to accomplish all this. And it could all happen in our generation!

## THE DESTRUCTION OF COMMERCIAL BABYLON

It sometimes appears to us as though God turns a blind eye to sin and injustice, that He just doesn't seem to care about human wickedness. How often have we asked, as did the prophet, "O Lord, how long shall I cry, and You will not hear? Even cry out to You, 'Violence!' and You will not save. . . . Why do You look on those who deal treacherously, and hold Your tongue when the wicked devours one more righteous than he?" (Habakkuk 1:2, 13).

The Bible makes it clear that finite perceptions like this are very human but never accurate. As the apostle Peter reminds us, "He is patient with you, not wanting anyone to perish, but everyone to come to repentance" (2 Peter 3:9, NIV). And yet the time inevitably comes when the day of patience gives way to the day of recompense. So will it be for commercial Babylon.

Revelation 18 describes in graphic detail the destruction of Babylon, the Tribulation capital of worldwide commerce. Just read the following prediction of Babylon's ultimate destruction at the very end of the Tribulation, and you will see what we mean:

> The kings of the earth who committed fornication
> and lived luxuriously with her will weep and lament
> for her, when they see the smoke of her burning,

standing at a distance for fear of her torment, saying, "Alas, alas, that great city Babylon, that mighty city! For in one hour your judgment has come."

And the merchants of the earth will weep and mourn over her, for no one buys their merchandise anymore: merchandise of gold and silver, precious stones and pearls, fine linen and purple, silk and scarlet, every kind of citron wood, every kind of object of ivory, every kind of object of most precious wood, bronze, iron, and marble; and cinnamon and incense, fragrant oil and frankincense, wine and oil, fine flour and wheat, cattle and sheep, horses and chariots, and bodies and souls of men. The fruit that your soul longed for has gone from you, and all the things which are rich and splendid have gone from you, and you shall find them no more at all.

The merchants of these things, who became rich by her, will stand at a distance for fear of her torment, weeping and wailing, and saying, "Alas, alas, that great city that was clothed in fine linen, purple, and scarlet, and adorned with gold and precious stones and pearls! For in one hour such great riches came to nothing." (verses 9-17)

Such will be the end of commercial Babylon at the close of the Great Tribulation. But before her utter destruction, the world will see horrors we can now only dimly imagine. Let us now consider the final seven judgments of God.

## THE BOWL JUDGMENTS: THE WRATH OF GOD
Daniel chapter 3 tells the famous story of the three Hebrew men who refused to bow down and worship the image of

gold that King Nebuchadnezzar had set up on the plain of Dura. The king was so infuriated by their refusal that he had them tossed into a furnace heated seven times hotter than normal. But before he did so, he threatened them with exactly this punishment, then made an unwise challenge: "And who is the god who will deliver you from my hands?" (verse 15)

The foolish king soon found out the answer to his arrogant question, because the God of heaven not only spared the lives of His three faithful servants, He even prevented the smell of smoke from soiling their untouched clothes. And so Nebuchadnezzar, an ancient type of the Antichrist, discovered that his feeble hands were no match for the hands of God Almighty.

You might say that the seven last plagues of the Great Tribulation are God's final response to Nebuchadnezzar's insolent boast—yet this time, the question is reversed. Now God is asking the Antichrist, "What god will deliver you from My hands?" And the answer, of course, is, "No one." For although the Antichrist may proclaim himself to be God and though he may receive his power from Satan himself, in the end he is revealed to be nothing before the true God of the universe—and therefore he will be thrown not into a furnace heated seven times hotter than normal, but into the lake of fire, which burns forever and ever.

### 1. The first bowl: Foul and loathesome sores (Revelation 16:2)

When men choose to worship Antichrist rather than Christ and demonstrate their allegiance by accepting the mark of the Beast, God responds by sending on them a plague of "foul and loathesome" sores. The Greek word for these sores is the very term the Septuagint (the Greek translation of the Old Testament) used to translate the Hebrew term for "boils" in the story of the Egyptian plagues in Exodus 9. John makes it clear that these awful sores afflict only those who worship the Antichrist and who have accepted the mark of the Beast; no Tribulation saint suffers from the least hint of them.

## 2. The second bowl: The sea turns to blood (Revelation 16:3)

Earlier in the Tribulation God had turned a third of the sea into blood; now He commands that the entire sea become "blood as of a dead man"—that is, corrupt, decaying, stinking, putrid. No wonder "every living creature in the sea died"! How is it possible to imagine a disaster this enormous, this all-encompassing? Dead sea creatures rise to the surface, spreading their corruption to the four winds. Think of an ocean full of such filth! It staggers the imagination. And this is only the second of the seven bowls of judgment!

## 3. The third bowl: The rivers and springs turn to blood (Revelation 16:4-7)

By this point in the Tribulation the Antichrist and his forces have martyred millions of believers. Therefore God seems to say to him, "You like blood? Very well. Then you may have it to drink!" Is this literal blood? Who knows for sure? But if Jesus could turn water into wine at the marriage feast of Cana, surely He would have no problem turning water into blood. Whatever the case, because of its rebellious, murderous ways, the world will find itself without drinking water. And so the prayer of the martyred saints in Revelation 6:10 will be abundantly answered. They asked, "How long, O Lord, holy and true, until You judge and avenge our blood on those who dwell on the earth?" This plague of blood is God's answer.

## 4. The fourth bowl: The sun scorches men (Revelation 16:8-9)

Their mouths already parched from lack of water, those who are unrepentant suffer even more intense thirst when God causes the sun to "scorch" them with "great heat." But even this does not drive the rebels to their knees in repentance. Instead, they blaspheme the name of God "who has power over these plagues; and they did not repent and give Him glory." How right the angel was who said to God, "true and righteous are Your judgments" (16:7)!

## 5. The fifth bowl: Darkness on the Beast's kingdom (Revelation 16:10-11)

Is it God's mercy that causes Him to follow the plague of scorching heat with cooling darkness? Perhaps, but even this does not cause rebellious mankind to repent, for verse 11 says: "They blasphemed the God of heaven because of their pains and their sores, and did not repent of their deeds." This verse reveals that the sores of the first bowl still afflict the people, and verse 10 appears to indicate that the darkness exacerbates their pain: "And they gnawed their tongues because of the pain." This is a special judgment focused particularly on the "throne of the beast" and on his "kingdom," thus demonstrating to the whole world where the source of its trouble lies. When the Antichrist proclaimed himself God, he made himself the focus of

God's wrath. And now the world will see without question who the real God is.

### 6. The sixth bowl: The Euphrates dries up (Revelation 16:12)

The sixth bowl judgment comes in two stages:

1. The drying up of the Euphrates River, in preparation for the armies of the kings from the east (verse 12);
2. The activity of demonic forces in bringing the armies of the world to the valley of Megiddo, where they will try vainly to oppose the Lord Jesus (verses 13-14).

It is likely that when the Euphrates River—the natural boundary between east and west for sixteen hundred miles—is "dried up," the "kings from the east" will march a sizable army across to battle with the King of kings. That army will probably be three to five million strong. These forces will be joined in the valley of Meggido by huge armies from all over the world, and while that valley is vast (as Napoleon has said, "the most ideal, natural battlefield in the world"), even it has a limit to how many people it can hold.

These "kings from the east" have befuddled Bible prophecy scholars for many years, for few scholars mentioned anything about them. That is, until the communist takeover of China after World War II. Since then it has become apparent that this largest of all countries (by population) has a prophetic role, however minor it may be, in end-time events. While China had been content to stay within its vast borders for thousands of years and keep largely to itself, its communist dictators have changed all that. They seem to have the same obsession that character-ized Communists before them—world conquest.

One hundred eighty years ago Napoleon Bonaparte said, "When China awakens, the world will tremble." You don't have to be a prophet to recognize that time of trem-bling has already come to Asia and soon will probably come to the whole world.

No longer is China the paper tiger she was for almost five thousand years. In our lifetime she has startled the world and frightened many in the military complex with her enormous economic and military potential. Many ob-servers recognize that within ten or, at most, twenty years, China could very well threaten the entire world, even more than the Soviet Union did just a decade ago. She already has the nuclear bomb and a delivery system that alarms ev-ery country in the Orient. She traffics in arms beyond be-lief, buying them from Russia and any of the impoverished satellite countries that will sell them, then turning around and selling whatever she doesn't want to any of her oil-rich allies, like Iran or Iraq.

The Red Chinese demand for Taiwan and the Spratly Is-lands indicates that China has a strategy to control all of Asia. Whoever controls the Spratlys controls not only the oil checkpoints to the oil-dependent countries of the East like Japan, Taiwan, and the Philippines, but also Austra-lia, Indonesia, and Singapore—where 50 percent of the world's population lives. Basing their claims to these al-most uninhabitable islands on centuries-old documents, they are probably more interested in the suspected rich oil fields under them than in the islands themselves. They know that no country can prosper today or in the foreseeable future without oil.

But it is not merely the Orient the Chinese are interested in. In 1997 they almost negotiated an incredible coup in the Americas. It was disclosed they had leased an important pier in Long Beach, California, that was being vacated by the U.S. Navy. Their government-owned COSCO company wanted to speed their enormous imports into the United States. (The American balance of payments with China already shows a deficit of $50 billion and is expected to go as high as $70 or $100 billion—a tribute to the greed of American capitalists whose concern for profits exceeds their concern for human rights or the safety of our country).

Keep in mind, China is controlled by some of the most dedicated Communists in the world. They are not "agrarian reformers" or "progressives" as our media tried to represent them a few years ago. They are a ruthless group of elite gangsters who have never wavered in their plan to use China as a military platform from which to conquer the world. The events of the next two decades—if indeed we have that long—will prove that point.

Of one thing we can be certain: China is not going to go away. We cannot fail to recognize that the present leaders of China are real threats to the world—and 1.2 billion people will not be denied! More important, John the Revelator saw them as players on the world scene in the end times.

Even so, the Bible has very little to say about China. In fact, what is said includes more than just China, for the term "kings from the east" really means "kings from the rising sun," which would include Japan and possibly other

Asian countries. As Dr. John Walvoord, considered the dean of prophecy scholars living today, writes of this expression:

> There has been some tendency to take the expression "the kings of the east"—literally, "the kings of the sunrise"—as referring specifically to Japan where the rising sun is a symbol of its political power. However, it is more natural to consider the term "rising sun" as a synonym for east.[2]

Geographically, the Euphrates River, one of the first rivers mentioned in the Bible, has served for centuries as the natural dividing line between East and West. While Judaism and Christianity had an enormous impact on the world west of the Euphrates River, it had very little influence on the East. The story of missionary efforts in China during the eighteenth century is a heroic tale, but not nearly as successful as in other countries where the people were not so exposed to demons and spirits of devils. After over one hundred years of courageous efforts, there are an estimated 60 million Christians in China. We all rejoice at this number of born-again souls, but that is only about 5 percent of the population. Few countries boast of more continuous persecution of Christians than China—even today. There is a satanic struggle in the Orient today between the spiritual "powers of the air"—Satan against the Spirit of God.

When we were in Beijing, we secretly interviewed several Christians. They know what it is like to be persecuted and to live under the constant threat of persecution. Several of the Christians we talked with indicated they first heard the gospel over shortwave radio, through which the Spirit of

God witnessed to their empty hearts. Several were former Buddhists, one a committed Communist. All admitted emptiness in their hearts prior to turning on the shortwave radio to hear gospel broadcasts out of Hong Kong. There is something satanic to the opposition to which Christians are subjected behind the Bamboo Curtain. We learned that the Chinese have two kinds of churches:

1. The approved (or mainline) churches that agree not to teach the forbidden doctrines of the inerrancy of Scripture and the second coming of Jesus Christ (two doctrines Satan has always opposed!).
2. The underground (or house) churches whose leaders teach the whole Bible, until they are discovered and imprisoned. It is in these house churches that thousands are coming to Christ each week.

Joseph Lam puts it in perspective:

> In the West, we think of bomb-making instructions on the Internet as dangerous. Not to the dragon. To him, the "most dangerous" message on the Internet is the "Second Advent of Christ." The soon return of Christ is the message the thought-police most want to censor out. In fact, in many areas the police are registering modems and even fax machines in order to keep the end-time message of Christ's return from being circulated. You see, Chinese Christians believe passionately that Christ is coming again, not just someday—but "in this generation." The dragon knows he must stop this Apostolic message of hope. If somehow he can stop these New

Testament-style Bible studies, he knows he will cripple church growth in China.

The kingdom of God and the second coming of Christ are the rarest sermon topics preached in China's government-controlled pulpits. . . . The dragon persecutes the house churches because he is terrified of the end-time gospel they preach. This message liberates the people from bondage to their control and so it has to be denounced as "anti-revolutionary" superstition.

- Christians are consistently forbidden the right to do any public evangelism of any kind. Private worship is reluctantly permitted, but gospel preaching is banned.
- Directives to the state-controlled churches warn pastors not to preach the message of Revelation.
- Pastors in congregations of the "Three Self Patriotic movement" skip liturgical readings about the second coming of Christ such as Hebrews 9:28 and Revelation 19 and 22:20-21.
- Sunday school teachers are not allowed to discuss the "Day of the Lord" predicted in both the Old and New Testaments.
- The Olivet Discourse, recorded in three of the four Gospels, is forbidden (it's the most important outline of prophecy in Scripture).
- Many Chinese hymns of advent, missions, judgment, and the millennial reign of Christ are no longer sung in registered Chinese churches. Such music isn't politically correct.

Nothing so upsets the dragon as the mention of Christ's return, and nothing so comforts the Chinese church and missions.[3]

We could not help thinking that in America, where pastors have the freedom to preach anything they please, thousands of churches never hear that Second Coming message—not because they are forbidden by the government to preach it but because they were tricked by seminary professors into thinking it is "confusing" or "not relevant for today." Satan uses different tactics in different cultures—anything that will produce silence on the blessed hope of Christ's soon return. Why? Because there is no more spiritually motivating teaching in the Bible!

Instead, the master deceiver has damned the billions of souls of the peoples of the East with a succession of false religions. The dragon, the official symbol of China, overpowered its first settlers with the polytheism and pantheism common there today. Dr. Henry Morris writes of the Chinese:

> For ages they have been dominated by religions (Buddhism, Confucianism, Hinduism and others) which are fundamentally evolutionary religions. That is, they all envision an eternal universe, with no concept of a transcendent, omnipotent, personal God who created all things. Their emphasis is solely on present behavior. To them history consists mostly of interminable cycles, without beginning or ending.
>
> Associated with these pantheistic systems was (and is) always the worship of spirits. Whether these

are understood as spirits of ancestors or as the spirits of trees and other natural objects, such worship is in reality worship of demons, or fallen angels. Such religions thus are also commonly associated with idolatry. This eastern religion—whatever specific form it may assume in a particular time or place—is essentially the same old worship of idols, which God's prophets continually condemned. Comprising a monstrous complex of evolutionary, pantheistic, polytheistic, idolatrous, astrological, animistic humanism, it is merely a variant of the primeval religion introduced by Nimrod at Babel and promulgated throughout the world by the confusion of tongues and subsequent worldwide dispersion from Babel.

By its very nature, it lends itself to control of its devotees by demonic influence.[4]

Author Joseph Lam writes:

The Himalayan Mountains of Tibet and Nepal gave Lucifer the high ground he adores (Isaiah 14:13-14). He dwells in high places like the sacred mountains of Taishan in Shandong province. All his false temples are amazingly similar—reaching upward to heaven. Be it at the Tower of Babel, the pyramids of Egypt, the Inca copies of ancient Ziggurats in Mexico, Egypt, or the stupas of Burma—all exalt the concept of man and demons reaching upward. It is no surprise that so many forms of animism, demon worship, Hinduism, and Buddhism have been born in the Himalayan Mountains.[5]

It is not difficult to see how at the end of the Tribulation the master deceiver will easily deceive "the kings from the east" and their followers into making the long trek west to the Meggido Valley to do battle with the King of kings. Already steeped in pagan religions for centuries and currently controlled by humanistic Communists with an obsession for world conquest, their vision of spreading their might and culture over the entire world will make them easy targets for one last gigantic deception—Armageddon.

The rise of China as a dominant world force during the past decade has enormous significance from a prophetic point of view. Many students of prophecy believe it signifies a trend that world geopolitical conditions are shaping up for the world's last great conflict, described over nineteen hundred years ago by the Apostle John: "Then the sixth angel poured out his bowl on the great river Euphrates, and its water was dried up, *so that the way of the kings from the east might be prepared*" (Revelation 16:12, emphasis added).

The significance of the rise of China to become a principal player among the nations of the world was not lost on Dr. John Walvoord. He saw the prophetic significance of the Chinese rise to prominence back in 1967 when he wrote:

> The fact that the rise of Asia has occurred in our twentieth century with so many rapid and unexpected developments is another evidence that the world is moving toward its final climax and the end of the times of the Gentiles. In Asia, as in other parts of the world, the stage is being set for the final drama in which the kings of the east will have their important part.[6]

If he were writing on that subject today, he might be inclined to say the curtain is about to rise. We are the first generation to witness the sleeping giant of China reach the potential of fulfilling this prophecy. No one doubts that unless something drastic and unforeseen occurs soon, China will gain control of most of the countries of the East, with whom she shares many religious and cultural similarities. It is realistic to believe that she could be led in these very days by her master, the dragon, "that old serpent, the devil," to so rebel against God that she would actually join the armies of the world in opposition to the coming of Jesus Christ.

What is needed to bring her to that point? Very little! Merely the deceiving spirit forewarned by John the Revelator. She is almost there today and could gain control of the entire Orient in ten or twenty years. And remember, the events of Revelation 16:12 do not take place until seven years *after* the rise of Antichrist, which follows the Rapture of the church. More than enough time to be fulfilled—and just one more reason to believe Christ may return for His church in our generation.

### 7. The seventh bowl: The greatest earthquake in history (Revelation 16:17-21)

With the pouring out of this final bowl judgment, a voice from the heavenly temple cries out, "It is done!" But what a finish it is! The most severe earthquake the world has ever known "since men were on the earth" shakes the planet to its foundations, crumbling Babylon into three parts and leveling the cities of the world. Babylon is struck particularly hard, for it is "remembered before God, to give her the cup of the wine of the fierceness of His wrath" (verse 19). And that is not all! Enormous hailstones weighing about 135 pounds each rain out of the sky, striking men all over the planet. But do they repent? No. They "blasphemed God because of the plague of the hail, since that plague was exceedingly great" (verse 21).

And with that, the bowl judgments are over. With the cessation of this plague, only one significant event remains before the kingdom of Christ can be established. The most famous battle in history is about to be fought.

# FIFTEEN

## *The Glorious Appearing*

"THAT last half of the seven years is called the Great Tribulation, and if we are alive at the end of it, we will be rewarded by seeing the Glorious Appearing of Christ."

Loretta raised her hand. "Why do you keep saying, 'if we survive'? What are these judgments?"

"They get progressively worse, and if I'm reading this right, they will be harder and harder to survive. If we die, we will be in heaven with Christ and our loved ones. But we may suffer horrible deaths. If we somehow make it through the seven terrible years, especially the last half, the Glorious Appearing will be all that more glorious."

*LEFT BEHIND, 309*

Some news stories are so enormous that ordinary headlines and bold print just won't cut it. For outsized events and cataclysmic happenings, newspapers for decades have resorted to what came to be known as "Second Coming type"—that is, a style and size of lettering that jumps off the page, grabs a reader by the throat, and demands, **READ ME!**

Second Coming type has been used to announce such major events as the Allied victory over Hitler, the end of World War II, and even (in one of the biggest blunders in American journalism history) Thomas Dewey's "defeat" of Harry S. Truman in the 1948 presidential election.

But why give the name "Second Coming type" to the fonts used for such tremendous events? Why not just call it "Big News type" or "Major Event type" or "Can You Believe *This?* type"?

The reason, of course, is that there *IS* no bigger event than the second coming of Christ, and even the most irreligious journalist at the most liberal newspaper in the most ungodly city in the world knows it. Ironically, when He comes, Second Coming type will sit unused on the presses. Why? Because there will be no time left to put out a flash street edition to announce His return!

## THE SECOND COMING: THE CORNERSTONE
## OF PROPHECY

At the second coming of Christ, Jesus will come back to this earth to judge His enemies, set up His kingdom, and rule over the earth for one thousand years.

Among the 318 New Testament predictions of Jesus' return, the Holy Spirit used many terms to describe His second coming, from "the coming [again] of our Lord Jesus Christ" (1 Corinthians 1:7; 1 Thessalonians 3:13, KJV) to "coming . . . with great power and glory" (Mark 13:26) to our favorite, found in Titus 2:13, the "glorious appearing." This latter term seems to us to best describe that magnificent event.

The Glorious Appearing will end the time of Satan's deception of mankind and will usher in Christ's kingdom of peace on earth. It is the very cornerstone of Bible prophecy and is one of the most loved and believed doctrines in the Bible, accepted by almost every denomination that still considers itself Christian. It is so much a part of the Christian faith that a Gallup poll indicated 66 percent of the American people believe that Jesus Christ is physically coming back to this earth in the future—at least 25 percent more than claim to be "born again."

Belief in Christ's second coming is much more prevalent among those who profess to be Bible-believing Christians because it is basic to our faith and has been a significant declaration of all official church councils since the third century. Only the doctrine of salvation is mentioned in Scripture more than is the Second Coming—and salvation is the only way to prepare for His coming.

## HOW THE BIBLE VIEWS IT

The most detailed description of the Second Coming was given by our Lord Himself in Matthew 24:

> For as the lightning comes from the east and flashes to the west, so also will the coming of the Son of Man be. (verse 27)

> Immediately after the tribulation of those days the sun will be darkened, and the moon will not give its light; the stars will fall from heaven, and the powers of the heavens will be shaken. Then the sign of the

> Son of Man will appear in heaven, and then all the
> tribes of the earth will mourn, and they will see the
> Son of Man coming on the clouds of heaven with
> power and great glory. And He will send His angels
> with a great sound of a trumpet, and they will
> gather together His elect from the four winds, from
> one end of heaven to the other. (verses 29-31)

Notice several things about our Lord's description of
His return. First, it will be public, obvious, and not re-
stricted to some little group. He says His coming will be
like lightning that flashes from the east to the west—everybody will see it, and there will be no hiding it. Second, He
says it will occur "immediately after" the Great Tribulation. Therefore we never have to check out someone's
claim that Christ has really appeared in the desert somewhere before that time, for the Lord Himself said He
would return after the Tribulation, not before. Third, His
return will be accompanied by "mourning" on the part of
"all the tribes of the earth"—the mourning of sadness on
the part of the Jewish nation, that it so long rejected Christ
as Messiah (see Zechariah 12:10-12), as well as the
mourning of despair on the part of the ungodly, who reject
Him as King even as He appears in the sky.

Just before He was crucified, Jesus gave another thrilling
description of His second coming. At His illegal trial before
Caiaphas the high priest, false witness after false witness
was brought forward to accuse Jesus of many things, but
our Lord replied to none of the charges. A frustrated
Caiaphas asked Jesus, "Do You answer nothing? What is it
these men testify against You?" (Matthew 26:62). But still
Jesus remained silent. Finally the high priest demanded, "I

adjure You by the living God that you tell us if You are the Christ, the Son of God!" Jesus said to him, "It is as you said. Nevertheless, I say to you, hereafter you will see the Son of Man sitting at the right hand of the Power, and coming on the clouds of heaven" (26:63-64). Immediately Caiaphas tore his clothes (a way of signaling his horror) and exclaimed, "He has spoken blasphemy!" (26:65).

Now, why did Caiaphas claim that Jesus had spoken blasphemy? Because he and everyone else in the room instantly recognized Jesus' claim to be the divine person described in Daniel 7:13-14:

> I was watching in the night visions, and behold,
> One like the Son of Man, coming with the clouds of
> heaven! He came to the Ancient of Days, and they
> brought Him near before Him. Then to Him was
> given dominion and glory and a kingdom, that all
> peoples, nations, and languages should serve Him.
> His dominion is an everlasting dominion, which
> shall not pass away, and His kingdom the one
> which shall not be destroyed.

In His exchange with the high priest, Jesus was claiming to be Daniel's "Son of Man"—that is, God in human flesh who would return to earth with the "clouds of heaven" to be worshiped and be given a kingdom that would never pass away. Neither Daniel nor Jesus had in mind here a mere "spiritual" coming, and if the disciples were at all confused on that point, their questions were erased the day the resurrected Christ was taken up into heaven. Luke writes that on that amazing day, Jesus "was taken up, and a cloud received Him out of their sight. And while they looked steadfastly toward heaven as He went up, behold, two men stood by them in white apparel, who also said, 'Men of Galilee, why do you stand gazing up into heaven? This same Jesus, who was taken up from you into heaven, will so come in like manner as you saw Him go into heaven'" (Acts 1:9-11). The angels made it plain that our Lord would "come" in the same way the apostles saw Him "go"—physically, visibly, and with clouds. Interestingly, He will also "touch down" on the same mountain from which He left, the Mount of Olives. Zechariah 14:3-5 says,

> Then shall the Lord go forth, and fight against those nations, as when he fought in the day of battle.
>
> And his feet shall stand in that day upon the mount of Olives, which is before Jerusalem on the east, and the mount of Olives shall cleave in the midst thereof toward the east and toward the west, and there shall be a very great valley; and half of the mountain shall remove toward the north, and half of it toward the south.
>
> And ye shall flee to the valley of the mountains; for the valley of the mountains shall reach unto Azal; yea, ye shall flee, like as ye fled from before the earthquake in the days of Uzziah king of Judah: and the Lord my God shall come, and all the saints with thee. (KJV)

When Jesus returns to our planet, His feet will touch down on the Mount of Olives, and it will split in two. Geological reports indicate there is a fault under the Mount; the touch of our Lord's feet upon the ground will cause that fault to split the mountain wide open, yet another powerful announcement of His coming.

But what of His "fight against those nations"? The apostle John gives dramatic details of this one-of-a-kind future event in Revelation 19:11-21:

> I saw heaven standing open and there before me was a white horse, whose rider is called Faithful and True. With justice he judges and makes war. His eyes are like blazing fire, and on his head are many crowns. He has a name written on him that no one knows but he himself. He is dressed in a robe dipped in blood, and his name is the Word of God. The armies of heaven were following him, riding on white horses and dressed in fine linen, white and clean. Out of his mouth comes a sharp sword with which to strike down the nations. "He will rule them with an iron scepter." He treads the winepress of the fury of the wrath of God Almighty. On his robe and on his thigh he has this name written: King of kings and Lord of lords.
>
> And I saw an angel standing in the sun, who cried in a loud voice to all the birds flying in midair, "Come, gather together for the great supper of God, so that you may eat the flesh of kings, generals, and mighty men, of horses and their riders, and the flesh of all people, free and slave, small and great."
>
> Then I saw the beast and the kings of the earth and their armies gathered together to make war against the rider on the horse and his army. But the beast was captured, and with him the false prophet who had performed the miraculous signs on his be-

half. With these signs he had deluded those who had received the mark of the beast and worshiped his image. The two of them were thrown alive into the fiery lake of burning sulfur. The rest of them were killed with the sword that came out of the mouth of the rider on the horse, and all the birds gorged themselves on their flesh. (NIV)

John here calls Jesus a righteous Judge, a righteous Warrior, and a righteous King. He is accompanied by the armies of heaven—but they are dressed as no other army in history. Usually soldiers are clothed in camouflage fatigues, but here they are all in white, symbolizing both their purity and Jesus' unconcern that their "uniforms" would be soiled. There is no fear of this, for they will not lift a finger in the battle to come; Jesus will accomplish all by the power of His almighty word.

John saw in this vision the most famous engagement in history, the battle of Armageddon. The Antichrist and the false prophet and all the godless armies of the world will gather there to fight each other, but when they see Christ "coming on the clouds of heaven," they will turn their feeble weapons against the King of kings and Lord of lords. The word *battle* in this text really means "campaign" or "war," and several other Bible passages indicate that the "battle of that great day of God Almighty" (Revelation 16:14) actually consists of at least four "campaigns" and spreads over almost all the land of Palestine:

1. The Lord first goes to Edom to rescue Israel from the hand of the Antichrist; here He soils His clothing in the blood of His enemies (Isaiah 63:1-6).

2. The Lord then goes to the Valley of Megiddo, where He defeats many of the armies of the world (Revelation 16:12-16).
3. Next the Lord defeats most of the remainder of the world's evil forces in the Valley of Jehoshaphat (Joel 3:1-2, 9-17; Revelation 14:14-20).
4. Last, the Lord will come to Jerusalem to defeat the advance guard of the Antichrist, who will attempt to wipe out the Holy City (Zechariah 12:1-9; Revelation 16:17-21).

On the great day of His return, Christ will defeat all His enemies, capture alive the Antichrist and the false prophet, and cast them into the lake of fire, where they will be tormented day and night forever and ever (Revelation 20:1-3). The birds of the air and the beasts of the field will feast on the corpses of the slain, and no one who resists Christ will remain alive.

When you read those passages, you can understand why Paul called the return of Christ to earth the "Glorious Appearing" and why we prefer that title to all others! Yet even that designation does not adequately describe this most magnificent happening in human history, for it will change the course of this world forever.

## DIFFERENT FROM THE FIRST

During His first coming our Lord endured persecution, mockery, rejection, and physical abuse, leading up to His crucifixion. He purposely humbled Himself and made Himself a human servant so that He could taste death for all human beings. In His first coming He made himself "lower than the angels" (Hebrews 2:7). Even so, He was more than a mere man, for He was God in human flesh. And though He had supernatural powers, He permitted himself to be persecuted, rejected, abused, and finally crucified, so He could become "the sin bearer" of God and thus save the world.

His Glorious Appearing will be a much different story, for then He will come in "power and great glory." He will never come in weakness again! All men will bow before Him; He will be "the King of kings" and "Lord of lords," and "every tongue will confess that He is Lord" (see Philippians 2:11)! All the angels and even Satan himself will be subject to His authority.

The Bible gives many incredible details of that Glorious Appearing—and all 318 predictions must be analyzed to fully understand this awesome event that we believe may well take place in the early part of the twenty-first century.

## The Glorious Appearing

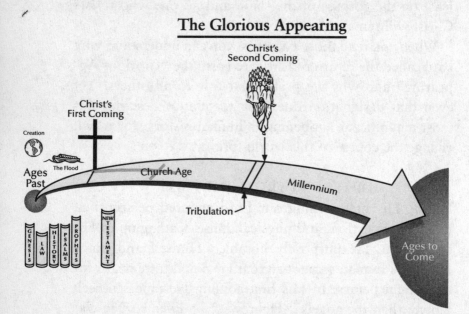

The world will never be the same after Jesus' glorious appearing! After he destroys the armies of the Antichrist on the mountains of Israel, He will chain Satan in the bottomless pit for the duration of the Millennium, judge the nations of the world according to the way they have treated His chosen people (Matthew 25), and finally usher in a time of peace that men and women of goodwill have yearned for throughout the centuries.

## THE MARRIAGE SUPPER OF THE LAMB

The church will already have enjoyed a taste of that kingdom to come at what the Bible calls "the marriage supper of the Lamb," described in Revelation 19:7-10. After the Rapture and following the judgment seat of Christ, where the members of the church will be rewarded for their faithful service (see 1 Corinthians 3:10-15; 2 Corinthians 5:10), a marriage will take place. The church ("the bride of Christ") and our Lord Jesus Christ will be officially married in heaven. While the earth is suffering through the last throes of the Tribulation, the church will enjoy a heavenly wedding. And then a feast!

Revelation 19:9 says, "Then he said to me, 'Write: "Blessed are those who are called to the marriage supper of the Lamb!"' And he said to me, 'These are the true sayings of God.'"

Who are these guests invited to the marriage supper of the Lamb? Not the members of the church, for they are the bride. We get one clue from John 3:29, where John the Baptist identified himself as a "friend of the bridegroom." We believe the guests will be faithful Old Testament saints, including those who died or were martyred in the Tribulation. All these will glory in what God has done through Christ in bringing to Himself a people for His name.

## EVEN SO, COME QUICKLY

The apostle John ends the book of Revelation with several pointed reminders of Christ's return:

> Behold, I am coming quickly! (22:7)

> And behold, I am coming quickly, and My reward is with Me, to give to every one according to his work. (22:12)

> Surely I am coming quickly. (22:20)

Friends, He is coming again, and He will do so quickly! Are you ready? John was, so he could write with gladness, "And the Spirit and the bride say, 'Come!' And let him who hears say, 'Come!'" (22:17). But he wasn't content to leave it at that. He knew some might be reading his book who weren't ready for the Lord's return. So to them he writes, "And let him who thirsts come. And whoever desires, let him take the water of life freely" (22:17).

Are you thirsty? Then come to Christ, so that you will be ready for Him when He comes. Do you desire to quench your thirst at the great fountain of God? Then come and take that water "freely." Drink deeply of His cool, refreshing waters. Cast yourself wholly upon His grace, and ask Jesus to satisfy your soul.

Then you, too, will be ready to say with John, "Even so, come, Lord Jesus!"

# SIXTEEN

## *The Millennium*

"IF we somehow make it through the seven terrible
years, especially the last half, the Glorious Appearing will be all that more glorious. Christ will
come back to set up his thousand-year reign on
earth."

"The Millennium."

"Exactly."

*LEFT BEHIND, 309*

Right idea, wrong timing.

When the United Nations was established by charter on
October 24, 1945, the leaders of the world hoped it would
help to end the kinds of wars that had so recently devastated the planet. They were so hopeful that they had the
following words of the Old Testament prophets inscribed
on their building in New York:

> They shall beat their swords into plowshares, and
> their spears into pruning hooks; nation shall not lift
> up sword against nation, neither shall they learn
> war any more (Isaiah 2:4 and Micah 4:3).

As we said—great idea, bad timing. Despite half a century of effort, the UN has not been able to teach the nations to beat their swords into plowshares nor their spears into pruning hooks. Nation has lifted up sword against nation, and they continue to eagerly learn war.

So were the prophets deceived? Mistaken? Did they somehow get the wrong message?

No, there's nothing wrong with the message. The problem is that neither the United Nations nor any other merely human organization will be able to bring in the peace envisioned by Isaiah and Micah. That peace will come only when the Prince of Peace, Jesus Christ, returns to this world to establish His kingdom of peace. Then and only then will the kingdom of harmony foreseen by the prophets take shape.

Jesus Christ is the only one who has been given the authority to bring such a kingdom into being—and He is the only one who has the power to enforce that peace from the first day and throughout eternity. His coming kingdom will truly be the utopia that has eluded mankind since the Fall. It will be a time of peace, righteousness, prosperity, and conversion and will abundantly fulfill all that the prophets have said about it.

## SATAN CHAINED IN THE PIT

Before such a kingdom can begin, however, the one who has for long ages caused so much devilish mischief must be put out of commission. And that is exactly what happens immediately after the glorious appearing of Jesus Christ. The apostle John tells us that an angel will descend from heaven with "the key to the bottomless pit and a great chain in his hand." This mighty angel will lay hold of Satan, bind him with the chain, cast him into the bottomless pit, imprison him there, and place a seal over his jail cell "so that he should deceive the nations no more" (Revelation 20:1-3).

Can you imagine what the world would be like without the deceiver around to whisper his lies into susceptible human ears? What would life be like if the tempter were not skulking nearby to prod us into this or that sin? How much would our lives improve if the accuser were not present to cast his accusations in our faces? Gone would be counterfeit truths, counterfeit promises, counterfeit angels, counterfeit gods! What a world that would be!

And that will be the world of the Millennium.

## HOW LONG WILL IT LAST?

We are not left in doubt about the duration of the kingdom age, for Revelation 20 mentions six times that it is to last for "one thousand years"—a millennium (from the Latin, *mille* = thousand and *annum* = year). One thousand years of peace on earth!

Hundreds of verses throughout the Bible describe different aspects of Christ's coming kingdom—far too many to consider here. But to gain some understanding of the basic outlines of the Millennium, let's briefly look at a few passages from both Testaments. Daniel 2:44 says:

> The God of heaven will set up a kingdom which
> shall never be destroyed; and the kingdom shall not

be left to other people; it shall break in pieces and consume all these kingdoms, and it shall stand forever.

Just before this, Daniel had seen a golden image, representing the four world kingdoms to come, smashed into nothingness by "a stone . . . cut out without hands" (Daniel 2:34). This stone was none other than the coming kingdom. And who will lead this kingdom? Psalm 2 gives the answer. That passage has long been known as a "messianic psalm," that is, a prediction about the Messiah. The Lord says to His Son in this psalm:

Ask of Me, and I will give You the nations for Your inheritance, and the ends of the earth for Your possession. You shall break them with a rod of iron; you shall dash them in pieces like a potter's vessel. (2:8-9)

In the book of Revelation the apostle John has this text in mind at least three times, first when he reports the words of Jesus to the one "who overcomes": "'He shall rule them with a rod of iron; they shall be dashed to pieces like the potter's vessels'—as I also have received from My Father" (Revelation 2:27). In 12:5 John speaks of a "male Child who was to rule all nations with a rod of iron," who "was caught up to God and to His throne"—an obvious allusion to Jesus. And last the apostle pictures Jesus on a white horse coming to conquer His enemies and says of Him, "He Himself will rule them with a rod of iron" (19:15).

The astonishing thing is that Jesus will invite His people to rule His kingdom with Him. That is the message of

Revelation 2:27 just quoted, and that is the message of Daniel 7: "A judgment was made in favor of the saints of the Most High, and the time came for the saints to possess the kingdom. . . . Then the kingdom and dominion, and the greatness of the kingdoms under the whole heaven, shall be given to the people, the saints of the Most High. His kingdom is an everlasting kingdom, and all dominions shall serve and obey Him" (verses 22, 27). And John says:

> And I saw thrones, and they sat on them, and judgment was committed to them. And I saw the souls of those who had been beheaded for their witness to Jesus and for the word of God, who had not worshiped the beast or his image, and had not received his mark on their foreheads or on their hands. And they lived and reigned with Christ for a thousand years. . . . Blessed and holy is he who has part in the first resurrection. Over such the second death has no power, but they shall be priests of God and of Christ, and shall reign with Him a thousand years. (Revelation 20:4, 6)

No wonder our Savior is called "King of kings and Lord of lords"!

## THREE COMPETING VIEWS

Not every Christian believes that Jesus Christ will literally return to this earth to set up a kingdom of peace and security that will last for a thousand years. At least two other views of the Millennium have arisen over the centuries.

*Amillennialism* is the belief that there is no future Millennium but that prophecy will be fulfilled in eternity. This belief crept into the church after Augustine introduced the practice of spiritualizing and allegorizing Scripture, which opened the door to many pagan doctrines and practices and helped to plunge the Western world into the Dark Ages for over eleven hundred years. Times were dark because people had little access to or knowledge of the Scriptures; consequently they lost the hope of Christ's second coming.

*Postmillennialism* is the notion that the church will evangelize this world, making it progressively better until it finally ushers in the kingdom. This belief was popularized by a seventeenth-century Anglican named Daniel Whitby. Since then it has waxed and waned in popularity according to the times. After the barbarities of World War I the doctrine suffered a sharp decline, and the catastrophe of World War II nearly finished it off. Today only a few groups still cling to the position, including those known as Reconstructionists. But the savagery of the twentieth century makes it difficult to maintain postmillennialism today.

Generally speaking, whenever people have taken the Bible at face value and interpreted it as it reads, they believe the second coming of Christ is scheduled before the Millennium unfolds; thus they are called *premillennialists*.

From the days of the apostles into the fourth century, the early church held to the premillennial view of future events. Before John wrote Revelation, his followers understood that Christ would establish His kingdom on this earth when He returned. In Matthew 24 our Lord's disciples asked a question that merged His coming with "the end of the age," indicating that Jews at that time expected their Messiah to set up His kingdom when He came. Since the first century church was predominantly Jewish, early on its members also merged Christ's coming with the establishment of His kingdom.

The following chart will illustrate:

## Early Church Pre-Millennial View

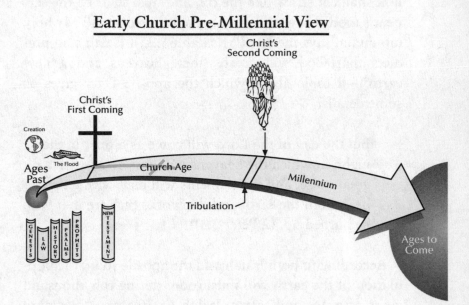

It is that King and kingdom that will reign over the earth for a thousand years, bringing in the peace that the prophets Isaiah and Micah so eloquently predicted thousands of years ago.

### A STAGGERING POPULATION

So many prophecies exist about the Millennium that we can only skim the surface here even in outline form. What will that kingdom be like?

Zechariah 14 tells us that Jerusalem will be the capital of the kingdom and that the world's peoples will regularly journey there to worship the king. The last two chapters of Isaiah tell us that major changes in the earth's climate, geography, flora, and fauna will occur. Of the latter change Isaiah says, "The wolf and the lamb shall feed together, the lion shall eat straw like the ox, and dust shall be the serpent's food. They shall not hurt nor destroy in all My holy mountain, says the Lord" (Isaiah 65:25). Isaiah also predicts that God will create "new heavens and a new earth"—a topic about which the apostle Peter gives us some details:

> But the day of the Lord will come as a thief in the night, in which the heavens will pass away with a great noise, and the elements will melt with fervent heat; both the earth and the works that are in it will be burned up. (2 Peter 3:10)

According to both Isaiah and the apostle John, the population of the earth will mushroom during this thousand years of peace and safety. Isaiah 65:20 says, "No more shall an infant from there live but a few days, nor an old man who has not fulfilled his days; for the child shall die one hundred years old, but the sinner being one hundred years old shall be accursed."

We believe this means that believers will live throughout the entire period but that the unregenerate will be given one hundred years to repent and accept Christ as their Lord; if they refuse to do so, they will die. This will result in an enormous population by the end of the Millennium, the vast majority of whom will be saved. In fact, we believe that because of the Millennium, there may be more people in heaven than in hell.

And so God will once more show His amazing grace in yet another breathtaking way!

### JESUS WINS!

The story is told of a humble Bible-believing custodian of a liberal seminary who was waiting for the students to finish a pickup basketball game so he could dust the gym floor. While the custodian was reading his Bible, one of these future ministers saw him and asked what he was reading. "Revelation," he replied. The young man, who evidently didn't believe anyone could understand prophecy—particularly a man who had never graduated from high school—asked, "Do you understand what you are reading?"

"I sure do!" the man replied.

Surprised at his answer, the seminarian asked, "What does it say?"

With a triumphant smile, the custodian declared, "Jesus wins!"

That is the premillennial message of all prophecy, especially the book of Revelation: "Jesus wins!" And we win with Him!

# SEVENTEEN

## *The Last Rebellion*

THERE is a reason that the study of prophecy is often called the examination of "last things." When we peer into the future through the lens of God's prophetic glasses, we see how events and movements and groups will "turn out" in the end. And while we like to focus on the attractive part of "last things," not everything that's called "last" is good.

So it is with the last rebellion.

### THE ANSWER TO A LONG DEBATE

For many years a debate has raged over what has the most influence on the behavior of human beings, "nurture" or "nature." Are human beings born basically good, only to have their environment corrupt them? Or are they born with a grave spiritual defect that no amount of good environment can cure?

Despite the Bible's many pronouncements about the corrupt nature of mankind since the Fall, many "experts" have claimed that human beings are basically good; the problem, they say, is that the human environment has been corrupted. If men and women lived in an environment free of such corrupting influences, they claim, such individuals would always display their inherent good nature.

The Millennium decisively proves the bankruptcy of such an unbiblical idea.

As astonishing as it may seem, Scripture teaches that when the thousand years of the Millennium have run their course, the unredeemed human beings alive at that time will rebel against His lordship and even try to attack His capital. John describes the troubling scene like this:

> Now when the thousand years have expired, Satan will be released from his prison and will go out to deceive the nations which are in the four corners of the earth, Gog and Magog, to gather them together to battle, whose number is as the sand of the sea. They went up on the breadth of the earth and surrounded the camp of the saints and the beloved city. (Revelation 20:7-9)

All it takes for the wicked hearts of the unredeemed to be exposed is the release of the deceiver from his thousand-year imprisonment. To that point millions of men and women probably will have concealed their true spiritual allegiance from public view. But when the devil is released, the desperate wickedness of their hearts suddenly becomes obvious. We believe this rebellion will be essentially a youth movement, since people in the Millennium will be given a hundred years to make their decision for the Savior. That means that everyone in this army will have to be under a hundred years old—and still their forces will be "as the sand of the sea"! Once again this points to the enormous population on earth by the end of the Millennium.

John tells us these young rebels will be deceived by the devil into believing that they can actually attack and overthrow the King of kings and Lord of lords. . . . But their deception will not last long. They will muster their forces from one corner of the globe to the other and will march on Jerusalem, where they will "surround the camp of the saints and the beloved city."

But there will be no battle. No call to arms. No defensive strategy or late-night negotiations or propaganda campaign or deploying of gigaton nuclear weapons.

There will, however, be massive destruction: "And fire came down from God out of heaven and devoured them" (Revelation 20:9).

And that's it. In a ball of celestial flame, the rebellion is over. There will be no repeat of the plagues of the Tribulation nor of the judgments of the Great Tribulation. Once and for all, human rebellion will have been wiped out of existence.

And once and for all, it will be crystal clear to a watching universe that the death and resurrection of Jesus Christ is absolutely essential for making the unrighteous human heart into a receptacle of God's holiness. The Millennium will prove that even the best of conditions—a thousand years of peace, prosperity, safety, long life, health, abundance—cannot change the wickedness of the unredeemed human heart. Only the Lord Jesus Christ can do that!

We believe that God may allow this final rebellion to go this far, and no further, to showcase one last time the centrality of the cross. The Millennium will make it clear that the only way for men and women to be made righteous is to put their trust in the Christ of Calvary, who shed His blood for their sins. And so the long argument of "nature" vs. "nurture" will be conclusively answered—to the glory of God and His Son, Jesus Christ!

### THE END . . . OF THE BEGINNING

With the obliteration of this final rebellion, God seizes Satan and throws him into the lake of fire and brimstone "where the beast and the false prophet are. And they will be tormented day and night forever and ever" (Revelation 20:10). This verse alone should give pause to those who think that eventually everyone will be saved. They will not! Jesus Himself spoke of a sin that would not be forgiven "either in this age or in the age to come" (Matthew 12:32), and this unholy trinity serves to illustrate the eternal fate of those who refuse to bow the knee before the Savior.

## The History of Man and God's Plan for His Future

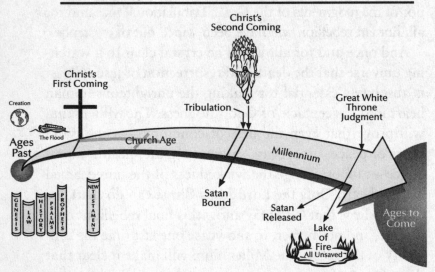

And so end both the final rebels against God and the first rebel who deceived them. Next on God's prophetic calendar: the final judgment at the great white throne.

# EIGHTEEN

## *The Great White Throne Judgment*

IF YOU had to vote for the most awesome passage in the Bible, what passage would you choose? Before you answer, consider that "awe" is defined as "an overwhelming feeling of reverence, admiration, fear, etc., produced by that which is grand, sublime, extremely powerful, or the like . . . fear or dread." What passage would you name as the most awesome in the Scriptures?

I know what passage would get my vote. Revelation 20:11-15 never fails to make my skin tingle and my heart beat a little faster:

> Then I saw a great white throne and Him who sat on it, from whose face the earth and the heaven fled away. And there was found no place for them. And I saw the dead, small and great, standing before God, and books were opened. And another book was opened, which is the Book of Life. And the

dead were judged according to their works, by the things which were written in the books. The sea gave up the dead who were in it, and Death and Hades delivered up the dead who were in them. And they were judged, each one according to his works. Then Death and Hades were cast into the lake of fire. This is the second death. And anyone not found written in the Book of Life was cast into the lake of fire.

This awesome passage describes the final judgment of unredeemed mankind. While the martyred Tribulation saints had been resurrected just before the Millennium, and Christians were resurrected at the Rapture, Revelation 20:5 tells us that "the rest of the dead did not live again until the thousand years were finished." Now is their time.

John includes all the unsaved in this passage, for he speaks of the "small" and the "great," of the dead who were in the sea and those who were in Death (the grave) and Hades (the place of torment)—that is, every unsaved person who ever lived. They will all be resurrected in order to stand for judgment before God at the great white throne.

## THE BOOKS ARE OPENED

John speaks of "books" being opened and of "another book" being opened. He tells us that "the dead were judged . . . by the things which were written in the books. . . . They were judged, each one according to his works" (20:12-13).

These statements immediately call our attention back to the words of the Lord Jesus: "What you have said in the dark will be heard in the daylight, and what you have whispered in the ear in the inner rooms will be proclaimed from the roofs" (Luke 12:3, NIV). And "There is nothing hidden that will not be disclosed, and nothing concealed that will not be known or brought out into the open" (Luke 8:17, NIV).

We also remember Ecclesiastes 12:14, which promises, "God shall bring every work into judgment, with every secret thing, whether it be good, or whether it be evil" (KJV), as well as Romans 2:5-6, where Paul speaks of the day of God's wrath "when his righteous judgment will be revealed. God will give to each person according to what he has done" (NIV).

It is a fearful thing even to imagine standing before God, "from whose face the earth and the heaven fled away" (Revelation 20:11), and have nothing but your own wicked works to show for the time on earth the Almighty had given you. I have often heard the ungodly boast that on the Day of Judgment they would demand that God justify Himself for the wrongs of the world, but this is sheer, wicked fantasy. It will never happen. If beloved Daniel collapsed in fear and utter weakness when he saw a vision of a heavenly being (and those with him did not even see it but still hid themselves in terror, Daniel 10:4-8); if the apostle John fell like a dead man when he saw a vision of the resurrected Christ (Revelation 1:10-17); if righteous Job, who had been demanding an audience with God, would say, "I have heard of You by the hearing of the ear, but now my eye sees You. Therefore I abhor myself, and repent in dust and ashes" when his demand was met (Job 42:5-6)—then what madness is this for the wicked to imagine they will justify themselves before God on the day they stand before Him at the great white throne!

No, on that day the words of Paul the apostle will come true: "Now we know that whatever the law says, it says to those who are under the law, so that every mouth may be silenced and the whole world held accountable to God" (Romans 3:19, NIV). The final word, of course, will be God's.

After these unsaved men and women are judged from the books of their works, another book is opened, the Book of Life. The New Testament refers to this book eight times, while three times the Old Testament mentions a book in which names are written. John says that "anyone not found written in the Book of Life was cast into the lake of fire" (Revelation 20:15). And so their story ends.

When this is completed, only one last event is scheduled for the Great White Throne Judgment. John writes, "Then Death and Hades were cast into the lake of fire. This is the second death" (Revelation 20:14). In this way the glorious words of the apostle Paul will be fulfilled: "The last enemy that will be destroyed is death" (1 Corinthians 15:26).

## "AWESOME" IS THE WORD

It probably is not humanly possible to meditate on these awesome truths for extended periods of time. Who can long ponder the lake of fire, an eternal place of torment, millions of unredeemed souls, a divine Person "from whose face the earth and the heaven fled away," or fearsome books of judgment that seal the fate of the unsaved?

And yet our Lord tells us of these awesome events. Why? *To give us every opportunity to escape the terrible judgment to come.* Remember, no believer in Christ will stand before God at the great white throne. That terrible spot is reserved for those who have rejected Christ as Savior, who have decided to crown themselves king, and who have refused to accept Jesus Christ as their true Lord.

Do not make that terrible mistake! Instead, place your faith in the Lord Jesus and ask Him to forgive your sins; then you will be ready "to stand before the Son of Man" (Luke 21:36) at the judgment seat of Christ.

One thing is sure: You *will* stand in one place or the other. Hell or heaven. Make sure it's the latter!

# NINETEEN

## The Eternal State

How do you describe eternity? How can you begin to picture an unending moment of happiness and contentment and joy in the presence of an eternally smiling God? When some bright youngsters were asked that question recently, here's what they said:[1]

*The best part of heaven is the party Jesus is going to give us. Lots of babies will be in heaven. If we need our dolls in heaven, Jesus will have them there.*

MICAH LEAKE, AGE 3

*There are roads of gold, gates of pearl, and after you have walked through the gates of pearl, I think you might see a humongous throne. I think the throne is made out of bricks of gold and outlined with pearls, decorated with emeralds—maybe even rubies! I don't know if I'm right, but I do know you will have to have bare feet.*

EMILY EDWARDS, AGE 7

*I think heaven would have fences in it with strawberries. David who fighted Goliath would be there too. I think heaven would have blueberries and gold in it. Old people will be there and God's angels. There also will be a big, big feast that keeps everybody full.*

ANDREW EDWARDS, AGE 3

*Heaven will be like living in the clouds with Christ and you can roller-blade on streets of gold. Peter will give you fishing lessons. We'll all be able to fly. We'll play tag in the sky. The trees will be made of gold and the leaves of silver. My point is, heaven is going to be wonderful!*

ISAAC ALLEN JONES, AGE 11

Yes, heaven is going to be wonderful (and who can tell about the strawberries?). We get our most expansive peek into what heaven will be like in Revelation 21–22, but other amazing hints and glimpses can also be found throughout the Scriptures.

For our purposes here, let's focus on a few of the highlights. For a more thorough exploration of what the Bible says about heaven, we suggest you refer to my book *Revelation: Illustrated and Made Plain* or one of several recent books on heaven (such as the one by Joni Eareckson Tada).

## THE SPLENDOR OF HEAVEN

The apostle John sets the stage for our contemplations of heaven in the first part of Revelation 21:

> Then I saw a new heaven and a new earth, for the first heaven and the first earth had passed away, and there was no longer any sea. I saw the Holy City,

the new Jerusalem, coming down out of heaven from God, prepared as a bride beautifully dressed for her husband. And I heard a loud voice from the throne saying, "Now the dwelling of God is with men, and he will live with them. They will be his people, and God himself will be with them and be their God. He will wipe every tear from their eyes. There will be no more death or mourning or crying or pain, for the old order of things has passed away." (verses 1-4, NIV)

What a place God has prepared for us from before the foundation of the world! John spotlights for us the best part of any description of eternity when he writes that a loud voice from the throne of God shouts, "Now the dwelling of God is with men, and he will live with them. They will be his people, and God himself will be with them and be their God."

What a wonder this will be—to continually see God's face (Revelation 22:4) and to walk in the light of His presence (21:23; 22:5)! No wonder John tells us there is no temple in heaven (21:22), for as Paul wrote, who hopes for what one already has (see Romans 8:24)? What need could you have for a temple when everywhere you go is God?

But a temple is not the only thing missing in heaven. What else does it lack? Consider the following short list:

- no more sea (21:1)
- no more tears, death, sorrow, crying, or pain (21:4)
- no more sinners (21:8)
- no more fear (21:12)
- no more sun or moon (21:23)

- no more night (21:25)
- no more sin or evil (21:27)
- no more disease or injuries (22:2)
- no more curse (22:3)

It would be enough to call this place "heaven" just from that list of what it *lacks*. But that wouldn't tell the half of the story! Now consider some of the remarkable features eternity will boast:

- unending fellowship with God (21:3, 7, 22)
- unending newness (21:5)
- unending water of life (21:6; 22:1)
- unimaginable beauty (21:11, 21)
- uncompromised security (21:12)
- unbroken unity between believers (21:12, 14)
- unlimited holiness (21:16)
- unparalleled size (21:16)
- untold wealth (21:18-21)
- unending light (21:23; 22:5)
- unrestricted access (21:25)
- unending fruit from the tree of life (22:2)
- unceasing service to God (22:3)
- unending reign (22:5)

Beyond these thrilling descriptions from the book of Revelation, we know from other Bible texts that heaven will be a place of:

- rest (Hebrews 4:1-11; Revelation 14:13)
- full knowledge (1 Corinthians 13:12)
- holiness (Hebrews 12:14; Ephesians 2:21)

- joy (1 Thessalonians 2:19; Jude 1:24)
- glory (2 Corinthians 4:17)
- worship (Revelation 7:9-12; 19:10)

With all that heaven and eternity have to offer, it is hard to see why anyone would deliberately choose to miss it. Yet many will, according to Revelation 21:8, 27 and 22:11, 15. Make sure you're not one of them!

## WE CAN HARDLY WAIT!

God has prepared a place for His children that is beyond their wildest imaginations. John the apostle and the other Bible writers could only hint at its true wonder, for the only way to fully appreciate the place will be to experience it personally. That's exactly what eleven-year-old Heather Knepper wants to remind all of us:

> Heaven will be the greatest place ever, but mainly because Jesus will be there. To get to this great place, though, you must believe in Christ our Lord.[2]

# PART THREE

## *Personalities*

# TWENTY

## *Satan, the Dragon*

BUCK had never been so close to the prophets and
had to resist the urge to touch them. "Show thyself
not to thine enemy," Eli said. "Be sober, be vigilant;
because your adversary the devil, as a roaring lion,
walketh about, seeking whom he may devour."

Buck could not speak. He tried to nod, to indicate
he had heard and understood, but he could not
move. Moishe leaned between him and Eli and
added, "Whom resist stedfast in the faith."
*APOLLYON, 191*

You've probably seen the television ads, perhaps in a
commercial for a national sandwich chain. A young man
seems torn between two options, one good for him, the
other bad. On one shoulder stands a tiny being in white,
complete with wings and halo, who urges the young man
to make a healthy decision. On the other shoulder stands a
tiny being in red, complete with horns and pitchfork, who

urges the young man to cast off restraint and choose a greasy alternative.

In the minds of the ad's creators, you've just witnessed another round in the conflict of the ages: good vs. evil, angels vs. Satan. According to this view, Satan is not much more than a mischievous imp, an almost cuddly little fellow who tempts us with chocolates and fatty foods.

*Really?*

The real Satan, the devil of the Bible, is far more than that. The Word of God tells us he is an immensely powerful, unutterably malevolent spirit being who lives to murder and deceive mankind. He will do everything he can to usurp the worship and glory that belong to God alone—and we do mean "everything."

## THE ORIGINAL SINNER

Satan is the original sinner. Although he was created as "the anointed cherub who covers" (Ezekiel 28:14), perfect in beauty and enormous in power and wisdom, at some point he despised his position as next to God and lusted after the place of God Himself. The prophet Ezekiel writes, "Your heart was lifted up because of your beauty; you corrupted your wisdom for the sake of your splendor; I [the Lord] cast you to ground" (Ezekiel 28:17). Isaiah further explains, "How you are fallen from heaven, O Lucifer, son of the morning! How you are cut down to the ground, you who weakened the nations! For you have said in your heart: 'I will ascend into heaven, I will exalt my throne above the stars of God; I will also sit on the mount of the congregation on the farthest sides of the north; I will ascend above the heights of the clouds, I will be like the Most High'" (Isaiah 14:12-14).

Much of the horror of the Tribulation directly results from the devil's desire to supplant God and to be worshiped as God. Satan is the guiding force behind the pagan religions of the world, as the apostle Paul makes clear: "The sacrifices of pagans are offered to demons, not to God" (1 Corinthians 10:20, NIV). The devil made it clear that his ultimate goal is to be worshiped when he said to Jesus in the wilderness, "All these things [the kingdoms of the world] I will give You if You will fall down and worship me"—to which our Lord responded, "Away with you, Satan! For it is written, 'You shall worship the Lord your God, and Him only you shall serve'" (Matthew 4:9-10).

Jesus called Satan a "liar and the father of lies" in whom is no truth, and a "murderer from the beginning" (John 8:44). The writer of Hebrews says the devil holds "the power of death" (2:14) while the apostle Peter says, "Your enemy the devil prowls around like a roaring lion looking for someone to devour" (1 Peter 5:8, NIV). John warned the church at Smyrna that "the devil is about to throw some of you into prison, that you may be tested, and you will have tribulation ten days" (Revelation 2:10), and commended the church at Pergamum because they held "fast to My name, and did not deny My faith even in the days in which Antipas was My faithful martyr, who was killed among you, where Satan dwells" (Revelation 2:13).

We learn a great deal about the nature and activities of Satan by looking at his various names as they appear in Revelation chapter 12. He is called:

• A "great red dragon" (verse 3, KJV). He is red because he is the motivating force behind much of the world's

bloodshed. He is a dragon because he is a vicious destroyer.
- An "old serpent" (verse 9, KJV). This name alludes to
his first appearance in the Bible in Genesis 3, when he
tempted Eve in the Garden of Eden, leading directly to
the fall of man.
- The "Devil" (verse 9). This name means "slanderer" or
"accuser," as in verse 10, where he is called "the accuser of our brethren, who accused them before our
God day and night."
- Satan (verse 9). This name means "adversary," the enemy of all God's people.

In other portions of Scripture Satan is called "the prince of
the power of the air" (Ephesians 2:2) and "the ruler of this
world" (John 14:30). Paul tells us Satan can disguise himself
"as an angel of light" (2 Corinthians 11:14, NIV) and warns
us to "put on the whole armor of God, that you may be able
to stand against the wiles of the devil" (Ephesians 6:11).

When you take all these descriptions together, you learn
that our adversary is a brutally strong, immensely intelli-
gent spirit being who every moment is consumed by intense hatred for God and all that belongs to Him. And yet
He is not God's rival! The Bible has no place for the eastern idea of two opposite but equal forces in the world, one
good and one bad. Although Satan was created as the pin-
nacle of all God's works, he is still infinitely below God Almighty. And although human history has been a contest
between the forces of good led by God and the forces of
evil led by Satan, there has never been any doubt about
how it will all turn out. And if you have any doubt about
that, read what Revelation 12 has to say:

> And another sign appeared in heaven: behold, a
> great, fiery red dragon having seven heads and ten
> horns, and seven diadems on his heads. His tail
> drew a third of the stars of heaven and threw them
> to the earth. (Revelation 12:3-4)

The seven heads described here probably refer to the seven heads of the Roman government, the epitome of human evil, that would appear through history. Five emperors had come and gone by the apostle John's time; one ruled during his time; and the seventh represents the Antichrist to come. The ten horns symbolize the ten kings at the time of the end who would rule the world under Antichrist.

When John tells us that the devil's tail drew a third of the stars of heaven and threw them to earth, he is probably describing the original demonic uprising against God. Satan somehow managed to convince a third of all God's angels to join him in his rebellion; these beings we now call "demons" or "fallen angels." They serve Satan and play an important role in the judgments of the Tribulation.

We are given a glimpse into the future of the devil and his evil forces starting in verse 7:

> And war broke out in heaven: Michael and his
> angels fought against the dragon; and the dragon
> and his angels fought, but they did not prevail, nor
> was a place found for them in heaven any longer. So
> the great dragon was cast out, that serpent of old,
> called the Devil and Satan, who deceives the whole
> world; he was cast to the earth, and his angels were
> cast out with him. Then I heard a loud voice saying
> in heaven, "Now salvation, and strength, and the

kingdom of our God, and the power of His Christ have come, for the accuser of our brethren, who accused them before our God day and night, has been cast down. . . . Woe to the inhabitants of the earth and the sea! For the devil has come down to you, having great wrath, because he knows that he has a short time." (Revelation 12:7-10, 12)

John tells us that even as tribulation breaks out on the earth below, a cosmic battle breaks out in heaven above. In a desperate attempt to overthrow God's throne, the devil and his angels make war on the armies of heaven, led by Michael the archangel. What kind of warfare this might be no mortal can imagine, but the result is never in doubt: Satan and his minions are defeated and thrown out of heaven permanently. Remember, until this very moment Satan has enjoyed access to the throne of God, where he accuses you and me before the Father. But the day is soon coming when even this access will be denied, and the devil and his demons will be ejected from heaven and confined to earth.

This is a cause of great rejoicing in heaven: "Now salvation, and strength, and the kingdom of our God, and the power of His Christ have come, for the accuser of our brethren, who accused them before our God day and night, has been cast down. . . . Therefore rejoice, O heavens, and you who dwell in them" (Revelation 12:10, 12)! But it is not a cause of great rejoicing on earth: "Woe to the inhabitants of the earth and the sea! For the devil has come down to you, having great wrath, because he knows that he has a short time" (Revelation 12:12).

We believe this great conflict occurs at the midpoint of the Tribulation. After Satan is defeated, evicted from heaven, and banished to earth, he personally indwells the Antichrist and through "the Beast" receives the worship he has always lusted after. This begins with the "abomination that causes desolation" when the Antichrist defiles the rebuilt temple by taking his seat there, declaring himself to be God. This event, as we have seen, triggers the "Great Tribulation" and the outpouring of the wrath of the Lamb. Satan knows that at this point he has but three and a half years before his incarceration and final doom, and that certain knowledge fills him with "great wrath."

Is it any wonder the second half of the Tribulation will be the most awful period in the history of humankind?

The special object of his hatred will be (as it has been throughout history) the chosen people of God. Why this blinding hatred for the Jews? Because it was through the Jews that the Lord Jesus Christ was born into this earth. Revelation 12:13 says, "When the dragon saw that he had been cast to the earth, he persecuted the woman [Israel] who gave birth to the male Child [Jesus Christ]."

Satan will try to finish in the Great Tribulation what he was unable to accomplish through Hitler's Holocaust, but once more he will be prevented from wiping out the Jews. Revelation 12:14-17 tells how God will miraculously protect the people of Israel for the last three and a half years of the Tribulation. This so enrages the devil that he goes off "to make war with the rest of her offspring, who keep the commandments of God and have the testimony of Jesus Christ" (12:17).

## THE END OF THE DRAGON

At the very end of the Tribulation Jesus returns to earth in the Glorious Appearing, defeats the armies of the Antichrist and the kings of the earth, and directs a mighty angel to seize Satan and bind him in the bottomless pit for a thousand years (Revelation 20:1-3). At the end of that period Satan is released for a little while, that he might go throughout the earth and deceive the unbelievers who have grown up at the end of the Millennium. These young people try to attack the Holy City, but fire from heaven destroys them all. And then, at long last, the devil himself—the deceiver, the tempter, the accuser, the liar, the murderer, the god of this world—is hurled into the lake of fire, where he will be tormented day and night forever and ever (Revelation 20:7-10).

Such is the end of Satan . . . not with a bang, but with a splash.

> Then He will also say to those on His left, "Depart from Me, you cursed, into the everlasting fire prepared for the devil and his angels." (Matthew 25:41)

# TWENTY-ONE

## *The Antichrist*

"SCRIPTURE indicates that there will be a great lie, announced with the help of the media and perpetrated by a self-styled world leader. Jesus himself prophesied about such a person. He said, 'I have come in My Father's name, and you do not receive Me; if another comes in his own name, him you will receive.'

"Let me warn you personally to beware of such a leader of humanity who may emerge from Europe. He will turn out to be a great deceiver who will step forward with signs and wonders that will be so impressive that many will believe he is of God. He will gain a great following among those who are left, and many will believe he is a miracle worker.

"The deceiver will promise strength and peace and security, but the Bible says he will speak out against the Most High and will wear down the saints of the Most High. That's why I warn you to beware now of a new leader with great charisma trying to take over the world during this terrible time of chaos and confusion. This person is known in the Bible as Antichrist. He will make many promises, but he will not keep them. You must trust in the promises of God Almighty through his Son, Jesus Christ."

LEFT BEHIND, 212–13

Here are two trivia questions for you:

1. Who are the only two characters in the Bible named "the son of perdition"?
2. Who are the only two persons in the Bible whom Satan himself is thought to possess?

If to both questions you answered, "Judas Iscariot and the Antichrist," you get a gold star.

### THE SON OF PERDITION

We all know who Judas Iscariot was—the traitor who with a kiss betrayed Jesus for thirty pieces of silver. Wherever the Gospels mention his name, some form of the phrase, "who betrayed him," is added.

It is not as well known that twice in the Gospels, Judas is said to be possessed by Satan:

Then Satan entered Judas, surnamed Iscariot, who was numbered among the twelve. So he went his way and conferred with the chief priests and captains, how he might betray Him to them. (Luke 22:3-4)

Jesus answered, "It is he to whom I shall give a piece of bread when I have dipped it." And having dipped the bread, He gave it to Judas Iscariot, the son of Simon. Now after the piece of bread, Satan entered him. Then Jesus said to him, "What you do, do quickly." (John 13:26-27)

For this satanic activity Judas is called "the son of perdition" in John 17:12 ("the one doomed to destruction," NIV). This Semitic phrase denotes "an abandoned character, one utterly lost and given over to evil."[1]

Interestingly, this same phrase is used to describe the Antichrist in 2 Thessalonians 2:3, where he is called "the man of sin . . . the son of perdition" ("the man doomed to destruction," NIV).

And while nowhere in Scripture does the Bible ever explicitly say that the Antichrist is indwelt by the devil, that has been the conclusion of many Bible scholars who have carefully compared the predicted events of Revelation 12 and 13. They believe that after the devil is defeated by the angelic forces and forcibly ejected from heaven at the midpoint of the Tribulation, he enters the body of the Antichrist and in God's temple declares himself to be God.

It should be obvious why both men are called "the son of perdition." Judas openly revolted against Jesus and set himself against our Lord at His first advent; the Antichrist will openly revolt against Jesus and set himself against our Lord just before His second advent. Of course, others during the days of Jesus' earthly ministry openly opposed Him—the Pharisees, the Sadducees, the scribes, the High Priest, Pilate, and the Romans—but the sin of these two is so awful and heinous and *personal* that their guilt is blatant—and so is their punishment. After Judas hanged himself, Scripture says, he went "to his own place" (Acts 1:25), and after the Antichrist is captured at the Battle of Armageddon, he will be thrown directly into the lake of fire (Revelation 19:20).

## THE LITTLE HORN

The wicked activities of the Antichrist were first foreseen by the prophet Daniel, who saw him as a "little horn." In the following passages note the character of this "little horn":

> There was another horn, a little one. . . . And there, in this horn, were eyes like the eyes of a man, and a mouth speaking pompous words. (Daniel 7:8)

> I watched then because of the sound of the pompous words which the horn was speaking; I watched till the beast was slain, and its body destroyed and given to the burning flame. (Daniel 7:11)

> I was watching; and the same horn was making war against the saints, and prevailing against them. (Daniel 7:21)

> He shall speak pompous words against the Most High, shall persecute the saints of the Most High, and shall intend to change times and law. Then the saints shall be given into his hand for a time and times and half a time. But the court shall be seated, and they shall take away his dominion, to consume and destroy it forever. (Daniel 7:25-26)

Several items stand out in Daniel's vision of the Antichrist, among them:

- He will speak pompously and arrogantly.
- He will persecute and "make war" against the saints of God for three and a half years.
- He will intend to change the times and laws.
- He will eventually be destroyed and his body thrown to the flames.

That is not the end of Daniel's vision of the Antichrist, however. In chapter 11 he is given a fuller picture of events that will take place at the very end of the age. In this vision the Antichrist is called "the king":

> Then the king shall do according to his own will: he shall magnify and magnify himself above every god, shall speak blasphemies against the God of gods, and shall prosper till the wrath has been accomplished; for what has been determined shall be done. He shall regard neither the God of his fathers nor the desire of women, nor regard any god; for he shall magnify himself above them all. But in their place he shall honor a god of fortresses; and a god which his fathers did not know he shall honor with gold and silver, with precious stones and pleasant things. Thus he shall act against the strongest fortresses with a foreign god, which he shall acknowledge, and advance its glory; and he shall cause them to rule over many, and divide the land for gain.
>
> At the time of the end the king of the South shall attack him; and the king of the North shall come

against him like a whirlwind, with chariots, horsemen, and with many ships; and he shall enter the countries, overwhelm them, and pass through. He shall also enter the Glorious Land, and many countries shall be overthrown; but these shall escape from his hand: Edom, Moab, and the prominent people of Ammon. He shall stretch out his hand against the countries, and the land of Egypt shall not escape.

He shall have power over the treasures of gold and silver, and over all the precious things of Egypt; also the Libyans and Ethiopians shall follow at his heels. But news from the east and the north shall trouble him; therefore he shall go out with great fury to destroy and annihilate many. And he shall plant the tents of his palace between the seas and the glorious holy mountain; yet he shall come to his end, and no one will help him. (Daniel 11:36-45)

In this passage we learn several more details about the Antichrist:

- He will "magnify himself above every god" (verse 36).
- He will blaspheme the true God (verse 36).
- He will be a thoroughgoing secularist who puts full confidence in his great military strength (verse 38).
- He will be a brutal conqueror (verses 39-42).
- He will control the world's finances (verse 43).
- He will meet his end "between the seas and the glorious holy mountain" (that is, in Israel, verse 45).

Daniel gives us a few more valuable pieces of information about the Antichrist in chapter 9. Verses 26-27 read, "And after the sixty-two weeks Messiah shall be cut off, but not for Himself; *and the people of the prince who is to come* shall destroy the city and the sanctuary. The end of it shall be with a flood, and till the end of the war desolations are determined. Then *he shall confirm a covenant with many for one week;* but in the middle of the week he shall bring an end to sacrifice and offering, and on the wing of abominations shall be one who makes desolate, even until the consummation, which is determined, is poured out on the desolate" (emphasis added).

From this crucial passage we learn that Antichrist will be of the racial stock of those who destroyed the city and the temple in A.D. 70 ("the people of the prince who is to come"). From history we know this "people" refers to the Romans, so Antichrist's heritage must also be "Roman," that is, from the eastern Mediterranean. (This is one of the main reasons why we believe it is impossible that a resurrected Judas Iscariot could be the Antichrist, as some have suggested. Judas was a Jew, not a Roman, and therefore he simply doesn't fit Daniel's prophecy.) In *Left Behind* we imagined that the Antichrist, whom we named Nicolai Carpathia, would come from Romania, a former eastern-bloc nation that retains much of its ancient Roman heritage.

This passage in Daniel 9 is also where we hear for the first time of the "abomination of desolation," in which Antichrist halts the sacrifices in the rebuilt temple and proclaims himself to be God, thus starting the Great Tribulation.

## THE MAN OF SIN

The apostle Paul tells us a little more about the coming Antichrist. His name for this wicked ruler is "the man of sin." To the Thessalonians who were worried that the Day of the Lord had already arrived, Paul wrote:

> That Day will not come unless . . . the man of sin is revealed, the son of perdition, who opposes and exalts himself above all that is called God or that is worshiped, so that he sits as God in the temple of God, showing himself that he is God. . . . The mystery of lawlessness is already at work; only He who now restrains will do so until He is taken out of the way. And then the lawless one will be revealed, whom the Lord will consume with the breath of His mouth and destroy with the brightness of His coming. The coming of the lawless one is according to the working of Satan, with all power, signs, and lying wonders, and with all unrighteous deception among those who perish. (2 Thessalonians 2:3-4, 7-10)

Paul agrees that the Antichrist will sit in the temple of God and there proclaim himself to be God. He also says the demonic influence that will sweep Antichrist to power is "already at work," although it is being kept in check by the Holy Spirit working through the church. Once the Rapture takes place (and the Holy Spirit is "taken out of the way"), the Antichrist will be revealed to the world. Soon after he will begin to astonish men and women through "lying wonders" and "signs" and "power"—all made possible by "the working of Satan." Most of the world will be deceived by his counterfeit miracles and will willingly follow and eventually worship the Antichrist. But in the end, the man of sin will be "consumed" with the breath of the Lord and "destroyed" with the brightness of His coming at the end of the Tribulation.

## THE BEAST

The apostle John gives us many more details about the Antichrist in the book of Revelation. John's special name for this godless world leader is "the Beast," although he first introduces the Antichrist not as a beast but as a conquering king:

> And I looked, and behold, a white horse. And he who sat on it had a bow; and a crown was given to him, and he went out conquering and to conquer. . . . Another horse, fiery red, went out. And it was granted to the one who sat on it to take peace from the earth, and that people should kill one another; and there was given to him a great sword. (Revelation 6:2, 4)

We have already seen that the rider on the first two horses of the Apocalypse is none other than the Antichrist. At first he conquers through diplomacy (the apparent meaning of the bow without arrows). He is a master diplomat and resolves disputes between countries by charisma and tact. But soon he turns his fearsome military machine on his enemies in a horrific World War III, and the result is a catastrophic loss of human life: a quarter of the world's population is wiped out. Can you see why he is called "the Beast"?

In Revelation 11 we meet "two witnesses" who arise to oppose Antichrist's evil activities; they prophesy against him for three and a half years. But John says, "When they finish their testimony, the beast that ascends out of the bottomless pit will make war against them, overcome them, and kill them" (Revelation 11:7).

Eventually the Beast turns this unbridled animosity toward all the people of God, as Revelation 13:5-7 makes clear: "And he was given a mouth speaking great things and blasphemies, and he was given authority to continue for forty-two months. Then he opened his mouth in blasphemy against God, to blaspheme His name, His tabernacle, and those who dwell in heaven. And it was granted to him to make war with the saints and to overcome them."

Earlier in that chapter John makes it plain that the beast's power and authority and kingdom are given to him by Satan (verse 2). And John also tells us something revealed to no one else:

> I saw one of his heads as if it had been mortally wounded, and his deadly wound was healed. And all the world marveled and followed the beast. So they worshiped the dragon who gave authority to the beast; and they worshiped the beast, saying, "Who is like the beast? Who is able to make war with him?" . . . And authority was given him over every tribe, tongue, and nation. And all who dwell on the earth will worship him, whose names have not been written in the Book of Life of the Lamb slain from the foundation of the world. (Revelation 13:3-4, 7-8)

The apostle predicts that the Beast will receive a mortal wound that is somehow healed. Some commentators stress that the wound only *seems* fatal (*"as if* it had been mortally wounded"), insisting that only God—and never the devil—could raise someone from the dead. We believe that the Beast really is killed, for John twice says that he "ascends out of the bottomless pit" (11:7; 17:8); we believe this means that the Beast is killed, descends to the pit, and ascends from there to the earth when he is resurrected—an evil counterfeit of the Lord's own death and resurrection. Whatever the truth, it is this event that causes the world to "marvel," to follow the Beast, and to worship him.

At this point in his career the Beast will have total control of the world, for he will command ten "kings" who rule the nations of the earth: "The ten horns which you saw are ten kings who have received no kingdom as yet, but they receive authority for one hour as kings with the beast. These are of one mind, and they will give their power and authority to the beast" (Revelation 17:12-13).

As the world careens wildly to the end of the age, staggering under the wrath-filled judgments of God, the Beast's kingdom starts to come apart. He hears rumors of insurrection, which fill him "with great fury to destroy and annihilate many," in Daniel's terminology (Daniel 11:44). He marches to the Valley of Megiddo, where he meets other armies of the world—and there they do an amazing thing. John describes the scene:

> And I saw the beast, the kings of the earth, and their armies, gathered together to make war against Him who sat on the horse and against His army. (Revelation 19:19)

These armies are no longer concerned about each other; now they are united in opposition to Jesus, the Lamb of

God! But the battle is swiftly over, and "then the beast was captured, and with him the false prophet. . . . These two were cast alive into the lake of fire burning with brimstone" (Revelation 19:20). They are still there, completely conscious, over a thousand years later when the devil himself is thrown into the lake of fire:

> The devil, who deceived them, was cast into the lake of fire and brimstone where the beast and the false prophet are. And they will be tormented day and night forever and ever. (Revelation 20:10)

## A POOR IMITATION

The Antichrist is scheduled to be the last ruler of this world—just before Jesus comes. While the unredeemed people of the world will fall down to worship him during the second half of the Tribulation, by the end of the Tribulation only one name will be worshiped: Jesus Christ, the King of kings and Lord of lords. At His return, the whole world will know it made a gargantuan error by mistaking Satan's cheap imitation for the Real Thing.

Aren't you glad that there is no reason for us to make such a colossal error? Even now we can join with the choirs of heaven and sing:

> Great and marvelous are Your works, Lord God Almighty! Just and true are Your ways, O King of the saints! Who shall not fear You, O Lord, and glorify Your name? For You alone are holy. For all nations shall come and worship before you. (Revelation 15:3-4)

# TWENTY-TWO

## *The False Prophet*

"You are using a title that has for generations been limited to religious leaders and royalty for Carpath—uh, Nicolae Carpath—, Potentate Carpathia."

"Yes, and I believe the time has come to refer to him in that manner. The potentate has contributed more to world unity than anyone who ever lived. He is beloved by citizens of every kingdom. And now that he has demonstrated supernatural power, *Excellency* is hardly too lofty a title."

*SOUL HARVEST, 142*

Every ruthless dictator has to have one. Joseph Goebbels served in the role for Adolph Hitler, becoming his minister of propaganda in 1933 when the Nazis came to power. From that point on, Goebbels increasingly began to rule Germany's cultural life. A brilliant orator and one of the original spin doctors, he masterfully shaped public opinion and must be credited with winning a great deal of Hitler's early popularity. Goebbels allowed only one vision of the future—Hitler's—to reach the masses. He once explained his intolerance of differing opinions by writing simply, "Politics corrupts the character."[1]

But as masterful as Goebbels was at encouraging the German nation to embrace the "glorious reich" envisioned by Hitler, Scripture indicates that his skills and charisma pale by comparison to another powerful and dangerous toady who is yet to burst upon the world scene.

## THE BEAST WITH TWO HORNS

The apostle John is the only prophet in either Testament who tells us about this coming Goebbels-like figure. The man he describes fits amazingly well with the warning Jesus gave His disciples in Matthew 24:24: "There shall arise false Christs, and false prophets, and shall shew great signs and wonders; insomuch that, if it were possible, they shall deceive the very elect" (KJV). Here is how John describes this greatest of false prophets, a master of "great signs and wonders":

> Then I saw another beast coming up out of the earth, and he had two horns like a lamb and spoke like a dragon. And he exercises all the authority of the first beast in his presence, and causes the earth and those who dwell in it to worship the first beast, whose deadly wound was healed. He performs great signs, so that he even makes fire come down from heaven on the earth in the sight of men. And he deceives those who dwell on the earth by those signs which he was granted to do in the sight of the beast. (Revelation 13:11-14)

This figure is elsewhere called "the false prophet" (Revelation 16:13; 19:20; 20:10). Most commentators believe he is of Jewish descent, since John says he comes up "out of the earth" (Palestine) rather than out of the "sea" (the Gentile world) as does the Beast. That he has two horns "like a lamb" suggests he will try to appear as gentle as "the Lamb of God," but this is nothing but a sham, for he speaks "like a dragon," eager to declare the very words of the devil. The false prophet will be the Antichrist's primary minister of propaganda, just as Goebbels was for Hitler. Unlike Goebbels, however, the false prophet will have the power to do "great signs" while in the presence of the Antichrist, even calling down fire from heaven—just as the two witnesses of Revelation 11 are said to do. In this way he will deceive the unregenerate masses of the earth to worship the Beast.

In fact, John says that in Babylon the false prophet will imitate the image vision of Nebuchadnezzar (Daniel 2) by building an image to the Antichrist, demanding that people around the world bow down and worship him through it.

## THE IMAGE THAT SPEAKS

And what an image this is! One of the most incredible prophecies in the book of Revelation predicts that in the middle of the Tribulation the false prophet—the number two man behind only the Antichrist himself—builds a great image, most probably in the likeness of the Antichrist. The population will be forced to bow down and worship this image. Then the incredible happens: "He was granted power to give breath to the image of the beast, that the image of the beast should both speak and cause as many as would not worship the image of the beast to be killed" (Revelation 13:15).

For centuries this passage has puzzled teachers of prophecy. Everyone knows Satan and his demons do not have the power to create life or human beings. This passage, however, says that "he was granted power to give breath to the image." There have been many fanciful suggestions of how Satan and the Antichrist would deceive the people with such a creature who could actually speak. But in the last few years the prophecy has come to appear a good deal less like science fiction than it used to.

I well remember twenty-five years ago visiting Independence Hall at Knott's Berry Farm in Buena Park, California, where I saw life-size images of the Founding Fathers of our country and heard them talking about what should go into the U.S. Constitution. That display was remarkably lifelike, using handmade replicas of the founders' bodies and best-known facial features together with electronically activated movement and recordings to provide them a means of speech. They were so lifelike I whispered to my wife, "That is the way the false prophet will get the Antichrist's image to speak during the Tribulation."

And that was a quarter of a century ago! Today technology has advanced to the point that we could make an image so lifelike that through voice-activated computers it could answer preprogrammed questions so convincingly that people (particularly the millions from technologically unsophisticated countries) would think they were actually talking to a living person.

And do not forget: People will not worship this image solely because it talks but because the false prophet will kill "as many as would not worship the image of the beast." Nebuchadnezzar's image in Daniel 3 didn't speak, but he had no trouble getting "all the people, nations, and languages" to fall down and worship the image at his command—all, of course, except for the three Hebrew young men who refused to go along with the king's program. Nebuchadnezzar tried to kill them, but the Lord preserved their lives . . . just as He will do for many of His choice servants during the Tribulation.

## THE MARK OF THE BEAST

It is interesting that the famous "mark of the beast" is actually administered by the false prophet. John writes:

> He causes all, both small and great, rich and poor, free and slave, to receive a mark on their right hand or on their foreheads, and that no one may buy or sell except one who has the mark or the name of the beast, or the number of his name. Here is wisdom. Let him who has understanding calculate the number of the beast, for it is the number of a man: His number is 666. (Revelation 13:16-18)

Everything the false prophet does is calculated to increase the power and authority of the Antichrist. That is not surprising, for he receives his own power and authority from the Antichrist. Since elsewhere in this book we considered at length the "mark of the beast," we will not say much about it here except to point out that this is yet another potent way to increase the might and control of the Antichrist. Total economic control is a potent motivator indeed.

## THE SATANIC TRINITY

Satan has always been a counterfeiter of spiritual realities, and in the Tribulation he hones his devilish art to a fine point. As God is a Trinity, so the devil tries to create his own kind of trinity: Satan in the role of the Father, Antichrist in the role of the Son, and the false prophet in the role of the Holy Spirit. Just as the Holy Spirit does not call attention to Himself but directs all worship to the Son, so the false prophet does not call attention to himself but directs all false worship to the Antichrist. The three members of this unholy trinity work together to accomplish their foul ends.

The best example of this evil cooperation is found in Revelation 16:13, where John writes, "And I saw three unclean spirits like frogs coming out of the mouth of the dragon, out of the mouth of the beast, and out of the mouth of the false prophet." These demons go forth to gather the kings of the earth to the final battle "of that great day of God Almighty" (16:14). The point to notice is that all three members of this unholy trinity act in concert; they function as a single unit, with a single goal and a single vile determination.

## A COMMON DESTINY

It is appropriate, then, that the members of this satanic trinity share the same destiny. At the conclusion of the Battle of Armageddon the false prophet and the Antichrist are plucked alive from the battlefield and tossed bodily into the lake of fire, where they are joined a thousand years later by Satan. There they will (together, but very much alone) be tormented day and night forever and ever—not ruling over the damned, as some think, but "punished with everlasting destruction from the presence of the Lord and from the glory of His power" (2 Thessalonians 1:9).

For three and a half short years the false prophet will force the unredeemed multitudes to worship the Antichrist; for eternity he will be punished. For three and a half short years he will seek to usurp Christ's glory; for endless ages he will be excluded from that glory. For three and a half short years he will wage war against the saints and take away their earthly lives; for an infinity of years he will suffer destruction and the agonies of the second death.

Not a very good trade, is it?

It never is.

# TWENTY-THREE

## *The Two Witnesses*

No one ever saw them come or go; none knew
where they were from. They had appeared strange
and weird from the beginning, wearing their bur-
lap-like sackcloth robes and appearing barefoot.
They were muscular and yet bony, with leathery
skin; dark, lined faces; and long, scraggly hair and
beards. Some said they were Moses and Elijah rein-
carnate, but if Buck had to guess, he would have
said they were the two Old Testament characters
themselves. They looked and smelled centuries old,
a smoky, dusty aroma following them. Their eyes
were afire, their voices supernaturally strong and
audible for a mile without amplification. . . .

Eli erupted again. "Tempt not the chosen ones,
for to come against the voices crying in the wilderness is to appoint one's own carcass to burn before
the eyes of other jackals. God himself will consume

your flesh, and it will drip from your own bones
before your breath has expired!"
*APOLLYON, 134–36*

Two of the most colorful characters in all of Bible
prophecy have to be the two supernatural prophets that
burst on the scene during the first 1,260 days of the Tribulation. God calls them "My two witnesses." They dress in
sackcloth, they prophesy, they dispense astonishing miracles, and they witness to the grace of God in a hostile Jerusalem culture.

Of course, this does not make them popular with the authorities or with the unredeemed multitudes. And it sets up
a final confrontation that leaves the world breathless.

### WHO ARE THEY?

Revelation 11:3-4 describes these two witnesses:

> "And I will give power to my two witnesses, and
> they will prophesy one thousand two hundred and
> sixty days, clothed in sackcloth." These are the two
> olive trees and the two lampstands standing before
> the God of the earth.

Some try to identify one of the witnesses with Enoch (because he never died, Genesis 5:24) and the other with either Elijah (who also never died, 2 Kings 2:11-12) or
Moses. For three reasons we are inclined to think they are
Moses and Elijah:

1. Moses and Elijah are the two most influential men in
   the history of the Jews. Moses introduced God's writ-

ten law to Israel and wrote the first five books of the Old Testament. Elijah was the first of the writing prophets and started the school of the prophets. Whenever the Jews said, "Moses and Elijah," they usually meant "the law and the prophets."

2. Moses and Elijah accompanied Jesus and the three disciples when He was "transfigured before them" on the mount and where He discussed His impending sacrifice on the cross (Matthew 17). How fitting that Moses and Elijah would return to Jerusalem to commence these last seven years of the Tribulation to "witness, testify and prophesy." Readers of the Left Behind series will recognize them as the two most intriguing characters in the first five volumes.

3. The two witnesses are said to reproduce the very miracles that Moses and Elijah performed while on this earth. John said of them, "And if anyone wants to harm them, fire proceeds from their mouth and devours their enemies. . . . These have power to shut heaven, so that no rain falls in the days of their prophecy; and they have power over waters to turn them to blood, and to strike the earth with all plagues, as often as they desire" (Revelation 11:5-6).

Elijah is famous for calling down fire from heaven. The most famous instance occurs in 1 Kings 18:36-38 in the account of the contest between the prophets of Baal and Elijah. The Lord sent fire on Elijah's altar on Mt. Carmel in response to his simple prayer: "Lord God of Abraham, Isaac, and Israel, let it be known this day that You are God in Israel, and that I am Your servant, and that I have done all these things at Your word. Hear me, O Lord, hear me, that this people may know that You are the Lord God, and that You have turned their hearts back to You again." Not so well remembered are the accounts in 2 Kings 1 in which two army captains, escorted by fifty soldiers each, arrogantly demand that Elijah come down off a hill where he's sitting, to accompany them to see the king. In both incidents Elijah says, "If I am a man of God, then let fire come down from heaven and consume you and your fifty men" (1:10, 12). And it does! That is why a third captain of fifty, along with his soldiers, carefully climbs the hill, falls on his knees before the prophet, and pleads, "Man of God, please let my life and the life of these fifty servants of yours be precious in your sight. Look, fire has come down from heaven and burned up the first two captains of fifties with their fifties. But let my life now be precious in your sight" (1:13-14).

The two witnesses have this kind of power, and then some. In *Tribulation Force* we imagined that one of these hostile encounters might happen like this:

> The two witnesses stopped preaching and stood shoulder to shoulder, glaring at the gunman as he approached. He ran full speed, firing as he ran, but the preachers stood rock solid, not speaking, not moving, arms crossed over their ragged robes. When the young man got to within five feet of them, he seemed to hit an invisible wall. He recoiled and flipped over backward, his weapon clattering away. His head smacked the ground first, and he lay groaning.
>
> Suddenly one of the preachers shouted, "You are forbidden to come nigh to the servants of the Most

High God! We are under his protection until the due time, and woe to anyone who approaches without the covering of Yahweh himself." And as he finished, the other breathed from his mouth a column of fire that incinerated the man's clothes, consumed his flesh and organs, and in seconds left a charred skeleton smoking on the ground. The weapon melted and was fused to the cement, and the man's molten necklace dripped gold through the cavity in his chest.[1]

Elijah is connected to divinely caused drought as well as to judgments of fire. In fact, the very first time he is mentioned in the Scriptures he is heard saying to wicked King Ahab, "As the Lord God of Israel lives, before whom I stand, there shall not be dew nor rain these years, except at my word" (1 Kings 17:1). And there wasn't; God honored the prophet's word.

Moses, of course, is intimately connected with the ten plagues that struck Egypt just before the Exodus (Exodus 7–12). In the very first plague God turned the waters of Egypt into blood—including the Nile, all streams, rivers, ponds, pools, and even the water in buckets of wood and stone. The water-turned-to-blood killed the land's fish and caused the water to stink, and conditions did not return to normal for a week.

The two witnesses of Revelation 11 will have awesome power and impact, together with the 144,000 witnesses, in producing the enormous soul harvest of the first forty-two months of the Tribulation described in Revelation 7. They will provide the millions of Jews in the Holy Land a theological and spiritual bridge to the Christian gospel. Many of the souls harvested at that time will be the sons and daughters of Abraham. We believe these two witnesses will also use some plagues to protect new believers from the Antichrist in the first half of the Tribulation.

The supernatural works entrusted to these two witnesses during the first half of the Tribulation is a testimony to the power of the living God. It is as though He once again demonstrates His mighty power and existence through these two witnesses, over whom the Antichrist has no power until the due time.

## THE ASSASSINATION OF THE TWO WITNESSES

We might wish that these two witnesses would oppose and finally overthrow Antichrist, as Moses did Pharaoh and Elijah did Ahab and Jezebel. But that is not their destiny:

> When they [the two witnesses] finish their testimony, the beast that ascends out of the bottomless pit will make war against them, overcome them, and kill them. And their dead bodies will lie in the street of the great city which spiritually is called Sodom and Egypt, where also our Lord was crucified. . . . And those who dwell on the earth will rejoice over them, make merry, and send gifts to one another, because these two prophets tormented those who dwell on the earth. (Revelation 11:7-10)

The two prophets make mortal enemies of the Antichrist and those who reject Christ and worship the Beast during the first half (or 1,260 days) of the Tribulation. For reasons known only to God, the Lord allows the Antichrist to overcome and kill the two witnesses once they "finish their testimony." Before that time they are untouchable; anyone who threatens them must be killed by flaming fire out of their mouths. But after they have accomplished the mission God entrusts to them, the Antichrist "makes war" on them and kills them.

And then the unsaved people of the world who so hate the witnesses commit an incredibly evil deed. They refuse them a decent burial, leaving their dead bodies to decay in the streets of Jerusalem. They even make a Christmas-like celebration out of their murders by sending and receiving gifts "in honor" of the occasion.

Then an even more incredible thing happens. John prophesies that "those from the peoples, tribes, tongues, and nations *will see their dead bodies three and a half days*" (Revelation 11:9, emphasis added). How could the whole world see their dead bodies? Ten years ago it was impossible to fulfill that prophecy—but today it could happen at any moment.

It took the Panama invasion for me to wake up to the fact that we are the first generation that could see the fulfillment of this prophecy. My wife and I were on vacation in Mexico and watched the whole invasion on CNN. During that brief attack, CNN proudly announced it was broadcasting in "fifty-five countries of the world, live."

In 1990 the world experienced an all-time first; TV news cameras broadcast the bombing of Baghdad, enabling billions of television viewers to experience it as it happened. This time CNN proudly announced that it was "live in 109 countries of the world." Today it claims to be in "210 countries," large and small.

It is now possible for CNN (or its successor) to let the world view the dead bodies of the two prophets of God killed by the Antichrist in the middle of the Tribulation. *We are the first generation ever to have that televising capability!* The prophetic significance of this fact cannot be overexaggerated. For the first time in history man has the technology to fulfill that Revelation prophecy. This, of course, did not take God by surprise—over nineteen hundred years ago He prophesied that such an event would be shared worldwide.

As the unredeemed "peoples, tribes, tongues, and nations" gaze on the putrifying corpses of the two witnesses, no doubt they will think, *Ha! Take* that, *you miserable troublemakers!*

But they rejoice too soon.

## THAT'S NOT ALL, FOLKS!

Why God allows the Antichrist to kill the two witnesses, we are not told. But we do know the story doesn't end with their deaths! God predicted that while the world is watching, He will do a mighty miracle:

> Now after the three and a half days the breath of life from God entered them, and they stood on their feet, and great fear fell on those who saw them. And they heard a loud voice from heaven saying to them, "Come up here." And they ascended to heaven in a cloud, and their enemies saw them. In the same hour there was a great earthquake, and a tenth of the city fell. In the earthquake seven thousand men were killed, and the rest were afraid and gave glory to the God of heaven. (Revelation 11:11-13)

The most supernatural event of those times will be televised instantly around the world—to the "peoples, tribes, tongues, and nations." Among other things, this will be a loving gesture by God Almighty, not only to resurrect and take to heaven His two prophets, but also to make known His existence and power around the world. We have no doubt that millions of souls to whom the 144,000 Jewish witnesses will be speaking and whom the Holy Spirit will be convicting will see this demonstration of the divine and respond to the Savior.

The people of Jerusalem will have even more reason to respond, for John tells us of a mighty earthquake that strikes at precisely that time, toppling a tenth of the ancient city and killing seven thousand persons. Very often in Revelation, after a divine judgment hits the earth, we read some version of "but they refused to repent and blasphemed the God who has power over these plagues." But not this time. John tells us that "the rest were afraid and gave glory to the God of heaven."

Please don't miss the significance of this verse! God intends that the terrible plagues and judgments of the Tribulation might cause the people of the world to repent and turn to Him. He tells us over and over in His Word that He has "no pleasure" in the death of the wicked (e.g., Ezekiel 18:32; 33:11) but instead desires that they turn from their sin and place their trust in Him. In our novel *Left Behind* we had a pastor make the following speech in a videotape intended for those who miss the Rapture:

> Strange as this may sound to you, this is God's final effort to get the attention of every person who has ignored or rejected him. He is allowing now a vast period of trial and tribulation to come to you who remain. He has removed his church from a corrupt

world that seeks its own way, its own pleasures, its own ends.

I believe God's purpose in this is to allow those who remain to take stock of themselves and leave their frantic search for pleasure and self-fulfillment, and turn to the Bible for truth and to Christ for salvation.[2]

God is a loving Father who is "not willing that any should perish but that all should come to repentance" (2 Peter 3:9). That "all" means those left behind after the Rapture as well as those who have the privilege of responding in faith before it occurs. And the two witnesses are a big part of God's means in the first half of the Tribulation to see that many men and women do, in fact, repent and enter into eternal life.

## ONE FINAL CHANCE

God's mercy is no weak thing. It is not some soft, fuzzy, warm trifle that merely overlooks human sin because it can't stand to see men and women suffer under the righteous judgments of God. No, God's mercy is a robust, strong, towering demonstration of His grace that reaches out to those who don't deserve it and uses any means necessary to bring them to their senses and into the glorious light of heaven.

In a very real sense, that is the ministry of the two witnesses of Revelation 11. The drought they bring and the plagues with which they smite the earth are really "severe mercies," to use author Sheldon Vanauken's striking phrase. So said the prophet Jeremiah long centuries ago:

It is good that one should hope and wait quietly for the salvation of the Lord. It is good for a man to bear the yoke in his youth. Let him sit alone and keep silent, because God has laid it on him. Let him put his mouth in the dust—there may yet be hope. Let him give his cheek to the one who strikes him, and be full of reproach. For the Lord will not cast off forever. Though He causes grief, yet He will show compassion according to the multitude of His mercies. For He does not afflict willingly, nor grieve the children of men. (Lamentations 3:26-33)

No, God will not willingly afflict or grieve the children of men. But He *will* do it, if that is the only way left for Him to get their attention. And the proof of that is the two witnesses of Revelation 11.

Call them the sons of Severe Mercy.

# TWENTY-FOUR

## The 144,000 Jewish Witnesses

"LADIES and gentlemen," Tsion continued, spreading his feet and hunching his shoulders as he gazed at his notes, "never in my life have I been more eager to share a message from the Word of God. I stand before you with the unique privilege, I believe, of addressing many of the 144,000 witnesses prophesied in the Scriptures. I count myself one of you, and God has burdened me to help you learn to evangelize. Most of you already know how, of course, and have been winning converts to the Savior every day. Millions around the world have come to faith already."

*APOLLYON, 47*

Every spiritual revival in history has shared some common features: earnest prayer, a deep sense of God's holiness, a chastened people of God. But every revival I know of has also featured something else: one or more "on fire" evangelists, men deeply committed to the truth of God's Word and zealous to bring that truth home to the hearts of those who listen, whether they be skeptics or seekers.

George Whitefield, one of the greatest evangelists of the eighteenth century, preached three or four times a day from the time he was twenty-two until his death at fifty-five. It was his habit to arise at 4 A.M., spend an hour with God and His Word, and begin preaching at 5 A.M. He evangelized throughout England, often to Wales, fifteen times to Scotland, twice to Ireland, and seven times to the American colonies, from New Hampshire in the north to Georgia in the south. His basic message to everyone—the poor and unlearned as well as the aristocracy of England—was, "Ye must be born again!" He preached it more than thirty thousand times in his lifetime, mostly in open-air meetings, and was a major reason for the success of the Great Awakening.

Imagine what might happen in this world if it were visited not by one or a dozen or even a hundred Whitefields, but by *144,000* of them! What kind of soul harvest might be reaped?

According to the Bible, the world may soon find out.

## EVANGELISTS BY THE THOUSANDS

One of our Lord's well-known promises about the end of the age is found in Matthew 24:14: "And this gospel of the kingdom will be preached in all the world as a witness to all the nations, and then the end will come." Most prophecy scholars locate this worldwide preaching of the gospel during the Tribulation.

It is assumed this feat will be accomplished through the ministry of the 144,000 witnesses described in Revelation 7, who reach a "multitude which no one could number, of all nations, tribes, peoples, and tongues" (verse 9). John tells us that God has a special ministry for these thousands of future Jewish converts to Christ, and that the Lord will prepare their way in a supernatural exercise of divine power:

> After these things I saw four angels standing at the four corners of the earth, holding the four winds of the earth, that the wind should not blow on the earth, on the sea, or on any tree. Then I saw another angel ascending from the east, having the seal of the living God. And he cried with a loud voice to the four angels to whom it was granted to harm the earth and the sea, saying, "Do not harm the earth, the sea, or the trees till we have sealed the servants of our God on their foreheads." And I heard the number of those who were sealed. One hundred and forty-four thousand of all the tribes of the children of Israel were sealed. (Revelation 7:1-4)

This passage suggests that before the world is plunged into the plagues and disasters ushered in by the sixth seal judgment at the end of the first quarter of the Tribulation, God will raise up an army of 144,000 Jewish evangelists to spread across the globe and bring in a soul harvest of unimaginable proportions. Each of these "servants" of God will receive a "seal" on his forehead. While we don't know exactly what this seal will be, the text seems to suggest it will be visible. Certainly the "mark of the beast" that unbelievers will receive is visible, and both are irreversible. In our novel *Soul Harvest* we speculated that the believer's mark would be visible to other believers but not to its owner or to unbelievers. And we imagined its sudden appearance might prompt an exchange between believers something like the following:

> "Look at me," Tsion said. He pointed to Buck's forehead.
>
> Buck said, "Well, look at yourself! There's something on yours, too."
>
> Tsion pulled down the visor mirror. "Nothing," he muttered. "Now you are teasing me."
>
> "All right," Buck said, frustrated. "Let me look again. OK, yours is still there. Is mine still there?"
>
> Tsion nodded.
>
> "Yours looks like some kind of a 3-D thing. What does mine look like?"
>
> "The same. Like a shadow or a bruise, or a, what do you call it? A relief?"
>
> "Yes," Buck said. "Hey! This is like one of those puzzles that looks like a bunch of sticks until you sort of reverse it in your mind and see the background as the foreground and vice versa. That's a cross on your forehead."
>
> Tsion seemed to stare desperately at Buck. Suddenly he said, "Yes! Cameron! We have the seal, visible only to other believers."
>
> "What are you talking about?"
>
> "The seventh chapter of Revelation tells of 'the servants of our God' being sealed on their foreheads. That has to be what this is!"[1]

Whatever the seal is, it affords these 144,000 Jewish witnesses "of all the tribes of the children of Israel" some kind of supernatural protection, at least until the great soul harvest of Revelation 7:9 can be accomplished. Oh, how we love that verse! Without question it leads off our favorite passage in all of Revelation:

> After these things I looked, and behold, a great multitude which no one could number, of all nations, tribes, peoples, and tongues, standing before the throne and before the Lamb, clothed with white robes, with palm branches in their hands, and crying out with a loud voice, saying, "Salvation belongs to our God who sits on the throne, and to the Lamb!"
>
> And all the angels stood around the throne and the elders and the four living creatures, and fell on their faces before the throne and worshiped God, saying: "Amen! Blessing and glory and wisdom, thanksgiving and honor and power and might, be to our God forever and ever. Amen."
>
> Then one of the elders answered, saying to me, "Who are these arrayed in white robes, and where did they come from?" And I said to him, "Sir, you know." So he said to me, "These are the ones who come out of the great tribulation, and washed their robes and made them white in the blood of the Lamb. Therefore they are before the throne of God, and serve Him day and night in His temple. And He who sits on the throne will dwell among them. They shall neither hunger anymore nor thirst anymore; the sun shall not strike them, nor any heat; for the Lamb who is in the midst of the throne will shepherd them and lead them to living fountains of

waters. And God will wipe away every tear from their eyes." (Revelation 7:9-17)

Some interpreters have a hard time believing that the Tribulation could usher in such an enormous soul harvest, but we are convinced this text shows that more men and women will be won to Christ in this period than at any time in history. That God could pour out His Spirit in a flood of conversions, even in an Old Testament setting, was proved in Jonah's day when the Lord spared the city of Nineveh after the prophet Jonah preached to its people, "Yet forty days, and Nineveh shall be overthrown!" (Jonah 3:4). The Bible says the inhabitants of that wicked Assyrian city heard Jonah and "believed God, proclaimed a fast, and put on sackcloth, from the greatest to the least of them" (verse 5). And how did God respond to such earnest repentance? "Then God saw their works, that they turned from their evil way; and God relented from the disaster that He had said He would bring upon them, and He did not do it" (verse 10).

And do not forget that it was another Old Testament prophet, Joel, who predicted a worldwide soul harvest for the time of the end:

> And it shall come to pass afterward that I will pour out My Spirit on all flesh; your sons and your daughters shall prophesy, your old men shall dream dreams, your young men shall see visions. And also on My menservants and on My maidservants I will pour out My Spirit in those days. And I will show wonders in the heavens and in the earth: blood and fire and pillars of smoke. The sun shall be turned

into darkness, and the moon into blood, before the coming of the great and terrible day of the Lord. And it shall come to pass that whoever calls on the name of the Lord shall be saved. (Joel 2:28-32)

A partial fulfillment of this prophecy took place on the day of Pentecost (Acts 2:16-21), but its full manifestation awaits the day of these 144,000 Jewish witnesses of Revelation 7. Their preaching of the everlasting gospel will be so clear and so powerful that it will result in the conversions of "a great multitude which no one could number" from every people group on the face of the earth!

## DANIEL AND THE TIME OF THE END

We are indebted to Daniel, the great Hebrew prophet, who asked the same questions we would ask about spiritual conditions during the end times. In his very important twelfth chapter he asked, "How long shall the fulfillment of these wonders be?" and "What shall be the end of these things?" He was told that "the words are closed up and sealed till the time of the end" (Daniel 12:9). Then he was told something often overlooked by prophecy students about end-time events: "Many shall be purified, made white, and refined, but the wicked shall do wickedly."

In other words, there is going to be an enormous divide at the time of the end between the many who shall become "purified, made white, and refined" and the "wicked." Of course, the only way to become purified and made white is by the "blood of the Lamb." The wicked will stubbornly reject the Savior and continue in their wickedness.

This passage will find its complete fulfillment in the Tribulation when the gospel will be preached around the world by the 144,000 witnesses and the angel with the everlasting gospel (Revelation 14:6), but even now it accurately describes our world. Sad to say, it is exactly the condition we see in the present day. Many are coming to Christ all over the world and turning from their wickedness, while many others reject the Savior and seem bent on continuing and even intensifying their wickedness. Can the end be far off?

## THE GOAL IS CLOSE

Jesus predicted in Matthew 24:14 that the gospel would be preached throughout the world during the Tribulation, yet already we are coming close to evangelizing all the world by the end of this decade! At the 1992 convention of the National Religious Broadcasters, the heads of three worldwide Christian shortwave radio ministries described their current evangelistic strategy. The presidents of Far Eastern Broadcasting ministries; HCJB in Quito, Equador; and Trans-World Radio, which covers Europe, announced a plan to take the gospel via shortwave radio to the entire world! Wycliffe Bible Translators expects to have the New Testament soon translated and printed in hundreds of additional languages throughout the world.

Dr. Bill Bright, a longtime visionary for Christ, is one of the most effective teachers of soul winning in the world today. He and the sixteen thousand workers under Campus Crusade for Christ have long had the goal of "helping to win the world for Christ." Recently they accelerated their plans.

The *JESUS* film, a dramatized version of the life of Christ narrated from the Gospel of Luke, has yielded incredible results. First produced in English, it had such remarkable effects that the script was translated into many other languages. My wife and I were present at the National Religious Broadcasters convention when Bill Bright, the film's originator, was presented a golden copy of the four-hundredth language translation of the film. He told me that Campus Crusade has recorded 500 million professions of faith in Christ from showing the film around the world. The film has been copied and presented in more countries than they can keep track of. Only God knows how many people have seen and responded to that film.

The church has produced many powerful soul winners and influential Christian leaders. We have had evangelists like George Whitefield, John Wesley, D. L. Moody, Billy Sunday, and many others. Yet the leading evangelist of the last half of this century, Billy Graham—frequent winner of the title "the most admired man in the world"—has preached the gospel to more people than any man in history. Because of his access to modern means of communication, he has probably preached the gospel to more people than all the evangelists of preceding centuries combined.

One of Graham's last messages was carried by video to more countries simultaneously than ever before; one reporter estimated that the evangelist preached the gospel that day to 281 million people. Even if that estimate was half right, that is an astonishing number. When you add that to the millions who have attended his crusades during the past fifty years, seen the TV programs of his crusades, watched his movies, read his books, or been influenced by his other efforts to get the gospel out, it is possible that he alone has presented the gospel to one billion or more souls.

The true missionary and evangelistic outreach of the

church is one of the best-kept secrets of our times. The prince of the power of the air, the god of this age, would have us believe that the whole world is following him. That is probably the biggest lie of our day. In reality, millions from all over the world are coming to Christ. Even in China, the Holy Spirit is bringing millions to faith in Christ through the ministry of faithful "house" churches. Still others are hearing good news via shortwave radio.

I read the *International World Religion Report* twice a month, and I am continually amazed at the moving of the Holy Spirit in leading millions of souls all over the world to the Savior. Since the fall of the Soviet Union, God is opening whole countries to gospel preaching, countries that have been closed for over seventy years.

Central and South America, too, have seen millions come to faith in Christ. During the Reagan years, when Communists tried to overpower the young democracies of Central America, all five countries elected conservative presidents who were either professing Christians or favorable to Christianity. One of those presidents told me that it was "the evangelicals that got me elected." The number of Christians had grown fourfold in his country, and it was the Christians who went to the polls and elected him over his communist opponent. Similar reports come from the other countries. It can accurately be said that the amazing soul harvest in Central and South America in the last two decades is what saved those regions from turning communist.

Even now we are seeing a new trend as hundreds of leaders in the body of Christ from all over the world are doing what Jesus commanded us to do: "Go therefore and make disciples of all the nations" (Matthew 28:19). Using available technology, these leaders and mission heads are multiplying their efforts in getting the gospel out as a prelude to "the time of the end."

## UNIVERSAL GOSPEL PREACHING YET TO COME

Matthew 24:14 is not now being fulfilled, and it won't be until the Tribulation. Yet even if present trends were allowed to continue, the task of worldwide evangelism could be accomplished in one or two decades! Technology is helping to spread the gospel. Thirty years ago it took a translator most of his lifetime to break down a tribal language into writing and then translate the New Testament into a tongue the people could understand. Now, with the aid of computers, one translator has been known to translate the New Testament into five languages! The task is getting smaller, not greater, even with an increasing world population.

Consequently, the rapid spread of the gospel is one more powerful evidence that we may be the generation that turns that task over to those who will complete it—the 144,000 Spirit-filled witnesses who will preach to the world shortly after Jesus raptures His church.

# TWENTY-FIVE

## Tribulation Saints and Martyrs

"REMEMBER my telling you about the 144,000 Jewish witnesses who try to evangelize the world for Christ? Many of their converts, perhaps millions, will be martyred by the world leader and the harlot, which is the name for the one-world religion that denies Christ."

Rayford was furiously taking notes. He wondered what he would have thought about such crazy talk just three weeks earlier. How could he have missed this? God had tried to warn his people by putting his Word in written form centuries before. For all Rayford's education and intelligence, he felt he had been a fool. Now he couldn't get enough of this information, though it was becoming clear that the odds were against a person living until the Glorious Appearing of Christ.

*LEFT BEHIND, 312*

In October 1998 the *Oregonian* newspaper did something unheard of among most U.S. metropolitan dailies. It began running a five-part, in-depth series on the persecution of Christians worldwide, focusing on the plight of believers in Pakistan, Burma, Sudan, Egypt, and China. The paper spent nine months in its investigation, turning to "people with the deepest ties to underground Christian movements around the world"[1] to help gain reliable information. The first installment of the remarkable series, headlined "Christian Persecution: Widespread, Complex," started like this:

> A Presbyterian pastor overlooks threats and builds the first Christian church in his region of Pakistan. A mob destroys the church. Masked men invade the pastor's home and stab him to death.
>
> A man leaves Islam to become a Christian. Egyptian secret police arrest him without a formal charge and torture him with an electric probe to make him inform them about other converts.
>
> A Roman Catholic boy in southern Sudan plays in the trees with his friends. Soldiers waging a holy war capture him and send him into slavery, where he is given an Islamic name and beaten with sticks by his master's wives. . . .
>
> Around the world, Christians are being tortured, beaten, raped, imprisoned, enslaved, forced out of their homes and killed—in large part because of what they believe.
>
> There are Christians clinging to their faith in countries where laws are stacked against them and

their beliefs. Yet they continue to praise and worship their God in the midst of extreme hardship.[2]

The entire eye-opening series brings true stories and actual faces and real people into focus and forces us to consider that although it still may be "safe" to be a Christian in America, in many other places around the world that is simply not true. Persecution and martyrdom are constant threats to millions of Christians around the world.

And the staggering truth is that it will only get worse. *Much* worse.

## BELIEVERS IN THE TIME OF WRATH

The Scriptures do not tell us much about believers in Christ during the time of the Tribulation, but what they do say both thrills and chills us. We thrill to the prophecies about millions of men and women coming to the Savior during this coming seven-year period of wrath—but a cold wind chills our soul when we read of the shocking persecution and martyrdom that will fill those years. Just consider a few prophesies from Daniel and Revelation:

> The same horn [the Antichrist] was making war against the saints, and prevailing against them. (Daniel 7:21)

> He . . . shall persecute the saints of the Most High, and shall intend to change times and law. Then the saints shall be given into his hand. (Daniel 7:25)

> When He opened the fifth seal, I saw under the altar the souls of those who had been slain for the word

of God and for the testimony which they held. And they cried with a loud voice, saying, "How long, O Lord, holy and true, until You judge and avenge our blood on those who dwell on the earth?" And a white robe was given to each of them; and it was said to them that they should rest a little while longer, until both the number of their fellow servants and their brethren, who would be killed as they were, was completed. (Revelation 6:9-11)

It was granted to him to make war with the saints and to overcome them. (Revelation 13:7)

Then I heard a voice from heaven saying to me, "Write: 'Blessed are the dead who die in the Lord from now on.'" "Yes," says the Spirit, "that they may rest from their labors, and their works follow them." (Revelation 14:13-14)

I saw the woman [the one-world church], drunk with the blood of the saints and with the blood of the martyrs of Jesus. And when I saw her, I marveled with great amazement. (Revelation 17:6)

Several important points should be emphasized from these texts to help us understand God's program for His people during the Tribulation.

**1. The Tribulation will see a great soul harvest.** Assumed by these passages and explicitly according to Joel 2:28-32, the Holy Spirit will be alive and well on planet Earth during the Tribulation, convicting all who are open to God with the gospel truth that Jesus died for their sins according to the Scriptures, that He rose again from the dead, and that they can be saved through faith in Him. The key then will be exactly what it is today and always has been—repentance and faith.

## 2. God is still in control.

Despite the horrific numbers of saints who will lose their lives in the Tribulation, God is still very much in control throughout the whole period. Note the careful language both Daniel and John use to describe the Antichrist's power over the people of God:

Daniel: "The saints shall be *given into his hand*" (Daniel 7:25, emphasis added).

John: "*It was granted* to him to make war with the saints" (Revelation 13:7, emphasis added).

Both of these texts stress that the Antichrist does nothing without the permission of God. The Beast does not tear the saints from God's grasp, nor does he somehow outmaneuver the Lord. The Tribulation saints are in the same position as was the Lord Jesus when He stood before the Roman governor Pilate. The arrogant Pilate demanded of a silent Jesus, "Do you refuse to speak to me? . . . Don't you realize I have power either to free you or to crucify you?" To which Jesus replied authoritatively, "You would have no power over me if it were not given to you from above" (John 19:10-11, NIV).

That is exactly the situation of these Tribulation saints. The Antichrist would have no power over them unless it had been given to him from above. In fact, God's control of His people's lives extends to the exact number of believers who will be martyred. That is what Revelation 6:11 has in mind when it reports that the martyred saints will be told in heaven to "rest a little while longer, until both the number of their fellow servants and their brethren, who would be killed as they were, was completed." Friends, *that* is total control!

### 3. The death of a believer is blessed.

"Blessed are the dead who die in the Lord," declares Revelation 14:13. The world will believe these martyrs are ignorant, foolish, idiotic. They will be thankful (if that word fits) that they are not among the ones marked for death. Some of the more tenderhearted (if there be any) may even pity these saints who would rather die than deny their Lord.

But God does not pity them. He blesses them! He will feel toward them just as He has felt all along toward all His people: "Precious in the sight of the Lord is the death of His saints" (Psalm 116:15). And this blessing of God comes with more than well-wishes. The apostle John says these martyrs will be granted "rest" (granted to no one living on earth) and that their works will "follow them" —that is, they will be richly rewarded for their perseverance even unto death.

### 4. God will avenge the death of His children.

When the slain saints cry out in heaven, "How long, O Lord, holy and true, until You judge and avenge our blood on those who dwell on the earth?" (Revelation 6:10), the Lord does not rebuke them. Instead He tells them to wait a little while longer. Our God is an avenging God, as the apostle Paul reminds us: "It is a righteous thing with God to repay with tribulation those who trouble you, and to give you who are troubled rest with us when the Lord Jesus is revealed from heaven with His mighty angels, in flaming fire taking vengeance on those who do not know God, and on those who do not obey the gospel of our Lord Jesus Christ" (2 Thessalonians 1:6-8). "The angel of the waters" makes a similar statement when God turns the seas and rivers and springs to blood near the end of the Tribulation: "You are righteous, O Lord, the One who is and who was and who is to be, because You have judged these things. For they have shed the blood of saints and prophets, and You have given them blood to drink. For it is their just due" (Revelation 16:5-6).

When the psalmist considered how the wicked prospered while he suffered, it almost broke his spirit. He admits he nearly lost his faith when he stewed over the seeming futility of faithfully serving God—"until I went into the sanctuary of God; then I understood their end. Surely You set them in slippery places; You cast them down to destruction" (Psalm 73:17-18). In other words, it encouraged this man to see that injustice would not always triumph.

The same encouragement is given at least twice in the book of Revelation. Revelation 13:9-10 says, "If anyone has an ear, let him hear. He who leads into captivity shall go into captivity; he who kills with the sword must be killed with the sword. Here is the patience and the faith of the saints." What gives persecuted saints "patience"? What assurance does their "faith" give them? That God is a righteous judge who will settle all accounts. The idea is found again in Revelation 14:12. After a graphic description of the eternal torments awaiting those who worship the Beast and receive his mark, the text says: "Here is the patience of the saints; here are those who keep the commandments of God and the faith of Jesus." In many such ways throughout Scripture God says, "It is mine to avenge; I will repay" (see Deuteronomy 32:35; Romans 12:19; Hebrews 10:30; et al.).

## VICTORY IS THEIRS

We should thank God that His Word does not leave the story of the Tribulation saints with their earthly demise, but loudly proclaims their ultimate victory through the blood of the Lamb. Consider first this stirring passage: "They overcame him by the blood of the Lamb and by the word of their testimony, and they did not love their lives to the death" (Revelation 12:11).

Often the Bible displays a logic that seems backwards to the world. Jesus says that whoever wants to be greatest must be least of all. He says that whoever is first will be last and that the last will be first. And in the book of Revelation He says that the overcomers are not those who wield the weapons of mass murder but those who lose their lives for Jesus' sake. Every time a faithful Tribulation saint depends upon the power of God and keeps his testimony to the end, he overcomes the Antichrist and the devil. These saints love the Lord more than they love their own necks, and for that they will be richly rewarded:

> But the saints of the Most High shall receive the kingdom, and possess the kingdom forever, even forever and ever. (Daniel 7:18)

> A judgment was made in favor of the saints of the Most High, and the time came for the saints to possess the kingdom. (Daniel 7:22)

But the court shall be seated, and they shall take away his [Antichrist's] dominion, to consume and destroy it forever. Then the kingdom and dominion, and the greatness of the kingdoms under the whole heaven, shall be given to the people, the saints of the Most High. His kingdom is an everlasting kingdom, and all dominions shall serve and obey Him. (Daniel 7:26-27)

And I saw something like a sea of glass mingled with fire, and those who have the victory over the beast, over his image and over his mark and over the number of his name, standing on the sea of glass, having harps of God. They sing the song of Moses, the servant of God, and the song of the Lamb, saying: "Great and marvelous are Your works, Lord God Almighty! Just and true are Your ways, O King of the saints! Who shall not fear You, O Lord, and glorify Your name? For You alone are holy. For all nations shall come and worship before You, for Your judgments have been manifested." (Revelation 15:2-4)

And I saw thrones, and they sat on them, and judgment was committed to them. And I saw the souls of those who had been beheaded for their witness to Jesus and for the word of God, who had not worshiped the beast or his image, and had not received his mark on their foreheads or on their hands. And they lived and reigned with Christ for a thousand years. . . . Blessed and holy is he who has part in the first resurrection. Over such the second death has no power, but they shall be priests of God and of Christ, and shall reign with Him a thousand years. (Revelation 20:4-6)

Whatever doubts might have plagued these saints during their trials on earth will vanish into nothingness the moment they stand before the King to rule and reign with Him in the millennial kingdom. Is it a reward vastly out of proportion to what they deserve? Of course! But that is the nature and the glory of our God. His grace knows no bounds, and His joy in blessing His people knows no limit.

So has it always been, and so shall it always be.

## NOT WORTHY TO BE COMPARED

The truths of Scripture do not change. Since God is its author, the message of the Bible can never show any "variation or shadow of turning" (James 1:17). So David said, "Your word, O Lord, is eternal; it stands firm in the heavens" (Psalm 119:89, NIV).

For that reason we suspect that the saints of the Tribulation will cling to one verse out of Romans with every bit of strength in them. It could well become the most important verse to them in all the arsenal of God's Word. As much as this verse comforts us now, we can imagine that it will bring untold comfort then. See if you agree.

For I consider that the sufferings of this present time are not worthy to be compared with the glory which shall be revealed in us. (Romans 8:18)

# TWENTY-SIX

## *The Unredeemed Multitudes*

**Moral Breakdown**
2 Peter 3:1-12

"On virtually every other channel, I saw—in that split second before the signal changed—final proof that society has reached rock bottom.

"I am neither naïve nor prudish. But I saw things today I never thought I would see. All restraint, all boundaries, all limits have been eradicated. It was a microcosm of the reason for the wrath of the Lamb. Sexuality and sensuality and nudity have been part of the industry for many years. But even those who used to justify these on the basis of freedom of expression or a stand against censorship at the very least made them available only to people who knew what they were choosing.

"Perhaps it is the very loss of the children that has caused us not to forget God but to acknowledge him in the worst possible way, by sticking out our tongues, raising our fists, and spitting in his face. To see not just simulated perversion but actual portrayals of every deadly sin listed in the Scriptures left us feeling unclean.

"My friend left the room. I wept. It is no surprise to me that many have turned against God. But to be exposed to the depths of the result of this abandonment of the Creator is a depressing and sorrowful thing. Real violence, actual tortures and murders, is proudly advertised as available twenty-four hours a day on some channels. Sorcery, black magic, clairvoyance, fortune-telling, witchcraft, seances, and spell casting are offered as simple alternatives to anything normal, let alone positive."

SOUL HARVEST, 325–26

Any rational person might assume that the people living at the time of the Tribulation would fall on their knees before God and call on Him for mercy. After all, that is one of the main purposes behind the severity of God's judgments, to get the attention of unsaved people so they would call on the name of the Lord and be saved.

But a careful analysis of the population figures given for that period in Revelation indicates that only about 25 percent will repent and turn to Christ. The majority will refuse to repent, for Scripture says of them, "But the rest of mankind, who were not killed by these plagues, did not repent of the works of their hands, that they should not worship demons, and idols of gold, silver, brass, stone, and wood, which can neither see nor hear nor walk; and they did not repent of their murders or their sorceries or their sexual immorality or their thefts" (Revelation 9:20-21).

These are the same people who "rejoice," "make merry," and "send gifts to one another" over the murders of God's two witnesses at the midpoint of the Tribulation (Revelation 11:10); the same people who "blasphemed the name of God who has power over these plagues; and they did not repent and give Him glory" (Revelation 16:9); the same people who "blasphemed the God of heaven because of their pains and their sores, and did not repent of their deeds" (Revelation 16:11); the same people who "blasphemed God because of the plague of the hail" (Revelation 16:21); and the same people whose "sins have reached to heaven," who are guilty of "the blood of prophets and saints, and of all who were slain on the earth" (Revelation 18:5, 24).

At least 75 percent of the people living during that incredible seven-year period will pit their will against God and reject His many calls for salvation. And so they will get what they fully deserve.

### THE TOP SEVEN SINS OF THE TRIBULATION

A passage we just reviewed, Revelation 9:20-21, lists the top seven sins of the Tribulation:

1. Rebellion against God ("they did not repent")
2. Worship of demons
3. Idolatry
4. Murders
5. Sorceries (drugs)
6. Sexual immorality
7. Thefts

It is interesting to compare this list with the one given by the apostle Paul in Colossians 3:5-6, which mentions "sexual immorality, impurity, lust, evil desires and greed, which is idolatry" (NIV). Paul then reminds his readers, "Because of these, the wrath of God is coming."

Is it ever!

We contend that even though these seven sins of the Tribulation will become rampant after the church has been raptured, already they are among the most dominant sins of our society. Note them briefly:

## REBELLION AGAINST GOD

Rebellion is a way of life today, both nationally and individually. Government, media, and education policy is relentlessly removing every vestige of our nation's heritage that relates to God, prayer, the Bible, and Christian values. For over fifty years faith in God and obedience to Him have been treated as vices rather than virtues and as national liabilities rather than assets.

The nation's capital is repeatedly embroiled in controversy over using tax funds to teach sexual abstinence to our children in the public schools—even though such teaching is the only training that has proven helpful in stemming the tide of sexual promiscuity. Secularizers insist that government can finance condoms for children, and if they get pregnant, provide them an abortion—but since teaching of abstinence is based on the Bible and the Jewish and Christian religions, it is therefore illegitimate. Such a prejudiced attitude not only ruins millions of our nation's youth but displays open rebellion against the will and laws of God.

## WORSHIP OF DEMONS

Twenty years ago Satan worship was scarcely heard of; today it is rampant. Satan worshipers are frequently on the evening news because of some satanic ritual that killed or maimed someone. Witchcraft, too, is becoming rampant, even respectable. A recent photo in *USA Today* pictured seven hundred witches dressed in black and wielding brooms, sweeping down the Matterhorn in Switzerland.[1] Add to that astrology, psychic readings, and other occult practices that seek information from satanic sources. Although mankind has a keen interest in the future, he refuses to go to the Word of God and the Holy Spirit, but instead often resorts to necromancy, tarot-card readings, voodoo, and other demonic practices. And it will only get worse during the Tribulation!

## IDOLATRY

Unredeemed man always resists worshiping God by faith but demands "aids to worship"—things made with human hands, from pictures to images to relics and icons. No wonder Vladimir Lenin concluded that "man is incurably religious." These days paganism is widespread not only in backward countries but also in America. Have you noticed the increasing worship of the mother goddess Gaia? A replica of the Parthenon located in a park in Nashville, Tennessee, features a huge statue to Gaia. To the Christ-rejecting mind, the worship of any female goddess is attractive, for she is nonjudgmental, gentle, and ever merciful. She would never banish people to hell for their sins, nor in most cases even punish them. She only blesses them—ever a preference for the God-rejecting sinner.

It is quite possible that we are on the verge of seeing a merging of the feminist movement, liberal Christianity (with its penchant for feminizing the Scriptures), and mother goddess worship. At the same time, many in the

Catholic church are trying to persuade the Pope to establish Mary worship as official church doctrine by naming Mary "co-redemptrix with Jesus" and the fourth member of the godhead. In all likelihood, as soon as all born-again Christians are raptured, there will be no restraining influence to keep such perverse doctrine from being made official. The next step, a very small one, would be for Gaia worshipers to become Mary worshipers. Perhaps that is why Babylon—the religious beast of Revelation 17 seen with a woman on its back—controls the Antichrist's kingdom during the first half of the Tribulation.

## MURDERS

One of the major social problems of our day is the rise in the murder rate. Already it has reached frightening proportions. Former Los Angeles police chief Bob Vernon told us that many in the younger generation have no respect for human life; witness the increasing number of murderers aged ten to eleven years old. The current violent crime rate—almost twenty-five thousand murders each year in America—is making this once-Christian nation the murder capital of the world. As deplorable as was the Vietnam War, more Americans lose their lives every two and a half years through murder than were killed in the entire ten years of that war.

The rise in drive-by shootings, rapes, muggings, and murders are horrible enough. But the greatest evidence that Tribulation-like living has already gripped our society is the government's attitude toward murdering the most innocent and weakest among us, the unborn. From the Supreme Court to the White House to Congress and throughout the nation, officials do nothing to halt the murder of more than one and a half million unborn babies every year—more than 40 million since 1973, when *Roe v. Wade* made abortion legal!

It is unfathomable that our great nation's president can veto a ban on partial-birth abortions. This is the murder of perfectly healthy babies, a procedure that two seconds later would be illegal. How can it fail to incur the wrath of God?

Considering our nation's attitude toward the wanton killing of the unborn, should it surprise us that many today are calling for the legalized killing of the elderly? The leaders of this world have forgotten that life is a creation of God; He alone should decide how long a person lives. The value of life, particularly of the weakest and most helpless among us, is a good test of the moral quality of a nation.

We shudder for our nation's future when already we have such a low regard for human life. When the unrestrained rebellion of the Tribulation is unleashed, the world will be a frighteningly dangerous place to live. No wonder God in His mercy plans to "shorten" the time.

## DRUGS

From the Greek word translated "sorceries" in the King James Bible we get the word *pharmacy*. Unfettered drug use will be common during the Tribulation. But even today, drug and alcohol use is skyrocketing out of control. Even our president admits to drug use in his youth, and it was he who appointed a surgeon general who considered the legalization of drugs.

Drugs and alcohol are a way of life for many nonbelievers. Adopting a drug-riddled lifestyle during the

Tribulation will not require any change for many inhabitants of the world—it will merely be intensified.

## SEXUAL IMMORALITY

From the White House to the movie theater, it is accepted policy today to disregard sexual purity before marriage and sexual fidelity afterward. Many educators have all but abandoned teaching virtue; instead they have made a virtue out of homosexuality and lesbianism, which for centuries were called "perversions" and in the Bible are called "an abomination" and "unnatural."

The sexual revolution of the sixties—based on the perverted sex studies of Alfred Kinsey in the fifties, followed by the explicit sex education of the seventies and eighties, and strengthened by the Supreme Court's 1972 decision that transformed pornography from an illegal business into a legally acceptable, ten-billion-dollar-a-year trade in the nineties—has turned the Western world into a sex-obsessed cesspool of immorality . . . just like that of the Tribulation. It is hard to believe that sexual immorality can get any worse than it already is—but it will!

## THEFTS

Gated communities and security systems are becoming a way of life today. Why? Because of the rise in theft. I can remember a time in southern California when I never locked my doors and could leave my keys in my car. Today there are bars on the windows of that community, and residents put The Club locks on their cars' steering wheels to keep their vehicles from being stolen.

Theft is with us today and will continue right into the Tribulation—although it will probably become much worse under Antichrist, who is opposed to everything Jesus Christ stands for.

During the Tribulation good will become evil, and evil will become good. Virtue will become "dangerous," and immorality will not only become commonplace, it will be officially endorsed.

But is this any different from our own day? The seven sins that will dominate the Tribulation are already here! From the standpoint of sinful practice, the world is ready to live under Antichrist. The only thing lacking is the Rapture of the church, which is the lone sin-restraining influence on today's society.

## A SECOND OPINION

In the world of medicine it is a wise and prudent practice to seek a second opinion when a physician's original diagnosis is both grave and troubling. That's not a bad thing to do here, either. We recommend consulting with the apostle Paul, who had something to say about how society and culture would deteriorate in "the last days":

> But know this, that in the last days perilous times
> will come: For men will be lovers of themselves, lov-
> ers of money, boasters, proud, blasphemers, disobe-
> dient to parents, unthankful, unholy, unloving,
> unforgiving, slanderers, without self-control, brutal,
> despisers of good, traitors, headstrong, haughty,
> lovers of pleasure rather than lovers of God, having
> a form of godliness but denying its power. And
> from such people turn away! For of this sort are
> those who creep into households and make captives
> of gullible women loaded down with sins, led away

by various lusts, always learning and never able to come to the knowledge of the truth. (2 Timothy 3:1-7)

Note the eighteen characteristics of a society in free fall as outlined by Paul. What is often lost on students of history is that such declining values have been a consistent part of Western culture since the First World War.

### 1. Selfish: "lovers of themselves"
As an experienced marriage counselor I can categorically state that the massive breakdown of marriage today has no greater single cause than selfishness. This is the natural result of two generations of teaching children and youth to "do your own thing" and get all the "gusto" out of life you can. Thanks to selfishness, the divorce rate in our country is above 51 percent.

### 2. Covetousness: "lovers of money"
How much is enough? We have a population that is never satisfied but is on a continual quest for more—more money, more things, and more gratification.

### 3. Boasters, proud
These are two traits God hates (Proverbs 16:18), yet they are both on prominent display today.

### 4. Blasphemers
The use of the Lord's name in vain is commonplace today. It used to be that it was prevalent only in the military, in bars, and on the athletic field but almost never in polite society. Today, thanks to Hollywood and others in the enter-

tainment industry, it has become universal in movies and even on TV. The fact that God not only disapproves of this kind of speech but also warns He "will not hold him guiltless who takes His name in vain" (Exodus 20:7) does not seem to deter millions from the sin of blasphemy.

It is hard to see what speech patterns need to be changed to fit the Tribulation. Imagine what will happen when the one group that almost never uses the name of God and His Son in vain is suddenly snatched out of this world, leaving all the blasphemers behind!

## 5. Disobedient to parents

Parents who are disobedient to God will raise children disobedient to their mothers and fathers. The rise in juvenile crime has reached epidemic proportions, worrying law enforcement officials as they contemplate the next generation. One police officer told us that child-and-youth-murder crime (ages 8–15) is escalating faster than any other crime category.

## 6. Rebellion

The spirit of rebellion is invading many Christian homes. Just today we heard a national youth speaker say, "Seventy percent of today's youth raised in Christian homes do not follow their parent's faith when they leave home." If he is right, that is up 25 percent in just twenty years. The music and lyrics popular with today's youth are built on rebellion to parents, police, and all authority figures. Although youth are naturally rebellious (the Bible teaches that "foolishness is bound up in the heart of a child but the rod of correction will drive it far from him," Proverbs 22:15), today's social workers and sociologists are trying to keep parents from disciplining their children! As a pastor I found there was a direct correlation between children who were not allowed to sass and disobey their parents in their very young years and those who followed their parents' faith in adulthood.

## 7. Unthankful

Rebellious people are unthankful people; that is why they are so miserable. We have never met a happy ingrate! The Bible teaches us to "be thankful," which produces a thankful attitude and thus a happy life—regardless of circumstances. That is not the mental attitude encouraged today. Instead, the disadvantaged are urged to complain about their terrible lot in life, even though it is measurably better than where they or their ancestors came from. Have you ever noticed that there are no lines to get out of America, Canada, and other Western countries? There are, however, long lines to get in. Regardless of their circumstances, people should be encouraged to thank God for their blessings rather than continually curse the darkness.

## 8. Unholy

Everywhere you turn today you see the hand of satanically inspired disrespect for God, and a worship of other gods. The worship of nature is an unholy form of pantheism famous for its intolerance of other religions. The worship of the occult does not foster holy living as taught in Scripture, but just the opposite. That may be one cause of its modern appeal: It panders to the immorality that has always been a part of pagan religions, many of which are invading the West.

## 9. Without natural affection

One of the most basic Judeo-Christian principles has been the natural and beautiful attraction between the sexes. The love of a mother and father for their children, the love of the extended family for each other, and the love of one's country were similarly considered "natural." Today we are living in a depraved Romans-chapter-one world that many fear God has given or will give up to "vile passions" that reverse the normal order of things (verses 26-27). Today homosexuality and lesbianism are accepted by many in officialdom as "normal." Promiscuity before and after marriage is assumed. Multiple marriages and divorces are said to be unrelated to integrity. We have reached a scary time when mothers have been known to abandon or drown their own children. Children have been known to kill their parents and then demand leniency from society because they are orphans. One unwed mother killed her own infant after giving birth in the bathroom. She stuffed the child in the trash can, then returned to the dance floor at her senior prom to dance the night away. We could call this decade the death of natural affection.

## 10. Truce breakers and false accusers

Whether it is Israel and the Oslo accords with the PLO, or Russia, China, or North Vietnam breaking treaties with America and the West, most people have lost confidence in nations and their leaders. A majority of citizens don't expect leaders to keep their officially written word, much less their spoken word. But it isn't just nations that break treaties and agreements at will; it is also private citizens. For example, our courts are filled with challenges to prenuptial agreements after the marriages blow up. We are a litigious society that boasts one lawyer for every three hundred people. Many lawyers are getting rich on the backs of broken agreements and false accusations.

## 11. Incontinent

The Greek word here means "without self-control." Although our country was built on self-discipline, industry, and personal integrity, today we are a nation of overweight, alcoholic drug abusers and sexual perverts who cannot control our desires and passions—and who don't even try.

## 12. Fierce

Society has turned hostile, so much so you are not sure you can avoid being insulted, berated, or assaulted by strangers who feel insulted by something you have done or said. "Road rage" is one of today's worst problems on the nation's highways—and women are as bad as men. When we lived in Washington, D.C., I was impressed with how seldom motorists paid any attention to common courtesies. While you tried to get into their lane, drivers would cut you off, causing you to miss your turn—costing you twenty minutes to get back to your corner, just to save them thirty feet. In other instances angry drivers have taken guns and shot other drivers, just so they won't lose their place in traffic.

In marriage, anger and hostility often result in spousal or child abuse. Police say that domestic conflicts are among their most dangerous calls. We are rapidly becoming a nation of "fierce" people.

## 13. Despisers

Esau is infamous for despising his birthright and selling it to his brother, Jacob, for a mess of porridge. Today we have a whole subculture of intellectual elitists who have rejected God and His wisdom. They not only embrace the "wisdom of this age" or the "wisdom of man," but they also demand that the rest of the nation do the same—and thereby despise their spiritual heritage.

## 14. Traitors

Who can deny that treachery is increasing in the Western world? People in lofty and influential positions have sold their country's secrets for money, influence, and more recently, ideology. When anyone in a position of influence puts his own ideology above loyalty to his country and betrays the nation's defense secrets, he or she is a traitor—another sign that the end is quickly approaching.

## 15. Heady and reckless

We have become a nation of reckless individuals who give little thought to making the decisions that will mold the rest of our lives. Recently we read that the national debt is above 6 *trillion* dollars. Additional borrowing has exceeded that amount, including 2 trillion dollars of credit charges alone, all at exorbitant interest rates. That totals at least *14 trillion dollars* of personal and national debt, plus corporate debts—and yet billions are invested on the stock market every day. Most economists believe there will be a day of reckoning and that a crash leading to a depression is inevitable.

It isn't in economic matters alone, however, that people are reckless. The same reckless condition is seen in the sexually permissive attitudes of both the heterosexual and homosexual communities. With sexually transmitted diseases (STDs), including the awful plague of AIDS, resulting in incredibly high death rates and painful illnesses, one can only marvel at the many reckless individuals who think, *It won't happen to me.* Unfortunately, for millions it does.

## 16. High-minded

The Greek word translated "high-minded" may also be rendered "haughty" or "puffed up" or "arrogant." It never ceases to amaze me that the purveyors of secular humanism, with their disgraceful track record of societal failure, can still be so autocratic as to assume the right to make decisions for others. We make no apology that we who hold to biblical doctrine and values are dogmatic—but not in our own wisdom or authority. We are convinced that obeying the principles of God is good for individuals, society, and the nations of the world. Wherever God's principles have been followed, they have elevated individuals and society. Wherever they are ignored, they have created cultural and moral depravity.

Yet high-minded people, usually those with advanced degrees, dogmatically oppose moral teachings and prefer the immmoral practices of humanism. Witness the recent pronouncements of Jane Fonda. She has announced a bold campaign to promote condom use while ridiculing abstinence programs in public education. Asserting that "80 percent of our youth are promiscuous," she is on a crusade to see that all young people have access to condoms, even though condoms have not proven to be safe either to avoid pregnancy or sexually transmitted diseases.

Such high-minded thinking reminds me of the forty-year tenured political science professor who was seated next to me on a trip to Amsterdam. He was on his first trip to Russia—the ultimate in national socialism. He admitted he believed a one-world socialist government would benefit all the downtrodden nations and improve life on this planet. We had an interesting discussion until I asked him, "Professor, how can you believe world socialism will improve life for many when you cannot give me a single example of one nation in the world that has ever been helped by socialism?" He became so incensed he hissed at me, "It's because of you capitalists! Socialism would work if we made it universal and adopted it worldwide." That kind of blind, high-minded, autocratic thinking is the last thing impressionable college students need to hear in the classroom. But in America this kind of high-minded thinking is common fare.

## 17. Lovers of pleasure

Who can deny that this world has gone crazy over pleasure? From topless dancers to Hollywood entertainment to sporting events, millions spend money they cannot afford on events that consume hours of their time and energy. The whole world is becoming addicted to entertainment—witness the crowds that attend rock and music concerts or major sporting events. Some fans go straight from one sport to another. Jerry Jones, owner of the Dallas Cowboys and a member of the communications and TV committee for the NFL, predicted to a *USA Today* reporter that there will be "17 new venues by the year 2002." That means that instead of thirty National Football League teams, there will be forty-seven.[1] Football has become the national sport and the most watched event on TV. As football fans ourselves, we can see where an ardent fan of several sports would get little fathering or husband-ing done.

## 18. No power with God

The Bible instructs leaders that "righteousness exalts a nation," yet all the nations of the world officially con-done immoral practices suicidal to their country's best interest. Our own nation has murdered so many unborn children that we have not only incurred the wrath of God but also destroyed our nation's social security system. Baby boomers are concerned there will not be enough taxpayers and wage earners in the nation when they start filing for social security benefits. It is time in these evil days for Christian leaders to lead their members into the voting booth and work to put a halt to the killing of inno-cent blood! It won't make America a righteous nation, but it will put a stop to the officially endorsed depravity that exists today.

## PAUL'S WARNING TO THE LAST DAYS' CHURCH

It would be wrong to conclude this section without high-lighting Paul's great warning to the church. Millions of our neighbors, friends, and relatives are committed to the im-moral lifestyle just outlined. While we should witness to them and share the gospel with them, Paul says on a per-sonal level, "from such turn away."

Christians should be careful not to be drawn into the last days' lifestyles. You don't have to participate in such lifestyles to win those who are open to the gospel. Even-tually, when their world begins to collapse around them, you will be available to offer hope and help through Christ. Like the people of Noah's day, most will not heed the warning of imminent judgment. But some who recognize the "perilous times" as a sign of the end will take advantage of the "ark of safety" and call on the name of the Lord!

## THE RETURN OF THE DAYS OF NOAH AND LOT

Jesus prophesied that "as it was in the days of Noah, so it will be also in the days of the Son of Man: They ate, they drank, they married wives, they were given in marriage, until the day that Noah entered the ark, and the flood came and destroyed them all. Likewise as it was also in the days of Lot: They ate, they drank, they bought, they sold, they planted, they built; but on the day that Lot went out of Sodom it rained fire and brimstone from heaven and destroyed them all. Even so will it be in the day when the Son of Man is revealed" (Luke 17:26-30).

Two of the most depraved periods in history were the days of Noah just prior to the Flood, and the days of Lot. In both cases the people were so sinful that God destroyed them from the face of the earth. In Noah's day it was the whole world that sinned; in Lot's day it was the cities of Sodom and Gomorrah.

It is instructive that our Lord Jesus chose to use the moral climate in which these ancient people lived as a warning about the lifestyles of men and women just before His return. It is our conviction that we are already living in the moral climate of the days of Noah and of Lot.

## WHAT KIND OF DAYS WERE THEY?

Even a casual reading of Genesis 6:1-9 shows that the people of Noah's day were sexually obsessed. In this case the sons of God were cohabiting with the "daughters of men"

and producing the "giants . . . mighty men . . . , men of re-
nown"—renowned doubtless for their wickedness. Some
prophecy scholars teach that "Nephilim," the Hebrew
word for "giants," doesn't mean merely tall men but supernatural creatures, the product of angels ("the sons of
God") and the daughters of men. Whatever the case, the
most important lesson we can learn from this passage is
that their wicked lifestyle caused God to unleash the flood.
Their lifestyle included three specific sins:

1. Sexual perversion.
2. "The thoughts of their hearts were [turned to] evil
   continually."
3. Routine living with disregard to the consequences of
   impending judgment.

These people were "eating and drinking, marrying and
giving in marriage." In other words, they ignored the
preaching of Noah for 120 years and violated the known
laws of God as if there were no accounting to come. They
were guilty of routine living in the light of impending
worldwide catastrophe—a sin much like that of our own
day.

Sexual sin has always been a problem with those who
forget God. As far back as human history can be traced,
prostitution has been a curse. What God intended as a
means of propagation of the race has always been under
satanic attack. Because of the strong sex drive God has
given husbands and wives for enjoyment and mutual pleasure, human beings have been vulnerable to the misuse of
that drive and have fallen into promiscuity, perversity, and
"sexual wickedness."

Present world conditions could very well be as bad or worse than those that existed in the days before the Flood and in the days of Lot. The most common sins of our day are sexual, from fornication to adultery to homosexuality. That is evidenced worldwide by the 50 million or more abortions perpetrated annually and the rampant sexually transmitted diseases, from STDs to AIDS—all diseases that, for the most part, do not afflict those who follow the sexual laws of God.

In the past generation, due to the increase in pornography via magazines, movies, TV, and videos, there has been an acceleration of sexual promiscuity and an ever lowering of the age of first sexual activity. The scourge of all sexual perversion is pedophilia and child molestation. Some have estimated that such sins against children have increased 300 to 500 percent since pornography was legalized by the Supreme Court in 1972. Pornography has caused the minds of both men and women to be obsessed with sex, or as the Bible predicted, "every imagination of the thoughts of his [man's] heart was only evil continually" (Genesis 6:5, KJV). Hollywood has polluted the most powerful communications vehicle the human mind ever invented—film—which has the ability to affect the mind, emotions, and will.

Divorce, homosexuality, and promiscuity have been encouraged and successfully cut free from integrity and character. One generation ago men or women who were unfaithful to their wedding vows were considered untrustworthy members of society. That standard is no longer in use. TV and Hollywood parade six- and eight-time marriage losers before the cameras to pontificate their moral values. It should surprise no one to hear their conclusions that marriage and sexual faithfulness is passé and that pro-miscuity (or as they call it, "sex with love" or "recreational sex") is meaningful and good. But sexual sinners are skilled liars and deceivers, so it should surprise no one that selfishly indulgent people will lie, cheat, and steal (or worse) to advance themselves in every other area of life.

## HOMOSEXUALITY, THE SIN OF LOT'S DAY

The sexual sins of Sodom and Gomorrah in Lot's time were so gross that men were driven with a passion not only for their own sex but even became disrespectful to the an-gels who visited Lot.

It is almost unbelievable in our day how those who re-ject the sexual laws of God have succeeded in making one of the basest of sexual sins—sodomy—respectable and even acceptable. Just a few years ago Hollywood stars kept their personal sex lives (which brought them to an early death) in the closet. But today homosexuals are "out" and demanding their "rights." What rights do they demand? The right to marry, the right to cohabit with the same sex, the right to teach school, where they could influence young minds, the right to adopt children, the right to serve in the military—and the list goes on.

Even though their dangerous lifestyle can shorten their expected life span by as much as 50 percent, it is consid-ered a "hate crime" to warn or speak out against it. And discrimination against a homosexual in job selection or dismissal is a violation of the law. If you refuse to rent your home to a homosexual couple, you are a lawbreaker! The secular world has turned the sexual laws of God upside down. A few years ago the American Psychological Associ-ation considered homosexuality a mental deficiency;

now the APA has endorsed it and proposed that their members no longer urge homosexuals to change their sexual lifestyle.

## THE FUTURE IS NOW

We have come to the place where officialdom demands that any sexual urge be permitted, regardless of its effects on marriage, the home, children, the human body, and the increased misery and suicide rate it causes. To them, anything that contributes to reducing the population is good. The only sexually bad thing is the propagation of traditional moral values. Until that elite officialdom is changed—and there appears to be no way to make that happen, short of a national spiritual revival—we can have no hope of improvement.

In other words, the moral conditions spoken of in the book of Revelation are already here. We are already living in days like those of Noah and Lot—days our Lord predicted would return just before His return to this earth. Morally speaking, *nothing* needs to happen before the Rapture, and any objective person assessing the rapidly declining moral standards of our day must admit that officialdom and millions of people worldwide are already living in Sodom-and-Gomorrah-like conditions.

## THE SIGN OF THE SCOFFERS

One final trait typical of the moral climate during the end times ought to be considered: the emergence of scoffers.

Modern skepticism has its roots in the empiricism of Descartes and has taken over the graduate schools of the world, especially through the uniformitarian theory that undergirds all of education today. Don't let the word *uniformitarian* throw you. It simply describes the theory that current processes of life are sufficient to account for the origin and development of all the earth's physical and biological phenomena. This, of course, eliminates divine revelation of catastrophic events designed by God to judge His creatures.

The theory of uniformitarianism, popularized in the mid-1800s by the English geologist Sir Charles Lyell, became a prominent foundation for Darwinism and evolution, Marxism and socialism, Freudianism and liberalism. It fostered many of the evils that beset our society today and is propagated by the most intellectually trained members of our society.

It is fascinating to note that almost two thousand years ago the apostle Peter, an untrained Galilean fisherman, predicted the exact thinking patterns that would characterize these scoffers. He prophesied that:

> Scoffers will come in the last days, walking according to their own lusts, and saying, "Where is the promise of His coming? For since the fathers fell asleep, all things continue as they were from the beginning of 'creation." For this they willfully forget: that by the word of God the heavens were of old, and the earth standing out of water and in the water, by which the world that then existed perished, being flooded with water. But the heavens and the earth which now exist are kept in store by the same word, reserved for fire until the day of judgment and perdition of ungodly men. (2 Peter 3:3-7)

Peter said these scoffers would deny the coming of the Lord because "since the fathers fell asleep, all things continue as they were from the beginning of creation" (2 Peter

3:4). The questions Peter said these scoffers would ask are based on their uniformitarian ideas.

If you eliminate the biblical worldwide flood, as uniformitarians do, you remove a vital proof for the second coming of Christ. But if in fact there was a flood, then God really does judge sinful men, and there is good reason to believe He will come again to judge the world. If man accepts the reality of the Flood, he is pressed to accept the likelihood of Christ's second coming.

To demonstrate this point, Peter reached back into history and with superb logic developed a line of reasoning too deep for some of the best-educated minds of our day. He highlighted five major historical events:

- *Creation:* God was the originator of all things, including man.
- *The Fall of Man:* Sometime shortly after creation man chose to disobey God and fell from innocence into sin. Death, disease, and human misery resulted.
- *The Flood:* Man's iniquity reached such depths that God destroyed all but eight people in the world's greatest cataclysm, the Flood.
- *The Life of Christ:* Jesus Christ came to die as a divine sacrifice for man's sin, to lift the curse on man and to prepare man for a future state of bliss where he could enjoy the unlimited blessings originally intended for him by his Creator.
- *The Second Coming of Christ:* The next major event in God's plan for man.

According to Peter's argument, the scoffers are thoroughly mistaken that things have continued in a state of uniformity. To the contrary, man has seen two major divisions of time, with a third to come. The first, terminated by the Flood, Peter calls "the world that then existed." The present world he calls "the heavens and the earth which are now preserved." The third, after the second coming of Christ, will provide a new heaven and earth, which are kept in place by the word (or power) of God.

Peter clearly teaches that the present order is not sufficiently similar to the one before the Flood to provide us with accurate indications of what that world was like. Scientists who draw conclusions from present conditions arrive inevitably at wrong conclusions.

## WHY ARE THEY SO BLIND?

Peter provides us with two reasons why scoffers are so blind. The first is found in 2 Peter 3:5, "For this they willfully forget." The unregenerate minds of unbelievers resist the idea of the intervention of God in human affairs. Their problem is spiritual—a matter of the will—and the unbeliever remains deliberately ignorant of the truth.

A great American whom I deeply admire once came to our city on a speaking engagement. I wrote ahead and invited him to have breakfast with me. As we ate, I shared with him the concern of my heart. "How is it that you have escaped liberalism in the fields of economics, government, history, philosophy, and education but have swallowed it in the area of religion?" He replied, "I settled the matter forty years ago on the subject of origins; I believe man is the product of evolution."

"But there have been amazing discoveries in geology, anthropology, archaeology, and other fields that discredit evolution," I replied.

With a voice of steel he announced: "The matter is closed!" Here is a man who can carefully weigh the evidence in worldly matters, but his mind is closed to spiritual realities. Is the problem lack of evidence? Oh, no! Peter understood the heart of men when he said they "willfully forget"!

Long before geologist Lyell promoted his theory of uniformitarianism, he was an atheistic humanist. As such, he rejected the biblical record, so it is unsurprising that he would arrive at conclusions diametrically opposed to the teachings of the Bible. Nor should we be surprised that Lyell's uniformitarianism, rejected by men like Pasteur, was accepted readily and advanced by the humanists of his day. All had one thing in common: They were "willfully ignorant" of the truth of God's Word.

All the evidence in the world—scientific and rational—will not convince the man who, like the Pharisees of Jesus' day, willed not to come to Him. Only when such a person comes to the end of himself will he seek the real and ultimate truth. Fortunately, many casualties of the scoffers are still open to truth. For these individuals we should daily be available to the Holy Spirit to share the promises of God.

Peter mentions a second reason for the scoffer's intellectual blindness in verse 3: They walk "according to their own lusts." The lovers of pleasure who fostered the "free love" movement, continue to advocate the use of marijuana, and lead rebellions against society, are bosom friends of uniformitarian philosophy! If we would learn from history instead of ignoring it, we would remember that the early humanists lived in exactly that way.

It is incredible, the moral depravity officially embraced

by today's educational community, from sexual permissivism to homosexuality to pornography to relativism. How well I remember when UCLA first instituted coed dormitories. I was so naïve that I said, "That is an idea that will not last; parents of girls will rebel." How wrong I was! Practically every college and university (except most Christian schools) today sanctions this immoral lifestyle. Who is to blame, the parents who pay the bills? The students? No—it is the educated scoffers who think our children are only little animals who should be permitted to "walk after their own lusts"—as do many of their professors.

There can be little doubt that this is a day of scoffers. Never have they grown so bold and blatant. They are not content to live after their own lusts, willfully ignorant of the claims of God in His Word; they also work tirelessly to pull the next generation into their Sodom-and-Gomorrah lifestyle. They are guilty of what Jesus predicted: "Woe to you, scribes and Pharisees, hypocrites [scoffers]! For you travel land and sea to win one proselyte, and when he is won, you make him twice as much a son of hell as yourselves" (Matthew 23:15). The scoffer-making industry today serves as one more sign that the Lord is coming soon.

## OUR MORAL HOLOCAUST

It was professor Alan Bloom who pointed out in his 1990 best-seller *The Closing of the American Mind* that the relativistic attitude of our best-educated youth today is: "Morals are no big deal!"

Such popular but erroneous thinking has resulted in the near death of virtue, in millions of fatherless children, and in millions of disease-plagued youth—much like the moral conditions described by the New Testament for the coming Tribulation. In fact, the present moral holocaust—based as it is on an evolutionary philosophy that rejects God, creation, and moral absolutes—exactly fulfills this sign of end-time moral conditions.

# TWENTY-SEVEN

## *The Role of Angels*

RAYFORD suddenly heard a voice, as if someone were in the car with him. The radio was off and he was alone, but he heard, clear as if from the best sound system available: "Woe, woe to the inhabitants of the earth, because of the remaining blasts of the trumpet of the three angels who are about to sound!"

*APOLLYON, 296*

At all the most crucial periods in the history of the world, angels were in the middle of the action. They were there at the creation of the earth when "the morning stars sang together and all the angels shouted for joy" (Job 38:7, NIV). They were there at the destruction of Sodom and Gomorrah (Genesis 19:1). They were there at the giving of the Law (Galatians 3:9). They were there in the time of the judges (Judges 21), in the time of David (2 Samuel 24:16), during the ministry of Elijah (1 Kings 19:5) and that of

Isaiah (2 Kings 19:35). They were there at the birth of Christ (Luke 2:8-14). They were there at our Lord's temptation (Matthew 4:11). They were there at the Garden of Gethsemane to strengthen Him (Luke 22:43). They were there at the empty tomb to announce His resurrection (Matthew 28:2). And they were there at the Ascension to announce His return (Acts 1:10-11).

In the last decade or so we have seen much nonsense about angels, utter foolishness about their appearance, their interests, and their ministry. But do not allow this contemporary silliness to obscure from view the very real and awesome role that angels are scheduled to play in the coming Tribulation. They are major players in the drama about to unfold.

## WHAT ARE THEY?

The first item to tackle is the identity of angels. Who and what are they? Are they glorified dead persons, as many books and movies imagine? Are they sweet, chubby cherubs who float along on fluffy clouds, dreaming of lazy afternoons?

The Bible presents no such saccharine pictures. It presents angels as powerful "ministering spirits" (Hebrews 1:14), created by God sometime before He called the universe into being (Job 38:7) to serve and worship Him (Hebrews 1:7).

Angels differ from one another in power and glory and function. Some, like Gabriel, serve primarily as messengers (Daniel 8:16; Luke 1:26), while others, like Michael the archangel, are said to have special protective responsibilities (Daniel 12:1; Jude 1:9). Angels called cherubim are closely associated with the throne of God (Ezekiel 10:20), while another class of angels, called seraphim, apparently guard the heavenly throne and lead in worship (Isaiah 6). We read of a destroying angel in the plagues sent on wandering Israel (1 Corinthians 10:10), and in 2 Kings 19:35 we learn that "the angel of the Lord" in a single night put to death 185,000 Assyrian troops who were besieging King Hezekiah's Jerusalem.

God's angels are powerful, wise, swift, efficient, and devoted to doing the will of the Lord.

## NOT ALL ANGELS ARE GOOD

Scripture distinguishes between "the holy angels" (Mark 8:38) who serve God, and the "demons" who answer to Beelzebub, the devil (Mark 3:22). Demons are apparently fallen angels (Revelation 12:4) who long ago chose to rebel against God and join Satan's unholy insurrection. Some of these fallen angels so heinously transgressed God's order that they are kept in darkness and bound in everlasting chains for their day of judgment (Jude 1:6; 2 Peter 2:4). Others are allowed to roam the earth and often seek to "possess" individuals by indwelling their bodies (Matthew 12:43-45). Individuals who are so possessed manifest a variety of odd and hurtful traits, such as dumbness (Luke 11:14), convulsions (Mark 9:18), or a refusal to wear clothing and a desire to live among the tombs (Luke 8:27).

During the days of His earthly ministry, Jesus had frequent confrontations with demons, whom He also called evil spirits. He forbade them from announcing His divine identity (Mark 1:34) and cast them out of those whom they were possessing (Luke 11:20). In the book of Acts a fascinating story tells of "seven sons of Sceva, a Jewish chief priest," who try to cast out demons "in the name of

Jesus, whom Paul preaches" (Acts 19:13, NIV). The text says that "one day the evil spirit answered them, 'Jesus I know, and I know about Paul, but who are you?' Then the man who had the evil spirit jumped on them and overpowered them all. He gave them such a beating that they ran out of the house naked and bleeding" (Acts 19:13-16, NIV).

What the Gospels make clear (and what Acts amplifies) is that these fallen angels are no match for Jesus Christ. In Matthew 8 Jesus is described ordering some demons out of a man and into a herd of pigs. But before He does so they cry out, "What do you want with us, Son of God? Have you come here to torture us before the appointed time?" (verse 29, NIV). In this connection the apostle James made a fascinating statement to his readers: "You believe that there is one God. Good! Even the demons believe that—and shudder" (2:19, NIV). Why do they shudder? Because they already know their awful doom. They can never forget that "eternal fire" is being "prepared for the devil and his angels" (Matthew 25:41, NIV).

## ANGELS IN REVELATION

Angels, both holy and fallen, are mentioned in the book of Revelation no less than seventy-seven times. They are seen acting in various capacities throughout the book and throughout the time periods outlined in the book. Many times a holy angel is pictured as making a proclamation:

> And I saw a mighty angel proclaiming in a loud voice, "Who is worthy to break the seals and open the scroll?" (5:2, NIV)

Then I saw another angel flying in midair, and he had the eternal gospel to proclaim to those who live on the earth—to every nation, tribe, language and people. (14:6, NIV)

A second angel followed and said, "Fallen! Fallen is Babylon the Great, which made all the nations drink the maddening wine of her adulteries." (14:8, NIV)

A third angel followed them, saying with a loud voice, "If anyone worships the beast and his image, and receives his mark on his forehead or on his hand, he himself shall also drink of the wine of the wrath of God." (14:9-10)

At other times angels are seen giving instructions or explanations:

Then I saw another angel coming up from the east, having the seal of the living God. He called out in a loud voice to the four angels who had been given power to harm the land and the sea: "Do not harm the land or the sea or the trees until we put a seal on the foreheads of the servants of our God." (7:2-3, NIV)

Then another angel came out of the temple and called in a loud voice to him who was sitting on the cloud, "Take your sickle and reap, because the time to reap has come, for the harvest of the earth is ripe." (14:15, NIV)

Then the angel said to me: "Why are you aston-
ished? I will explain to you the mystery of the
woman and of the beast she rides, which has the
seven heads and ten horns." (17:7, NIV)

At other times angels are heard to burst out in mighty
chorus to God:

Then I looked and heard the voice of many angels,
numbering thousands upon thousands, and ten
thousand times ten thousand. They encircled the
throne and the living creatures and the elders. In a
loud voice they sang: "Worthy is the Lamb, who
was slain, to receive power and wealth and wisdom
and strength and honor and glory and praise!"
(5:11-12, NIV)

All the angels were standing around the throne and
around the elders and the four living creatures. They
fell down on their faces before the throne and worshiped God, saying: "Amen! Praise and glory and
wisdom and thanks and honor and power and
strength be to our God for ever and ever. Amen!"
(7:11-12, NIV)

It is through the angels that God executes most of His
judgments in the Tribulation. They are the ones who blow
the seven trumpets that announce the second series of divine judgments; they are the ones who pour out the final
seven bowl judgments. It is an angel who is told to "take
your sharp sickle and gather the clusters of grapes from the
earth's vine, because its grapes are ripe" (14:18, NIV). It is

the angels who place "the seal of the living God" on the foreheads of the servants of God (7:2-3; 9:4). It is the angelic army that defeats Satan and his fallen angels, evicting them from heaven and casting them to the earth (12:7-9). It is an angel who comes down out of heaven at the end of the Tribulation, seizes Satan, and binds him in the bottomless pit for a thousand years (20:1-2). And angels are entrusted with the safety and security of the New Jerusalem in eternity (21:12).

According to the prophet Daniel, Michael the archangel has special duties in the Tribulation. He will be tasked with protecting the nation Israel. Daniel writes, "At that time Michael, the great prince who protects your people, will arise. There will be a time of distress such as has not happened from the beginning of nations until then. But at that time your people—everyone whose name is found written in the book—will be delivered" (Daniel 12:1, NIV).

God even uses fallen angels to accomplish His purposes in the Tribulation. Apollyon, the evil angel of the bottomless pit, is released at the fifth trumpet judgment to lead a demonic army of locustlike creatures who will torment unbelievers for five months (Revelation 9:1-11). In the sixth trumpet judgment, four fallen angels who have been bound at the river Euphrates are released to kill a third of mankind (Revelation 9:13-15). And just before the Battle of Armageddon, three evil spirits "that looked like frogs" proceed out of the mouths of the devil, the Beast, and the false prophet, to deceive the kings of the world and to gather them for "the battle on the great day of God Almighty" (Revelation 16:13-14, NIV). In all these things, the fallen angels merely carry out the will of God. They are never "on the loose."

## GOD OVER ALL

The book of Revelation offers us an awesome picture of the power and supernatural abilities of the angels, both holy and fallen. But it never allows us to be so taken with them that we forget the main personality of the book, God Almighty and Jesus, His Son. The apostle John was so overwhelmed by the sight of one of these mighty angels that twice he fell down at the angel's feet to worship him. And twice the angel's response was both immediate and forceful:

> Do not do it! I am a fellow servant with you and with your brothers who hold to the testimony of Jesus. Worship God! (19:10, NIV)

> Do not do it! I am a fellow servant with you and with your brothers the prophets and of all who keep the words of this book. Worship God! (22:9, NIV)

Worship God! Whether in prophetic studies or any other activity, that is always the best advice of all.

# EPILOGUE

## *It's Later Than It's Ever Been*

NO ONE knows for certain when Christ will return or whether we are really living in the end times. We believe, however, that Christians living today have more reason than those of any generation before us to believe that Christ could come in our lifetime. For example, all prophecy scholars agree that the generation that saw Israel restored to her land in 1948 could well be the "generation [that] will certainly not pass away until all these things have happened" (Matthew 24:32-34, NIV). In other words, before that strategic generation passes from the scene, time, as we know it, will come to an end.

When you examine all the "signs of the times" that have been fulfilled in our lifetime, you have to believe the coming of Christ is very near. As Jesus said, "Near, even at the doors." *This* generation does indeed have more solid reason to believe Christ could come in our lifetime than any before us. Yes, we could indeed be living in the end times!

Dr. John Walvoord, the most knowledgeable living prophecy scholar in the world today, said the following at a prophecy conference about the times in which we live:

> I have been studying prophecy for many years [over fifty], and while I do not believe it is possible to set dates for the Lord's return, I do sense in the world today an unprecedented time of world crises that can be interpreted as being preparatory for the coming of the Lord. If there ever was a time when Christians should live every day as though Christ could come at any time, it is today.

We could not agree more. We hope that everyone who reads this book will be prepared for His coming at any moment. Don't be like the majority, "ashamed before Him at His coming." We pray that you will "be ready" when He comes!

The story is told of a little girl who had trouble sleeping one night. Her bedroom was upstairs, and her parents were downstairs reading. First she asked for a glass of water, then a cookie, and then she wanted to know what time it was. Finally her parents' patience ran out, and they warned her to go to sleep, threatening to punish her if she called them again.

The best she could do was lie there, watching the ceiling and listening for the striking of the grandfather clock downstairs. When the clock struck eleven, something must have gone wrong mechanically, because as she counted the hours, the clock tolled eleven and kept on going: twelve, thirteen, fourteen. When the clock tolled eighteen, she threw caution to the wind, jumped out of bed, ran downstairs, and cried, "Mom, Dad—*it's later than it's ever been!*"

That is what we are saying to you—prophetically, it is later than it has ever been. We pray that you will live every day as though Jesus could come at any moment, because no generation of Christians ever had more reason for believing He could come in their lifetime than does ours!

# NOTES

## CHAPTER 2

1. Thomas Ice and Timothy Demy, *The Truth about the Signs of the Times* (Eugene, Oreg.: Harvest House, 1997), 8.

## CHAPTER 4

1. M. R. DeHaan, *Signs of the Times* (Grand Rapids, Mich.: Zondervan, 1951), 49.
2. Ibid., 50.
3. Richard Lacayo, "The Lure of the Cult" *Time*, 7 April 1997, 45.
4. Tim LaHaye, *The Beginning of the End* (Wheaton, Ill.: Tyndale House, 1972), 35–36.
5. See Isaiah 66:7-9; Jeremiah 4:23-31; Hosea 13:12-14; Micah 4:9–5:3.

## CHAPTER 5

1. John Walvoord, *Armageddon, Oil and the Middle East Crisis,* (rev. ed.) (Grand Rapids, Mich.: Zondervan, 1990), 105–6.
2. In fact, the prophets predicted two regatherings into the land: one as a nation in unbelief, after which they will be driven out again by the Antichrist in the middle of the Tribulation; and another when Christ returns three and a half years later, this time in belief, ready to inherit the kingdom with their newly accepted Messiah as king.
3. Arthur James Balfour, "The Balfour Declaration" January 30, 1996, http://www.lib.byu.edu/~rdh/wwi/1917/balfour.html (July 21, 1999).
4. Walvoord, *Armageddon,* 105-6.
5. Arnold Fruchtenbaum, *Footsteps of the Messiah* (Tustin, Calif.: Ariel Press, 1982), 445.

## CHAPTER 6

1. Patricia Klein, reviewer, on-line review, Amazon.com 1998.
2. Robert L. Thomas in *The Expositor's Bible Commentary,* vol. 11 (Grand Rapids, Mich.: Zondervan, 1978), 321–22.
3. Ralph Earle in *The Expositor's Bible Commentary,* vol. 11 (Grand Rapids, Mich.: Zondervan, 1978), 371.
4. D. Guthrie, J. A. Motyer, A. M. Stibbs, D. L. Wiseman, eds., *The New Bible Commentary: Revised* (Grand Rapids, Mich.: Eerdmans, 1970), 1172.
5. Earle, *The Expositor's Bible Commentary,* 411.

## CHAPTER 8

1. Tim LaHaye, *The Beginning of the End* (Wheaton, Ill.: Tyndale House, 1972), 65.
2. For a complete study of the identification of Russia, see LaHaye, *The Beginning of the End*, 63–87.
3. LaHaye, *The Beginning of the End*, 80.
4. *The Intelligence Digest*, September 19, 1997.

## CHAPTER 9

1. Thomas Ice and Timothy Demy, *Fast Facts on Bible Prophecy* (Eugene, Oreg.: Harvest House, 1997), 186–87.
2. *Our Hope Magazine*, August 1950, 50.
3. Tim LaHaye, *No Fear of the Storm* (Sisters, Oreg.: Multnomah, 1992), 41–42.
4. Ibid., 42–43.
5. Ibid., 45.
6. Grant Jeffrey, *Apocalypse* (Frontier Research Publication, 1992), 85–94.
7. Tim LaHaye and Jerry B. Jenkins, *Tribulation Force* (Wheaton, Ill.: Tyndale House, 1996), 53–54.

## CHAPTER 10

1. Thomas Ice and Timothy Demy, *The Truth about the Last Days Temple* (Eugene, Oreg.: Harvest House, 1997), 29.
2. Ibid., 30.
3. Ibid.
4. Ibid.
5. Ibid., 32.

## CHAPTER 11

1. Joe Chambers, *A Palace for the Antichrist* (Green Forest, Ark.: New Leaf Press, 1996), 66.
2. Charles H. Dyer, *The Rise of Babylon: Sign of the End Times* (Wheaton, Ill.: Tyndale House, 1991), 141.

## CHAPTER 12

1. Arnold Fruchtenbaum, *Footsteps of the Messiah*, 121–22.
2. Gleason L. Archer Jr., "Daniel" in *The Expositor's Bible Commentary*, vol. 7 (Grand Rapids, Mich.: Zondervan, 1985), 113.

3. Tim LaHaye and Jerry B. Jenkins, *Tribulation Force* (Wheaton, Ill.: Tyndale House, 1996), 64.

## CHAPTER 13

1. Tim LaHaye and Jerry B. Jenkins, *Tribulation Force* (Wheaton, Ill.: Tyndale House, 1996), 424–25.
2. Peter and Patti Lalonde, *The Edge of Time,* (Eugene, Oreg.: Harvest House, 1997), 92.
3. A more complete listing of paganism is found in Tim LaHaye, *Revelation: Illustrated and Made Plain* (Grand Rapids, Mich.: Zondervan, 1975).
4. LaHaye and Jenkins, *Tribulation Force,* 275.
5. *H du B Report* 40, from Paris, October 1997.
6. *Washington Times,* 12 October 1997.
7. Tim LaHaye and Jerry B. Jenkins, *Apollyon* (Wheaton, Ill.: Tyndale House, 1999), 334.
8. *Time,* 21 May 1965, 35.

## CHAPTER 14

1. Terry L. Cook, *The Mark of the New World Order* (Springdale, Pa.: Whitaker House, 1996), 203–4.
2. John Walvoord, *The Nations in Prophecy* (Grand Rapids, Mich.: Zondervan, 1976), 141.
3. Joseph Lam, *China: The Last Superpower* (Green Forest, Ark.: New Leaf Press, 1996), 102–3.
4. Henry M. Morris, *The Revelation Record* (El Cajon, Calif.: Institute for Creation Research, 1983), 310–11.
5. Lam, *China,* 56.
6. Walvoord, *The Nations in Prophecy,* 142.

## CHAPTER 19

1. Dave and Jan Dravecky, *Do Not Lose Heart* (Grands Rapids, Mich.: Zondervan, 1998).
2. Ibid.

## CHAPTER 21

1. Merrill C. Tenney, "John" in *The Expositor's Bible Commentary,* vol. 9 (Grand Rapids, Mich.: Zondervan, 1981), 164.

## CHAPTER 22

1. *The Random House Encyclopedia, New Revised,* 3rd ed., s.v. "Goebbels, Joseph."

## CHAPTER 23

1. Tim LaHaye and Jerry B. Jenkins, *Tribulation Force* (Wheaton, Ill.: Tyndale House, 1996), 323–24.
2. Tim LaHaye and Jerry B. Jenkins, *Left Behind* (Wheaton, Ill.: Tyndale House, 1995), 212.

## CHAPTER 24

1. Tim LaHaye and Jerry B. Jenkins, *Soul Harvest* (Wheaton, Ill.: Tyndale House, 1998), 193–94.

## CHAPTER 25

1. Mark O'Keefe, "Christian Persecution: Widespread, Complex," *Oregonian,* 25 October 1998, A7.
2. Ibid., A1, A7.

## CHAPTER 26

1. *USA Today,* 13 October 1997.

# ABOUT THE AUTHORS

**Jerry B. Jenkins** (www.jerryjenkins.com) is the writer of the Left Behind series. He is author of more than one hundred books, of which ten have reached the *New York Times* best-seller list. Former vice president for publishing for the Moody Bible Institute of Chicago, he also served many years as editor of *Moody* magazine and is now Moody's writer-at-large.

His writing has appeared in publications as varied as *Reader's Digest, Parade,* in-flight magazines, and many Christian periodicals. He has written books in four genres: biography, marriage and family, fiction for children, and fiction for adults.

Jenkins's biographies include books with Hank Aaron, Bill Gaither, Luis Palau, Walter Payton, Orel Hershiser, Nolan Ryan, Brett Butler, and Billy Graham, among many others.

Seven of his apocalyptic novels—*Left Behind, Tribulation Force, Nicolae, Soul Harvest, Apollyon, Assassins,* and *The Indwelling*—have appeared on the Christian Booksellers Association's best-selling fiction list and the *Publishers Weekly* religion best-seller list. *Left Behind* was nominated for Book of the Year by the Evangelical Christian Publishers Association in 1997, 1998, 1999, and 2000. *The Indwelling* was number one on the *New York Times* best-seller list for four consecutive weeks.

As a marriage and family author and speaker, Jenkins has been a frequent guest on Dr. James Dobson's *Focus on the Family* radio program.

Jerry is also the writer of the nationally syndicated sports story comic strip *Gil Thorp,* distributed to newspapers across the United States by Tribune Media Services.

Jerry and his wife, Dianna, live in Colorado.

**Dr. Tim LaHaye** (www.timlahaye.com), who conceived the idea of fictionalizing an account of the Rapture and the Tribulation, is a noted author, minister, and nationally recognized speaker on Bible prophecy. He is the founder of both Tim LaHaye Ministries and The Pre-Trib Research Center. Presently Dr. LaHaye speaks at many of the major Bible prophecy conferences in the U.S. and Canada, where his nine current prophecy books are very popular.

Dr. LaHaye holds a doctor of ministry degree from Western Theological Seminary and a doctor of literature degree from Liberty University. For twenty-five years he pastored one of the nation's outstanding churches in San Diego, which grew to three locations. It was during that time that he founded two accredited Christian high schools, a Christian school system of ten schools, and Christian Heritage College.

Dr. LaHaye has written over forty books, with over 30 million copies in print in thirty-three languages. He has written books on a wide variety of subjects, such as family life, temperaments, and Bible prophecy. His current fiction works, written with Jerry B. Jenkins—*Left Behind, Tribulation Force, Nicolae, Soul Harvest, Apollyon, Assassins,* and *The Indwelling*—have all reached number one on the Christian best-seller charts. Other works by Dr. LaHaye are *Spirit-Controlled Temperament; How to Be Happy Though Married; Revelation Unveiled; Understanding the Last Days; Rapture under Attack; Are We Living in the End Times?;* and the youth fiction series Left Behind: The Kids.

He is the father of four grown children and grandfather of nine. Snow skiing, waterskiing, motorcycling, golfing, vacationing with family, and jogging are among his leisure activities.

# THE FUTURE IS CLEAR

## Left Behind®
### A novel of the earth's last days . . .
In one cataclysmic moment, millions around the world disappear. In the midst of global chaos, airline captain Rayford Steele must search for his family, for answers, for truth. As devastating as the disappearances have been, the darkest days lie ahead.

0-8423-2911-0 Hardcover      0-8423-1675-2 Audio book—Cassette
0-8423-2912-9 Softcover      0-8423-4323-7 Audio book—CD

## Tribulation Force
### The continuing drama of those left behind . . .
Rayford Steele, Buck Williams, Bruce Barnes, and Chloe Steele band together to form the Tribulation Force. Their task is clear, and their goal nothing less than to stand and fight the enemies of God during the seven most chaotic years the planet will ever see.

0-8423-2913-7 Hardcover      0-8423-1787-2 Audio book—Cassette
0-8423-2921-8 Softcover      0-8423-4324-5 Audio book—CD

## Nicolae
### The rise of Antichrist . . .
The seven-year tribulation period is nearing the end of its first quarter, when prophecy says "the wrath of the Lamb" will be poured out upon the earth. Rayford Steele has become the ears of the tribulation saints in the Carpathia regime. A dramatic all-night rescue run from Israel through the Sinai will hold you breathless to the end.

0-8423-2914-5 Hardcover      0-8423-1788-0 Audio book—Cassette
0-8423-2924-2 Softcover      0-8423-4355-5 Audio book—CD

## Soul Harvest
### The world takes sides . . .
As the world hurtles toward the Trumpet Judgments and the great soul harvest prophesied in Scripture, Rayford Steele and Buck Williams begin searching for their loved ones from different corners of the world. *Soul Harvest* takes you from Iraq to America, from six miles in the air to underground shelters, from desert sand to the bottom of the Tigris River, from hope to devastation and back again—all in a quest for truth and life.

0-8423-2915-3 Hardcover      0-8423-5175-2 Audio book—Cassette
0-8423-2925-0 Softcover      0-8423-4333-4 Audio book—CD

## Apollyon
**The Destroyer is unleashed . . .**
In this acclaimed *New York Times* best-seller, Apollyon, the Destroyer, leads the plague of demon locusts as they torture the unsaved. Meanwhile, despite growing threats from Antichrist, the Tribulation Force gathers in Israel for the Conference of Witnesses.

0-8423-2916-1 Hardcover
0-8423-2926-9 Softcover

0-8423-1933-6 Audio book—Cassette
0-8423-4334-2 Audio book—CD

## Assassins
**Assignment: Jerusalem, Target: Antichrist**
As a horde of 200 million demonic horsemen slays a third of the world's population, the Tribulation Force prepares for a future as fugitives. History and prophecy collide in Jerusalem for the most explosive episode yet of the continuing drama of those left behind.

0-8423-2920-X Hardcover
0-8423-2927-7 Softcover

0-8423-1934-4 Audio book—Cassette
0-8423-3682-6 Audio book—CD

## The Indwelling
**The Beast takes possession . . .**
It's the midpoint of the seven-year Tribulation. As the world mourns the death of a renowned man, the Tribulation Force faces its most dangerous challenges yet. Time and eternity seem suspended, and the destiny of mankind hangs in the balance.

0-8423-2928-5 Hardcover
0-8423-2929-3 Softcover

0-8423-1935-2 Audio book—Cassette
0-8423-3966-3 Audio Book—CD

## The Mark
**The Beast rules the world . . .**
His Excellency Global Community Potentate Nicolae Carpathia, resurrected and indwelt by the devil himself, tightens his grip as ruler of the world. The battle is launched for the very souls of men and women around the globe as sites are set up to begin administering the mark.

0-8423-3225-1 Hardcover
0-8423-3228-6 Softcover
(available fall 2001)

0-8423-3231-6 Audio book—Cassette
0-8423-3968-X Audio book—CD

**Watch for book 9 in this best-selling series to arrive fall 2001**

### Left Behind®: The Kids
Four teens are left behind after the Rapture and band together to fight
Satan's forces in this series for ten- to fourteen-year-olds.

#1 *The Vanishings* 0-8423-2193-4      #7 *Busted!* 0-8423-4327-X
#2 *Second Chance* 0-8423-2194-2     #8 *Death Strike* 0-8423-4328-8
#3 *Through the Flames* 0-8423-2195-0     #9 *The Search* 0-8423-4329-6
#4 *Facing the Future* 0-8423-2196-9     #10 *On the Run* 0-8423-4330-X
#5 *Nicolae High* 0-8423-4325-3     #11 *Into the Storm* 0-8423-4331-8
#6 *The Underground* 0-8423-4326-1     #12 *Earthquake!* 0-8423-4332-6

**Watch for the next Left Behind®: The Kids books,
available spring 2001**

### Have You Been Left Behind®?
Based on the video that New Hope Village Church's pastor Vernon Billings
created for those left behind after the Rapture. This video explains what
happened and what the viewer can do now.

0-8423-5196-5 Video

### An Experience in Sound and Drama
Dramatic broadcast performances of the first four books in the best-selling
Left Behind series. Original music, sound effects, and professional actors
make the action come alive. Experience the heart-stopping action and
suspense of the end times for yourself. . . . Twelve half-hour episodes, on
four CDs or three cassettes, for each title.

0-8423-5146-9 *Left Behind®: An Experience in Sound and Drama* CD
0-8423-5181-7 *Left Behind®: An Experience in Sound and Drama* cassette
0-8423-3584-6 *Tribulation Force: An Experience in Sound and Drama* CD
0-8423-3583-8 *Tribulation Force: An Experience in Sound and Drama* cassette
0-8423-3663-X *Nicolae: An Experience in Sound and Drama* CD
0-8423-3662-1 *Nicolae: An Experience in Sound and Drama* cassette
0-8423-3986-8 *Soul Harvest: An Experience in Sound and Drama* CD
0-8423-3985-X *Soul Harvest: An Experience in Sound and Drama* cassette
0-8423-4336-9 *Apollyon: An Experience in Sound and Drama* CD
        (available spring 2001)
0-8423-4335-0 *Apollyon: An Experience in Sound and Drama* cassette
        (available spring 2001)
0-8423-4338-5 *Assassins: An Experience in Sound and Drama* CD
        (available spring 2001)
0-8423-4337-7 *Assassins: An Experience in Sound and Drama* cassette
        (available spring 2001)

Discover the latest about the Left Behind series
and interact with other readers at **www.leftbehind.com**

For information regarding additional prophecy books
by Dr. Tim LaHaye, visit
**www.timlahayeministries.org**